T0136129

Artificial Intelligence for Cyber Defense and Smart Policing

The future policing ought to cover identification of new assaults, disclosure of new ill-disposed patterns, and forecast of any future vindictive patterns from accessible authentic information. Such keen information will bring about building clever advanced proof handling frameworks that will help cops investigate violations. *Artificial Intelligence for Cyber Defense and Smart Policing* will describe the best way of practicing artificial intelligence for cyber defense and smart policing.

Salient Features:

- Combines AI for both cyber defense and smart policing in one place.
- Covers novel strategies in future to help cybercrime examinations and police.
- Discusses different AI models to fabricate more exact techniques.
- Elaborates on problematization and international issues.
- Includes case studies and real-life examples.

This book is primarily aimed at graduates, researchers, and IT professionals. Business executives will also find this book helpful.

S. Vijayalakshmi is currently working as an Associate Professor in the Data Science Department in Christ (Deemed to be University), Lavasa Campus, Pune, India. She has many academic portfolios associated with the current position. Her research area is on image processing and Internet of Things (IoT).

P. Durgadevi has been working as an Assistant Professor in the Department of Computer Science and Engineering at the GITAM University (Deemed to be University), Bengaluru, India. She is currently doing research in medical image processing and IoT.

Lija Jacob is an Assistant Professor at the Department of Data Science, Christ (Deemed to be University), Lavasa, Pune, India. She has more than 17 years of teaching experience and 8 years of research experience. Her research interests are computer vision, machine Learning, and deep learning.

Balamurugan Balusamy is currently working as a Professor in the School of Computing Sciences and Engineering at Galgotias University, Greater Noida, India. He has published 30-plus books on various technologies and visited 15-plus countries for his technical course. He has several top-notch conferences in his resume and has published over 150 of quality journal articles, conference papers, and book chapters combined.

Parma Nand has a PhD in Computer Science and Engineering from IIT Roorkee, M. Tech and B. Tech in Computer Science and Engineering from IIT Delhi. Prof. Parma Nand has more than 27 years of experience both in industry and in academia. He has received various awards like Best Teacher Award from the Union Minister, Best Students Project Guide Award from Microsoft in 2015 and Best Faculty Award from Cognizant in 2016. He has successfully completed government funded projects and has spearheaded the last five Institute of Electrical and Electronics Engineers

(IEEE) International conferences on Computing, Communication and Automation (ICCCA), IEEE students chapters, Technovation Hackathon 2019, Technovation Hackathon 2020, International Conference on Computing, Communication, and Intelligent Systems (ICCCIS-2021). He is a member of Executive Council of IEEE, UP section (R-10), a member of Executive Committee IEEE Computer and Signal Processing Society, a member of Executive India Council Computer Society, and a member of Executive Council Computer Society of India, Noida section, and has acted as an observer in many IEEE conferences. He also has active memberships in ACM, IEEE, CSI, ACEEE, ISOC, IAENG, and IASCIT. He is a lifetime member of Soft Computing Research Society (SCRS) and ISTE.

Artificial Intelligence for Cyber Defense and Smart Policing

Edited by
S. Vijayalakshmi, P. Durgadevi, Lija Jacob,
Balamurugan Balusamy, and Parma Nand

CRC Press
Taylor & Francis Group
Boca Raton London New York

CRC Press is an imprint of the
Taylor & Francis Group, an **informa** business

A CHAPMAN & HALL BOOK

Designed cover image: thinkhubstudio/Shutterstock

First edition published 2024
by Chapman & Hall
2385 NW Executive Center Drive, Suite 320, Boca Raton FL 33431

and by Chapman & Hall
4 Park Square, Milton Park, Abingdon, Oxon, OX14 4RN

Chapman & Hall is an imprint of Taylor & Francis Group, LLC

© 2024 selection and editorial matter, S. Vijayalakshmi, P. Durgadevi, Lija Jacob, Balamurugan Balusamy, and Parma Nand ; individual chapters, the contributors

Library of Congress Cataloging-in-Publication Data
Names: Vijayalakshmi, S. (Associate professor), editor. | Durgadevi, P., editor. | Jacob, Lija, editor. | Balusamy, Balamarugan, editor.
Title: Artificial intelligence for cyber defence and smart policing / edited by S. Vijayalakshmi, P. Durgadevi, Lija Jacob and Balamarugan Balusamy.
Description: First edition. | Boca Raton, FL : Chapman & Hall, 2024. | Includes bibliographical references and index. | Summary: "The future policing ought to cover the identification of new assaults, the disclosure of new ill-disposed patterns and forecast of any future vindictive patters from the accessible authentic information. Such keen information will bring about building clever advanced proof handling frameworks that will help cops investigate violations. Artificial Intelligence for Cyber Defence and Smart Policing will describe the best way of practising artificial intelligence for cyber defence and smart policing"-- Provided by publisher.
Identifiers: LCCN 2023029665 | ISBN 9781032170930 (hbk) | ISBN 9781032170947 (pbk) | ISBN 9781003251781 (ebk)
Subjects: LCSH: Law enforcement. | Computer crimes. | Artificial intelligence.
Classification: LCC HV7921 .A77 2024 | DDC 363.20285--dc23/eng/20231020
LC record available at https://lccn.loc.gov/2023029665

ISBN: 9781032170930 (hbk)
ISBN: 9781032170947 (pbk)
ISBN: 9781003251781 (ebk)

DOI: 10.1201/9781003251781

Typeset in Times
by Deanta Global Publishing Services, Chennai, India

Contents

Contributors vii

Chapter 1   Machine Learning in Cyber Threats Intelligent System... 1

                W. Jaisingh, Preethi Nanjundan, and Jossy P. George

Chapter 2   Cybercrimes in the Associated World.. 21

                R. Gunavathi and K. Mani Bharathi

Chapter 3   Recent Developments in Threat Intelligence and Challenges................................... 32

                S. Kannadhasan, R. Nagarajan, R. Prabhu, and K. Chandramohan

Chapter 4   AI in Forensics: A Data Analytics Perspective 41

                Lija Jacob, K.T. Thomas and M. Savithri

Chapter 5   Big Data for Intelligence and Security... 61

                S. Vijayalakshmi, Savita, P. Durgadevi, and A.S. Mohammed Shariff

Chapter 6   Deep Learning Decision Support Model for Police Investigation 76

                Arun Mozhi Devan, V. Raghul, Urvashi Dhasmana, Asutosh Rath and Lija Jacob

Chapter 7   Big Data Paradigm in Cybercrime Investigation 91

                Rohan Harchandani, Palak Bansal, Shreyans Jain, Jasleen Kaur Sondhi, and Lija Jacob

Chapter 8   Low-Cost High-Impact AI Tools vs Cybercrime... 110

                P. Durgadevi, A.S. Mohammed Shariff, S. Nagaraj, M. Dinesh Babu, and Savita

Chapter 9   Computer-based (AI) Intelligence in the Field of Defence 121

                T Akilan, U Hariharan, and P. Durgadevi

Chapter 10   Assembly of Cyber and Illegal Intimidation.. 135

                Jaya Sinha, M. Chandraprabha, and T. Akilan

Chapter 11 Computer-based Intelligence and Security 160

Sushma Tanwar, S. Vijayalakshmi, P. Durgadevi, and R. Girija

Chapter 12 Case Study: Artificial Intelligence and Machine Learning in Cybersecurity 172

Girija R, Abiram G, P. Durgadevi, and Savita

Index... 177

Contributors

G. Abiram
SRMIST
Chennai, India

T. Akilan
Department of IQAC, Amity University
Kolkata, India

M. Dinesh Babu
Galgotias College of Engineering and
    Technology
India

Palak Bansal
Department of Data Science, Christ University
Pune, Lavasa, India

K. Mani Bharathi
CSUITE TECH LABS
Chennai, Tamil Nadu, India
India

K. Chandramohan
Department of Computer Science and
    Engineering, Gnanamani College of
    Technology
Tamil Nadu, India

M. Chandraprabha
Department of Computer Science and
    Engineering, Galgotias College of
    Engineering and Technology
Greater Noida, Uttar Pradesh, India

Savita
School of Engineering & Technology,
    Maharishi University of Information
    Technology
Noida, India

Arun Mozhi Devan
Department of Data Science, Christ University
Pune, Lavasa, India

Urvashi Dhasmana
Department of Data Science, Christ University
Pune, Lavasa, India

P. Durgadevi
GITAM University (Deemed to be University)
Bengaluru, India

Jossy P. George
Department of Data Science, Christ University
Delhi NCR Campus, India

R. Girija
Manav Rachna University
Faridabad, India

R. Gunavathi
Department of Data Science,
    Christ University
Pune, Lavasa, India

Rohan Harchandani
Department of Data Science,
    Christ University
Pune, Lavasa, India

U. Hariharan
Department of CSE, Apex Institute of
    Technology, Chandigarh University
Mohali, Punjab, India

Lija Jacob
Department of Data Science,
    Christ University
Pune, Lavasa, India

Shreyans Jain
Department of Data Science,
    Christ University
Pune, Lavasa, India

W. Jaisingh
Presidency University, Bengaluru, India

S. Kannadhasan
Department of Electronics and Communication
    Engineering, Cheran College of
    Engineering, Anna University
Karur, Tamil Nadu, India

S. Nagaraj
Jain University
Bangaluru, India

R. Nagarajan
Department of Electrical and Electronics
    Engineering, Gnanamani College of
    Technology, Anna University
Namakkal, Tamil Nadu, India

Preethi Nanjundan
Department of Data Science,
    Christ University
Pune, Lavasa, India

R. Prabhu
Assistant Professor, Department
    of Electronics and Communication
    Engineering, Gnanamani College of
    Technology
Tamil Nadu, India

V. Raghul
Department of Data Science,
    Christ University
Pune, Lavasa, India

Asutosh Rath
Department of Data Science, Christ University
Pune, Lavasa, India

A.S. Mohammed Shariff
Galgotias College of Engineering and Technology
India

M. Savithri
Department of Data Science, Christ University
Pune, Lavasa, India

Jaya Sinha
Department of Computer Science and
    Engineering, Galgotias College of
    Engineering and Technology, Greater Noida,
    U.P., India

Jasleen Kaur Sondhi
Department of Data Science, Christ University
Pune, Lavasa, India

Sushma Tanwar
Manipal University
Jaipur, India

K.T. Thomas
Department of Data Science, Christ University
Pune, Lavasa, India

S. Vijayalakshmi
Department of Data Science, Christ University
Pune, Lavasa, India

1 Machine Learning in Cyber Threats Intelligent System

W. Jaisingh, Preethi Nanjundan, and Jossy P. George

1.1 INTRODUCTION

Organizations share information about cyber attacks as a crucial component of cyber threat intelligence, in order to enhance their understanding of potential threats and proactively safeguard their systems and networks. Cyber-attacks and defenses both rely heavily on machine learning, but neither of them achieve their goals when they rely on it completely. A malware sniffer can detect malware in encrypted traffic based on an analysis of encrypted traffic elements in network telemetry. The algorithms of machine learning uncover threats hidden in encryption, instead of decrypting them. Since machine learning can recognize patterns in massive datasets and predict threats automatically, it excels in this area. By automating their threat detection, cyber teams can identify threats more quickly and can isolate situations that need to be manually investigated.

The emergence of Internet of Things (IoT) applications has greatly contributed to the surge in internet usage in recent years, particularly with the widespread adoption of IoT devices. Utilizing the internet has become increasingly prevalent, as indicated by the latest Data Report, which delivers information on Internet users around the world. Moreover, according to the Data Report's data, 1 million Internet users log in each day. A breakdown of Internet usage by year is presented according to the Data Report. (See Figure 1.1 [1]).

By cumulative net practice, numerous safety vulnerabilities have been created. Several security technologies are used to close these gaps, including firewalls, data encryption, and user authentication. Using these technologies, many attacks can be prevented. The technology cannot, however, analyze packet content at the packet level. Accordingly, attacks will not be detected to the desired level. As a response to these shortcomings, intrusion prevention systems (IPSs) and intrusion detection systems (IDSs) have been developed. The algorithms used in these security systems, for example machine learning, deep learning, and artificial intelligence, allow them to perform deeper data analyses than when using other security systems. IDSs, on the other hand, are primarily used for detecting and analyzing intrusions, whereas IPSs use both intrusion detection and prevention mechanisms [2].

Information transfer speeds and Internet usage have increased as well, causing several anomalies [3]. As a result, there are increasingly more attacks on the Internet. Figure 1.2 shows common vulnerabilities and exposures observed year wise. In 2019, new vulnerabilities were discovered and there was an increase of 3.8% in comparison with last year [4] (see Figure 1.2).

In order to prioritize the safety and stability of their users, organizations and institutions are ramping up their investments in cyber security technologies. According to a recent report by Crystal Market Research (CMR), the cyber security industry is projected to reach a spending of USD 173.57 billion by 2022. In 2012, USD58.13 billion was spent on cyber security. The report highlights the increase in cloud storage and IoT knowledge, as well as the USD58.13 billion spent on cyber security in 2012. The graph in Figure 1.3 displays the scope of cybersecurity market available by CMR according to years is represented [5].

DOI: 10.1201/9781003251781-1

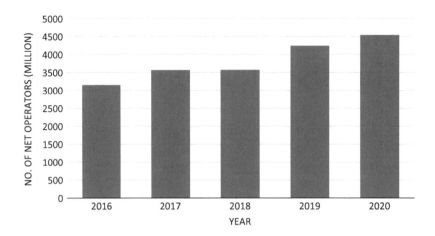

FIGURE 1.1   Yearly changes in the number of net operators (in millions) [1].

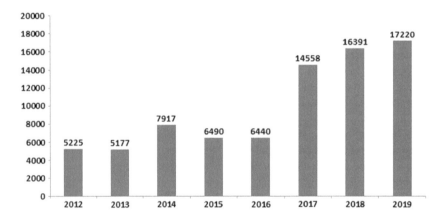

FIGURE 1.2   Novel common vulnerabilities and exposures by year [4].

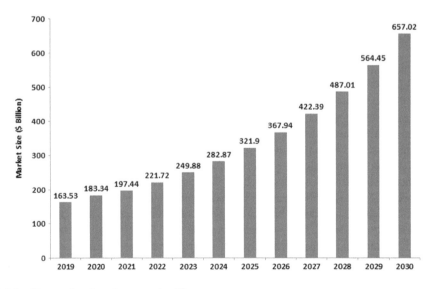

FIGURE 1.3   The market for cyber security [5].

As Internet usage increases, cyber security businesses have to develop more subtle security schemes. Cyber security businesses must develop more sophisticated security schemes as Internet usage rises. One way to ensure cyber safety is by conducting studies on net conduct. IDSs are among the skills that organizations are using today to be more alert to cyber threats.

Rules or signatures are used by IDSs after finding and investigating occurrences, depending on the system type. The signature-based interference detection system compares the information in the net with the spell designs stored in its file. The system generates an alarm if a match is discovered. These signature-based IDSs have a major disadvantage of not being able to detect attacks that are not in their database. Rules-based IDS, also called anomaly-based IDS, keeps track of usual conduct conditions in the IDS file. The system continuously monitors all network activities. If the specified rules are not being followed, an alarm will be generated. It is their ability to detect unknown attacks that makes anomaly-based intrusion detection systems so attractive [6-8].

1.2 RELATED WORKS

Almost every day, attackers are updating their software and their knowledge, and they are coming up with new attack scenarios. As a result, interference uncovering schemes are being established day by day for net schemes to be safe and to counter rising malware issues. Many literature studies have been conducted for this purpose, and novel lessons are being conducted every day to make IDSs more effective.

In their study, Inayat et al. [8] analyzed the project limits of the current interruption reply system (IRS). In the results of their study, it was determined that there was much literature in this field, but most of them lacked attacks interpretation and used a reply metric in place of a dynamic one. Consequently, more false alarms were generated. The study by Ferran et al. [9] used several deep learning approaches, including recurrent neural networks (RNN), deep neural networks (DNN), restricted Boltzmann machines (RBM), deep belief networks (DBN), convolutional neural network (CNN), and deep Boltzmann machines (DBM). Both datasets are encoded using deep autoencoders (DA) CSE-CIC-IDS 2018 and Bot-IoT. Deep learning performance is compared to the time required to classify data sets. Furthermore, the authors examined 35 about discovery data set in the works based on deep learning-based intrusion detection systems.

The CSE-CIC-IDS-2017 dataset was developed by Sharafaldin et al. [10] since the available datasets were not sufficient to meet the interruption discovery needs at that time. To collect data, a test set with system assailants and wounded individuals was established. The test environment was used to conduct brute force attacks, heartbeat attacks, botnet attacks, DDoS attacks, web attacks, and infiltration attacks. Additionally, machine learning methods were used to evaluate system performance. In their study, Patil et al. [11] planned the hypervisor equal dispersed network security (HLDNS) security outline for cloud computing. This method is used to monitor a virtual machine server for intrusions. A similarity-based feature extraction algorithm, classifier accuracy, and a fitness function are used to extract features. Using the datasets UNSW-NB15 and CICIDS-2017, the proposed method was evaluated for performance. Researchers compared two deep learning algorithms – CNN and RNN algorithms – using the CSE-CIC-IDS 2018 dataset. Kim et al. [12] used CNN and RNN deep learning algorithms in their study.

Kanimozhi et al. [13] used Artificial Neural Network (ANN), Random Forest (RF), k-NN, support vector machines (SVM), ADA BOOST, and Naive Bayes (NB) machine learning techniques for categorizing CSE-CIC-IDS 2018 dataset. Khammassi et al. [14] planned a feature assortment strategy based on logistic regression and the Non-Dominated Categorization Genetic Algorithm II (NSGA-II). In this study, a Multinomial Logistic Regression approach (NSGA2- MLR) and a Binomial Logistic Regression approach (NSGA2-BLR) were used to evaluate the recommended solution. A combination of C4.5, Random Forest (RF), and Naive Bayes (NB) algorithms was used to classify the best subsets. A total of three datasets were used in education: NSL-KDD, UNSW-NB15, and CIC-IDS2017. An extensive review of intrusion detection systems was conducted by Ring et al. [15]. According to this study, network-based intrusion detection systems use various data formats. A further 15 criteria for determining the suitability of data sets were developed. Data quality, volume, recording environment, and evaluation made up the remaining five categories. Kamiozhi et al. [16] classified the CSE-CIC-IDS-2018 dataset using artificial intelligence (AI). A success rate of 99.97% was achieved based on the classification.

A test environment developed by Moustafa et al. [17] is more relevant to real-world network traffic. Data collection from the UNSW-NB15 test environment is generated by IXIA PerfectStorm. The data collection was made using programs such as Perfect-Storm, Tcpdump, Argus, and Bro-IDS developed by IXIA. In the test environment, nine different bout scenarios were designed using the IXIA tool: Fuzzers, Analysis, Backdoors, denial of service (DoS), Exploits, Generic, Reconnaissance, Shellcode, Worms. In an additional study, Moustafa et al. [18,19] evaluated the UNSW-NB15 data set for complexity. For this purpose, an arithmetical examination of experiences was performed in the initial phase. The next step was to examine the correlations between the features. In the final stage, we evaluated and compared the data set's performance with five classifiers of KDD99. Testing was conducted on the NSL-KDD and UNSW-NB15 datasets. Zhang et al. [20] have developed a unified approach that integrates the Multiscale Convolutional Neural Network (MSCNN) and the Long Short-Term Memory (LSTM) techniques. The main stage of the technique involved examining the spatial possessions of the information set. Transitory characteristics were handled using the LSTM network in another phase of the technique. Training and testing of the type were performed on the UNSW-NB15 dataset. As far as correctness, untrue fear degree, and false-negative speed are concerned, the method outperforms traditional neural network models. Gottwald and colleagues developed a technique based on multivariate correlation (MC) for identifying network anomalies based on multivariate correlation and feature selection. These tests were conducted on the UNSW-NB15 and NSL-KDD datasets.

Khambasi et al. [21,22] point out that for categorizing IDSs in less time and with better accuracy, exposing features that represent the whole dataset is important. The researchers used wrapper logistic regression in conjunction with genetic algorithms to select the best intrusion detection system attributes. Datasets used in the tests included KDD99 and UNSW-NB15, which were likened to additional education. As part of their study, Kamongo et al. [23] analyzed the AWID and UNSW-NB15 datasets by using Wrapper-based Feature Extraction Unit (WFEU) feature extraction techniques and Feed-Forward Deep Neural Networks (FFDNNs). Rashid et al. [24] classified the NSL-KDD and CIDDS-0001 datasets using SVM, Naive Bayes (NB), KNN, and Neural networks as well as DNN. Before using the classification algorithms, hybrid feature assortment and categorization procedures were continued to be used to increase classifier performance.

David et al. [25] used an empirical method based on a Dynamic Threshold algorithm to detect DDoS attacks. This method was validated using datasets from DARPA. A comparison of the proposed approach with existing approaches shows that it has higher detection rates and requires fewer dispensation periods. The KDD Cup 99 data set was categorized by Ertam et al. [26] using NB, BayesNet (bN), Random Forest (RF), Multilayer Perceptron (MLP), and Sequential Minimal Optimization (SMO) algorithms. To investigate 802.11 network attacks in depth, Kolias et al. [27] developed the AWID dataset. In the next step, the AWID data set was kept strictly secret by using the techniques like AdaBoost, Hyperpipes, J48, NB, OneR, RF, and Xero algorithms. Using the k-nearest neighbor classification and k-mean clustering methods, Verma et al. [28] categorized the flow-based and labeled data set CIDDS-001. We evaluated data from OpenStack servers and data from external servers separately. The CIDDS-001 dataset was classified by Verma et al. using techniques such as k-Nearest Neighbor (kNN), SVM, Decision Tree (DT), RF, NB, DL, Artificial Neural Network (ANN), Self-Organizing Maps (SOMs), and Expectation-Maximization (EM).

1.3 CYBERSECURITY ATTACK TYPES USED IN PUBLIC IDS DATASETS

In this section, we will discuss some of the most commonly used IDS datasets and bout types within them.

1.3.1 DATASETS

To detect cyber security threats, data sets from various sources can be used. Public data sets are divided into seven categories based on their content, according to Ferran et al. See Figure 1.4 for a list of available datasets and classifications.

Datasets generated by the MT Lincoln Laboratory were part of the DARPA project, which was generated as a network-based dataset in 1998. Data on various network attacks were collected in the seven weeks of training. Two-week attacks were also included in the test data [29]. This data collection was inspired by the DARPA data collection effort of 1998. There is a simulated renunciation of the facility, hacker to user (U2U), and remote to local (R2L) battle. Five million lines of network activity were recorded over seven weeks in the dataset. Tests of intrusion detection algorithms were often conducted using this dataset [30].

Dataset NSL-KDD: The NSL-KDD dataset was created to address data issues associated with the KDD 99 dataset. Owing to the unique KDD 99 data collection, it covers no redundant or unnecessary information. Record numbers are sufficient. Duplicates and redundant entries were removed, resulting in a decrease in data collected, from 5 million to 150,000 records. Subsequently, the intrusion detection system data was divided into training and testing subgroups. Both KDD CUP 99 and NSL-KDD use the same assets and lessons. A variety of attacks such as DoS, Remote to Local (R2L), User to Root (U2R), and searching are replicated in the KDD 99 data set [30].

Kyoto Dataset: The dataset contains 24 characteristics. To construct these characteristics, 14 of the KDDCup99 datasets were used. Using honeypot systems at Kyoto University, these 14 data characteristics were selected from 41 features of the KDD Cup 99 data set. Further ten capabilities were added to make the intrusion detection system even more effective [31–33].

In a network intrusion detection system that used anomaly detection, CIDDS-001 (Coburg Network Intrusion Detection Dataset) was developed as a data collection tool. In the data collection, scripts were written in the map and Python languages.

Attacks included are port scans, ping scans, denial-of-service attacks, and brute-force attacks. The data usually includes the following classifications: Normal, Attacker, Victim, Suspicious,

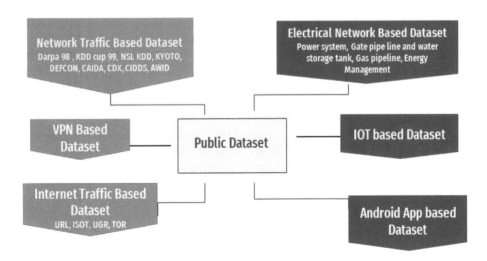

FIGURE 1.4 Datasets available to the public and their classifications [9].

and Unknown. An external server provides traffic statistics from OpenStack as well as data collected by the OpenStack project [32–33].

A seven-day network data set was used for the ISCX-2012 data collection. Data on authenticated as well as unauthorized network communications were collected. Malicious network activity may involve stealing confidential information, launching denial of service attacks, or employing brute force Secure Socket Shell (SSH) attacks. The classes are Normal and Attacker [34].

Dataset CSE-CIC-IDS 2017: The Communications Security Establishments (CSEs) and the Canadian Institute for Cybersecurity collected this information in 2017. The dataset was designed using a violent and prey network created in the testing environment. We collected the data in a lab environment, with both attackers and victims. At the location where the bouts took place, a change was made, a CPU running Kali Linux, and three Windows 8 PCs. One Windows Server 2016, one server with an Ubuntu 16 operating system, and one attendant with an Ubuntu 12 operating system, as well as a router and firewall are present in the target network. All strategies in the victim network were then added to the Active Directory domain on Windows Server 2016. To keep track of all activity on the target network, the router's uplink harbor was additionally reflected [35].

The java-B-profile scheme was used to design an agent for the CSE-CIC-IDS dataset that generated regular traffic. We duplicated several protocol-based characteristics by using machine learning and statistical techniques, including HTTP, HTTPS, FTP, SSH, and e-mail. For building attack traffic data, Patator, Slowloris, Slowhttps, Metasploit, and Ares technologies were cast-off. In addition to brute force attacks, botnets, DDoS, Web assaults, and penetrations, these attacks were all premeditated. This dataset describes 14 attack types in total. The following types of attacks have been tagged: DoS Golden Eye, Heartbleed, DoS hulk, DoS Slow HTTP, DoS Slowloris, DDoS, SSH-Patator, FP, Patator, Brute force, XSS, Botnet, infiltration, PortScann, and SQL injection.

Data collection for the 2018 CSE-CIC-IDS dataset shared many of the characteristics with those of the 2017 collection. Assaults were better simulated in the test set, however, by employing more devices. There were 50 computers in the attacker's network while 420 types of machinery and 30 attendants were in the prey's network. Additionally, the prey system was alienated into six sections: R&D (Department 1), Management (Department 2), Technician (Department 3), Secretary and Operations (Department 4), and Computer and Information Technology (Department 5). Aside from the IT department, all departments had Windows operating systems installed (Windows 8.1 and Windows 10). The IT department had all computers running the Ubuntu operating system. The server room had been installed with various attendant operating systems, including Windows Server 2012 and Windows Server 2016. The result was the creation of a topology that resembled a real-world network with machine diversity. Seven different attack scenarios were used to collect this data: brute force, heartbeat, botnets, DoS, DDoS, Web assaults, and penetrations [36].

The dataset was shaped by ACCS (Australian Centre aimed at Cyber Security). This dataset was created by combining IXIA Perfect-Storm, Tcpdump, Argus, and Bro-IDS. There are three virtual servers in IXIA, which simulate normal and abnormal traffic. This tool was used to create fuzzes, shellcode, backdoors, DoS attacks, exploits, generics, reconnaissance, and worms. To create a current threat environment, the tool uses the Common Vulnerabilities and Exposures (CVE) website. Routers are linked to the firewall to simulate the test environment. The firewall is arranged to allow all circulation to pass through, both regular and abnormal. During the simulation, tcpdump was used to capture the data packets received on one of the routers. Argus and Bro-IDS gears remained cast-off to break down the information into 49 features, and 12 C # algorithms were used to further break down the data.

1.3.2 TYPES OF ATTACKS

Various attack types have been used in IDS literature studies, with this section covering a few of them. System vulnerabilities are found through vulnerability scans. Aside from vulnerability scanning, this approach can also gather information about the target, such as its network map. Common tools for performing this operation include Nmap, Nessus, and OpenVAS. The first phase of a cyber-attack entails a vulnerability identification process. Next, the attack method is decided [37, 38].

By exploiting the target system's resources, such as RAM or CPU, a denial of service (DoS) attack is launched. DDoS attacks (Distributed Denial of Service) disable the target system faster because the target system is deactivated and unable to assist in such an attack [39]. DoS attacks are launched simultaneously from multiple locations. To disable the board system, a massive number of connection attempts are sent at the same time in a DDoS attack. This prevents the system from accepting new connections. A few of the methods used in this attack scenario are HTTP flooding, ICMP flooding, and Transmission Control Protocol (TCP) flooding [40, 41].

The objective of a brute force attack is to gain total control of the target system. Specifically, the attacker tries to discover the user's password. Data is posted to the target system to obtain login information. The method uses a range of username and password combinations if no information is provided in the request. Telnet, SSH, RDP, FTP, and HTTP systems are most commonly targeted by this attack type [42, 43].

The attack increases a system's authority by exploiting the vulnerability of the target system. Taking advantage of software or hardware vulnerabilities, malware infects the system. The system is infected as soon as a system safety susceptibility is found and the system administrator is unaware of it [44, 45].

The majority of SQL injection attacks are server-side attacks. By exploiting vulnerabilities in website databases, hackers are able to hack the database. In this way, websites can collect users' private information. According to the OWASP (Open Web Application Security Project) [46, 47], which contracts through web submission safety, this type of attack is the most common.

Other types of attacks included in the widely used DARPA, KDD99, and NSL-KDD data sets include Remote to Local (R2L), User to Root (U2R), and Searching. U2R bouts take advantage of susceptibilities to gain root access through the takeover of a common user account. In an R2L attack, a packet is sent across the network to the target system and an attempt is made to gain local access to that machine as its user. Furthermore, searching bouts are used to uncover susceptibilities in the target network, similarly to the susceptibility scan described above [48].

1.4 CYBER-PHYSICAL SYSTEMS (CPS)

With the ever-increasing usage of network-related services, there is more sensitive data available on the web. Unauthorized users with malicious intent gain access to network systems and attempt to get important information or destroy it, leaving networks vulnerable. Network security measures do not completely prevent cyber-attacks from occurring. In turn, the threat of network infiltration has increased, necessitating the use of network intrusion detection systematists to counter such attacks. During assaults, packet data analysis provides useful information that can help identify future attacks. Furthermore, we would be able to better prevent such assaults if we knew how they were classified, such as DoS attacks, Cross-Site Scripting attacks, and so forth. If you construct aids, keep in mind that a non-intrusion misdiagnosed as an intrusion can be more damaging than an untrue warning (non-interruption classified as an interruption).

Cyber-physical systems utilize feedback loops to connect computers and physical processes through these network services. Networks are used to connect sensors, actuators, and other components in these systems. TCP/IP and wireless protocols are used on the communication network at a lower level than those on a computer network. Thus, cyber-physical systems may be attacked just as easily as a regular computer network. By contrast, cyber-physical systems are safety-critical, and an unexpected disappointment, whether caused by a cyber-attack or something else, and can harm both the physical systems involved and the people relying on them. Because of this, such assaults must be avoided at all costs. Computer and physical resources are integrated into a cyber-physical system (CPS) to enable meaningful control through computation and communication [49]. Many industrial contexts make use of it to control equipment, devices, and systems remotely. Despite this, extensive use of CPS can cause a variety of security problems, including catastrophic damage to goods controlled by CPS and danger for individuals dependent on them. The installation of NIDS on these systems is therefore essential to take preemptive action before the damage caused by these assaults becomes irreversible.

Recent technological advancements have presented several new problems when it comes to network monitoring, even though it has long been utilized for security, forensics, and other purposes [50]. The following are among the most important issues:

- Data volume – Increasing adoption of the Internet of Things, cloud-based services, and other technologies has led to an increase in data volume. Analyzing such vast datasets efficiently and effectively requires the development of new methods.
- Accuracy – Accurate performance requires more granularity and contextual awareness to provide an all-inclusive and complete view.
- Variety – This is due to the development of new and diverse procedures, as well as the variety of data passing through systems today. It is therefore difficult to identify the characteristics that distinguish normal from irregular traffic.
- Low-frequency bouts – When these types of bouts occur, such inequity results in low detection precision because the AI training set is unbalanced.

Additionally, most IDSs classify attacks based on machine learning. By identifying valuable features that differentiate invasions, supervised learning can identify attacks. Unfortunately, when adequate and suitable traffic data are not obtainable, feature learning is difficult. Additionally, the number of incursions is relatively small compared to non-intrusions, which makes training more difficult.

It might be possible to solve these subjects using network circulation data obtained from a variety of bases, and unsupervised feature learning might be used to create suitable pictures of the data. The following features may be cast-off to train a classifier by means of a branded (then, uncertainty necessary, smaller) dataset that includes benign and irregular traffic. A constrained, isolated, and private network environment can be used for gathering traffic data for tagged datasets. Our paper proposes a method for extracting just the most important features from a feature vector and then categorizing invasions using these features.

1.4.1 Study of Cyber-Physical Systems

Throughout the years, machine learning-based techniques have been developed for network interruption detection. Because the CICIDS2017 dataset is still new, it has only been tested with a handful of approaches. The chapter begins with a detailed overview of the IDS methods, including general methods such as feature selection, ensemble models, and deep learning methods. The last part of the article examines strategies similar to the recommended strategy, with a focus on the CICIDS2017 dataset.

In IDS, the most important aspect is to select and maintain the best characteristics that define the data while removing duplicates or redundant attributes to reduce its dimensionality. A hybrid approach that uses support vector machines (SVMs) and genetic algorithms (GAs) to improve SVM performance is presented in [51–52]. Features subsets are selected in this alternative approach. Lightning attachment procedure optimization (LAPO) is combined with SVM to select features, beating GA. Numerous studies have shown that multiple classifiers outperform a single classifier. Multiple classifiers are frequently used to enhance intrusion detection accuracy. This dataset was used in [53]'s ensemble approach combining artificial neural networks (ANNs), support vector machines (SVMs), and multivariate adaptive regression splines (MARS).

This field is gaining traction fast with deep learning. As the use of large data and processing power increases, researchers are more interested in deep learning approaches. In recent years, numerous research studies have demonstrated how deep learning outperforms standard approaches in detecting various objects. NIDS methods and deep learning methods have been compared in research [54], and deep learning-based methods are shown to produce better discovery correctness for a variety of sample sizes and traffic anomaly categories. Using the Synthetic Minority Oversampling Technique (SMOTE), they have shown how to bridge the class gap.

There have been numerous deep learning-based approaches developed to safeguard a secure environment in a range of areas, such as detecting malware in IaaS clouds [55–56], providing a safe and secure travel experience for drivers through Intelligent Transport Systems (ITS), and providing access to cloud platforms for the Internet of Things (IoT) [57]. For system interruption detection, deep autoencoders are used in combination with perceptrons in [58]. We used samples from KDD 1999 for this study. Mirsky et al. [59] proposed an ensemble of autoencoders. As part of Kitsune, the authors developed an ensemble of autoencoders that extracts features.

A few deep learning-based approaches have been developed to guarantee a secure environment in a variety of domains, including the detection of malware in IaaS clouds [55], ensuring a safe and secure driving experience through Intelligent Transportation Systems (ITS), and connecting to cloud platforms for the Internet of Things (IoT) [57, 58] combines deep autoencoders with perceptrons for network intrusion detection. For this study, samples from KDD 1999 were used. A collaboration of autoencoders was proposed by Mirsky et al. [59]. They developed a set of autoencoders that extract features as part of Kitsune.

A novel approach uses bio-inspired deep neural networks to identify intrusions on communication networks in cyber-physical systems.

1.5   BIOINSPIRATION DEEP NEURAL NETWORKS IN CYBER-PHYSICAL SYSTEMS

Integrated computer, communication, and control technologies have become commonplace in industries such as manufacturing switch schemes, power grids, transportation networks, and vehicle social networking [60–62]. This addition also uses message systems for nursing and controlling processes. Thus, multiple recent research studies point to sophisticated attacks such as Stuxnet Worm, Rejection of Service (DoS), Distributed Denial of Service (DDoS), Secret, Repetition, Honesty, Botnet, Furtive, Trick, and various attacks targeting these communication networks [63]. In [64], the impact of disruptive attacks on CPS networks is explored. CPS networks monitor and manage physical processes in transportation schemes, water treatment plants, smart grids, and biochemical plants, and attacks on these infrastructures are likely to have catastrophic results [65].

CPSs' ecosystem is structured so that there is a message system at the center of all connections between the bodily and cyber layers [66]. Physical processes can be controlled by CPSs by using sensors, actuators, computers, and message systems [67]. Controllers acquire sensor data through communications networks. The actuators receive commands from the controllers based on these measurements. Auxiliary actuators also translate controller commands into physical action. When these actions occur, measurements from sensors are transmitted to controllers, and instructions from controllers are transmitted to actuators for real-time processing to take place. During these operations, data flows across message systems, which are frequently the board of cyberattacks (Figure 1.5).

Cyber-physical systems pose distinct threats and impacts because of their unique characteristics, according to [69]. DDoS and DoS attacks on smart grids might exhaust resources, according to [70]. According to [71], other possible implications of these attacks include a system's inability to avert catastrophic destruction, as well as a loss of critical physical processes in an open loop. An exploit could be used to exploit a software weakness and launch a shellcode attack on the CPS network. Alternatively, worm attacks can spread rapidly over CPS networks via replication, especially if the

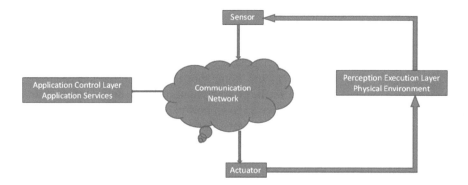

FIGURE 1.5   The CPS ecosystem as a miniaturized model [68].

targets have security vulnerabilities. This is achieved using the growth concept, which utilizes a recursive technique to make this bout feast over the message system of the CPS network [72,73]. There are several additional difficulties when dealing with the safety of CPSs, as outlined in the miniaturized model [74].

A majority of strategies fail to anticipate these attacks very accurately, so picking one that can adapt to a variety of attacks is essential. The high harshness of these bouts, as well as their possibility to intensify and compromise the privacy, truth, and convenience of CPS courses and message systems, leads us to suggest a cross model for interruption forecast on CPS networks. A bio-inspired method of hyperparameter search is cast-off in the model to select the optimal deep neural network structure suitable for anticipating any bout on the message systems of CPSs. Bio-inspired search combined with deep learning was selected for a variety of reasons. These are some of them:

   i) Bio-inspired algorithms are also effective for solving problems requiring optimization to achieve a desired or optimal outcome.
  ii) In bio-inspired algorithms, there is a stochastic optimization algorithm that is computationally realistic and uses randomization and resident hunt to find a solution to an assumed optimization problem with an unruly function.
 iii) In addition to being used to solve exceedingly complex problems, bio-inspired algorithms are rummage-sale to generate solutions in real-time, even in the face of dynamic problem definitions, shifting constraints, and unbalanced datasets.
  iv) Cyber-attack detection and prediction are among the bulk of studies focusing on deep learning in cybersecurity [75]. Deep learning is among the bulk of studies focusing on cyber-attack detection and prediction [75].
   v) Data representations can be learned through deep learning and attacks can be modeled from attack data.
  vi) Meanwhile, deep learning buildings are overall purpose estimate copies that can discover the association amid contribution data and productions of a neural network regardless of its difficulty, and they can be used to solve attack prediction problems.

1.5.1 Existing Works using Bioinspiration Deep Neural Networks

Computer-based algorithms and processes regulate and monitor CPS mechanisms. Data transmission across the communication networks of CPSs entities is vulnerable to attack because of the implementation of these algorithms. CPS security has been the subject of several research projects, including [76]. With supervised machine learning methods, prediction models are generated from control data streaming from power systems and gas pipelines.

Before revealing the real class label, the learner guesses the class label of the inward instance based on given criteria. The loss measured here is the change between the predicted true label and the exposed factual label, and it plays an important role in updating the model for good results on binary and multiclass datasets. Although cost-sensitive and potentially resolving class injustice, hyperparameters are selected based on skilled knowledge, which might impact the accuracy of learning algorithms.

Orojloo H et al. [77] suggest a technique for assessing the impact of assaults on a CPS both directly and indirectly. The impact of attack proliferation is explored by examining how systems behave both during normal operation and under attack. By comparison with usual and irregular CPS conduct, attacks on the CPS are graded based on either their straight or unintended effects on the system's bodily subtleties. As a result, sensitive assets and system control settings can be detected. The proposed technique may provide a higher level of accuracy.

An integrated model-based technique is used by Tantawy et al [78] to assess the security risk of a CPS. By determining the physical dangers to the CPS networks, this paper proposes a robust security strategy. Models for network and data flow are used to explore cyber-attacks in the environment of CPS, which can have a range of effects on the CPS. As a result of the technique, cost-effective and secure designs could be developed, but it was based on the assumption that every occurrence was certain, with a possibility of one, which might lead to insufficient designs. As a result, the risk assessment model overlooked the attacker profile, which is essential for the risk assessment process.

Mo researchers Sinopoli [79] and Yin [80] investigated honesty bouts on CPSs using separate line time-invariant schemes. The researchers analyzed the system's robustness to integrity attacks, identifying accessible methods and approximating the attack mistake. A technique based on the ellipsoidal distribution was used to compute the outer estimates of the accessible set. Under certain circumstances, an attacker may be able to undermine the system if the accessible set is unbounded.

In [80], the use of a hidden Markov chain model and a finite state model were proposed for identifying malicious attacks on CPSs. A multi-stage attack on a CPS could be identified using this approach to safeguard critical resources and infrastructure. This approach was successful in 86.2% of cases. Considering that these hits are incapacitating, precision must be enhanced. Additionally, [81–82] proposed a system-based approach to determining if covert deception attacks are successful. The study examined three different types of furtive dishonesty bouts based on the ability of the attacker to damage the organization, knowledge of its dynamics, and available hypothesis testing tools. It is crucial to increase the accuracy of this system because its usefulness is influenced by its accuracy.

Using a different set of circumstances, Nizam et al examined the identification and deterrence of physical system intrusions in a cyber-physical system. To detect and categorize DDoS and untrue data injection attacks (FLAC), they used the Chi-Square detection algorithm, as well as the fuzzy logic-based attack classifier. Their efforts were successful 96% of the time. Due to the variety of techniques used to resolve a categorization problem, fuzzy logic usually does not produce accurate results.

For determining onward trails after an attacker to a prey location during a DoS attack situation, [83] examined a unique probabilistic packet marking mechanism. The study found that an average of 23 packets might be misused by an attacker to build a forward channel. By contrast, this method is slow. An attack requiring a deep understanding of the system, such as a covert one or a zero-dynamic one, is extremely difficult to carry out. As discussed in [84], modulation matrices were introduced into the route of the regulator variable star to influence the effort performance of the process and reveal an adversary's attacks. A modulation matrix was designed to identify covert attacks. Although this method produced promising results, it was vulnerable to adversarial attacks because it required perfect system knowledge.

A novel adaptive design was developed by Jin et al [85] to secure CPS sensors and actuators against attacks. To enhance safety and care in CPSs, an adaptive controller was developed that ensured consistent final finiteness when the sensor and actuator were assaulted. The design appears to be capable of handling nonlinearities and uncertainty in a way that can be integrated into the verification and validation of system performance and adversarial attacks, but this is yet to be explored.

For identifying new CPS attacks, [86–87] proposes a semi-supervised method. An automatic detection process may include both unlabeled and labeled data for the detection of unknown malware. According to the SVM employed in this analysis, the accuracy of static malware data analysis is 95.79%, while dynamic malware analysis is 100%. SVM training and convergence may take a long time when dealing with large datasets, however. Hyperparameters were designated using expert information, which included some trial and error. A technique developed by Beg and colleagues to identify false-data inoculation bouts on cyber-physical DC microgrids was published in 1987. An attack to identify a false-data inoculation attack was recognized as a discrepancy between the candidate and the real invariants. A high level of computational complexity was required for their model to perform well.

Detecting kinetic cyberattacks is suggested as a novel approach in [88]. According to statistical estimation of functions mapping equivalent releases to cyber area information, the scheme's behavior could be predicted with an accuracy of 77.45%. The accuracy shows poor performance, and keeping up with the growing cyber-physical attack situation will be difficult. The authors [89] presented a new architecture for intrusion detection in a CPS that relied on a distributed blind approach. A modified Bayesian likelihood ratio test was used in the proposed method, and closed-form formulations were developed for the test statistic. Even with its complexity and high accuracy, the model achieved a 99.75% accuracy.

An examination of confrontational attacks on the IoT is discussed in [90]. Using generative adversarial networks (GANs) as a distributed intrusion detection technique, after performing 5000 iterations on privacy-preserving IoT networks, the authors discovered highly impressive results. GANs, on the other hand, is based on the idea of confrontational learning, which, according to Mo et al. [91], provides the opportunity for balancing and synchronizing two adversarial networks during the exercise procedure. In the nonappearance of this balance and synchronization, achieving excellent training results may be difficult. GANs are also susceptible to mode collapse in Mobile Ad Hoc Networks (MANETs) and Wireless sensor networks (WSNs), making them challenging to train and necessitating substantial data and adjustments [92].

As an intrusion detection system, deep learning architectures such as Convolutional Neural Networks (CNNs) and their derivatives are offered [93]. A high-level representation of high-level feature sets could be charted to a low-level representation of system traffic. The CNN three-layer RNN network obtained the greatest accuracy of 96.9% by utilizing multiple network topologies of a CNN ranging from 1 to 3 layers. These topologies included recurrent neural networks (RNN), Long Short Term Memory (LSTM), and Gated Recurrent Units (GRU). However, these models have some drawbacks. As a starting point, the network topology is decided using expert knowledge, thereby requiring a great deal of feature engineering to achieve convergence in a short period. This method also relies on outdated datasets that don't accurately depict the diversity of attacks and overall network architecture that exist in a real-world network. As a consequence, the method needs to be enhanced.

There is a mechanism presented in [94] for detecting both shallow and deep network intrusions. The low and deep networks are trained for binary classification tasks and multi-class classification tasks using the KDD Cup '99 and NSL-KDD datasets. Conferring to the trials, deep networks are more effective than shallow networks.

The heftiness of deep intrusion recognition representations is examined in [95]. Analyzing the presentation of each model in a non-adversarial and an adversarial setting takes advantage of the NSL-KDD dataset. A wide variety of deep learning and machine learning models remain to be less accurate when hostile samples are used. Moreover, their modes of operation have given poor results when compared with advanced technologies.

Deep neural networks are used to build intrusion detection systems that can detect damaging activity, such as DDoS and malware cyber threats. Malware attacks are detected with a 99.44% accuracy, while DDoS attacks are detected with a 99.79% accuracy. Results recommend this security solution to small and medium businesses. The method uses binary classification of assaults, making it impossible to determine the kind or class of attack.

To build a flow-based anomaly IDS in a multiclass environment, [96,97] built a multilayer, fully connected neural network. Data from the CICIDS2017 dataset was rummaged to authenticate the model. However, the model was not sophisticated enough to deal with today's sophisticated attacks or to be able to identify the type of attack by analysis. The authors proposed a hybrid strategy for detecting IoT network attacks based on two levels of detection. To categorize network traffic as abnormal or normal, flow-based irregularity detection was used at the first level. The second level of feature selection was achieved using Recursive Feature Elimination (RFE).

Ensemble deep learning is used to detect and localize physical layer threats in a cyber-physical grid.

1.6   DETECTING PHYSICAL LAYER ATTACKS USING DEEP LEARNING ENSEMBLES

Different wireless communication technologies and protocols (CPS) are used to facilitate the two-way flow of information in today's dangerous substructures (known as Cyber-Physical Systems). Wireless communication networks in CPSs provide several advantages, including unrestricted access to information, low connection and upkeep costs, and distant request provision [99]. Health care, transportation, industry, and critical infrastructure are all affected by CPS technology. Often referred to as the smart grid, a cyber-physical smart grid is a good example of CPS.

Communication networks and sensors are integrated into electricity infrastructure as part of a "smart grid". This system uses IoT plans and progressive metering infrastructure (AMI) to monitor and control feeding behavior and gather ingesting statistics. It is skillful and monitored by a Supervisory Control And Data Acquisition (SCADA) organization. By allowing two-way communications within the system's infrastructure, wireless network technology improves the competence of the control cohort and distribution [100]. A smart meter and sensor network linked to the power grid network can provide real-time data about power consumption to production centers, which can be rummaged to plan an effective cohort and delivery plan [101].

Some various resources and technologies have been integrated into the smart grid system, including keen rhythms to collect incoming data and the SCADA system to screen and switch control cohorts. Using a two-way communication system, SCADA works with Advanced Metering Infrastructure (AMI) to identify detailed power consumption and distribute power accordingly. There are various systems available for two-way announcements, including Home Area Networks (HANs), Neighborhood Area Networks (NANs), and Wide-Area Networks (WANs), which connect power stations, substations, and operation centers. Additionally, SCADA allows for the expansion of national distribution sites as well as large geographic areas [102]. Through the smart grid, broadcast and delivery networks, structure supervisors, and diverse forms of energy cohort, including green energy, can interact. The smart grid enables interaction between broadcast and delivery networks, structure supervisors, and various energy producing sources, including green energy.

However, even though the smart grid is advantageous in many ways, its communication network's integration into any system leaves it vulnerable to cyberattacks. This vulnerability has been identified by several organizations throughout the world. These include the National Institute of Standards and Technology (NIST), the Energy Expert Cyber Security Platform (EESCP), and the European Commission's Smart Grids Taskforce [103]. Communications infrastructures could be harmed substantially by adversaries who take advantage of vulnerabilities in communication networks [104]. Several instances of control theft probed by the FBI [105] as well as the Black Energy virus that caused power outages in Ukraine in 2016 are examples of contemporary cyber-attacks.

1.6.1 PRESENT LEVEL OF KNOWLEDGE

A large number of approaches to keen grid safety and attack discovery have been presented in works [106], since smart grids are vulnerable and have a significant impact on human lives. State estimation algorithms have been proposed as models for attack detection [107]. algorithms. One way to speed up the search for viable sensor sets is to employ a Satisfiability Modulo Theory (SMT)-based search algorithm [108]. There is also literature discussing how to control tactics that can be used to locate an assault. An analysis of a methodology for determining the assault site based on an entire amount of nursing devices equivalent to double the number of cooperated sensors [109] was offered in one study. An additional study [110] presents a method to counter zero-dynamic assaults that take place when actuators are compromised, and not sensors.

Hadziosmanovic et al. [111] used Modbus-based detection as well. They showed how to identify assaults using Modbus, an industrial communication protocol, by monitoring the system's state variables. However, another article [112] shows that the Modbus protocol is vulnerable to flooding assaults. Several articles provide attack applications for Modbus, exposing its susceptibility to a variety of assaults. Chen et al. suggested an actual cyber-physical testbed [113] that combined communication and power system simulations. They also successfully deployed man-in-the-middle and overflowing assaults to expose its susceptibility to cyber-attacks. In addition to replay assaults, another work [114] shows these attacks and proposes a unique role-based access control (RBAC) paradigm for safe authorization. Another study [114] illustrates these attacks and suggests a new role-based access control (RBAC) paradigm for secure authorization in addition to replay assaults. Because of their complexity and unpredictability, cyber-physical grids have security weaknesses. Because attackers can access networks through a range of endpoints, research into the security of such systems examines a variety of defense mechanisms in addition to the detection and classification of bouts. Attacks on RFID networks [115] and denial of service (DoS) attacks on generic systems [116] have both been mitigated using game theory and Nash equilibrium.

The works focus on identifying susceptibilities and potential bout conditions that can circumvent current security measures, in addition to identifying occurrences and extenuating circumstances. Unobservable attacks, for sample, are assaults in which a sub-status network's and topological data are altered to conceal a physical attack [117]. Assaults like these can overburden a network line, leading to disruptions and breakdowns. Another study [118] examines bouts that board both the physical and cyber at the same time and launch a novel attack method that is undetected by current defaces. As part of this assault, the control center is physically disconnected from a transmission connection before launching an attack on another part of the scheme. Additional attacks against the countryside are planned for the future. These coordinated cyber-physical attacks are described in detail by Chung et al [118].

Attack detection strategies that are purely based on models will not suffice to ensure the security of the smart grid [119], and attack categorization methods need to be scalable for larger systems.

For this reason, intelligent systems and machine learning have been promoted as means of detecting cyber-attacks [120]. Researchers have found that supervised learning techniques result in better overall classification of assaults in general than unsupervised learning techniques. There have been many supervised learning algorithms developed that perform well. Study results compare several different learning techniques and prove that a Gaussian-based Support Vector Machine (SVM) performs better at classifying bigger test systems. Additionally, numerous studies have found that the margin setting algorithm (MSA) outperforms SVM and ANN. Other machine learning methods, such Artificial Immune Systems (AIS) and Support Vector Machines (SVM), can be used to detect bouts in a network. In addition to identifying where the assaults originate, this study also tries to determine what is fueling them. However, despite its positive results, simulations have largely been used to identify and localize threats on the network layer rather than those on the operational technology layer. This research used recurrent neural networks (RNNs) to analyze temporal changes in past information. A variety of other techniques have been used, such as AdaBoost, random forest, and joint trail mining. Similarly Extreme Learning Machines (ELMs) and Margin Setting Algorithms (MSAs) are used to identify data integrity problems. Rather than pinpointing specific system metrics, all of the above research focuses on detecting assaults or identifying types of attacks.

Detecting threats to smart grids and control systems has also been done using deep learning. The use of deep neural networks together with state estimation has been demonstrated for identifying nonlinear structures in electrical weight information. The Phasor Measurement Units (PMUs) provide real-time readings that can be analyzed for an actual finding of False Data Injection (FDI) attacks for cyber-attack mitigation using deep learning. Among the common measures for detection and data handling are deep autoencoders. Even though deep learning techniques enhance detection and classification accuracy as well as processing efficiency in some cases, they lack approaches that link occurrences to specific sites in physical schemes.

1.7 CONCLUSION

Information security teams are increasingly dependent on artificial intelligence to augment their efforts. Humans are incapable of adequately protecting the dynamic enterprise attack surface, so AI provides valuable analysis and threat identification that help cybersecurity practitioners reduce breaches and improve security postures. A growing role for artificial intelligence (AI) is being played by IT security teams as they seek to improve their efficiency. As a result, it detects intrusions before they occur, identifies and prioritizes risk, spots malware immediately on a network, guides incident response, and identifies malware before it spreads. To reduce breach risks and improve security posture, security professionals can use artificial intelligence to analyze and detect threats at an enterprise-level attack surface, which humans are incapable of safeguarding. Artificial intelligence can assist in identifying and prioritizing risks, directing incident response, and detecting malware attacks before they occur. Cybersecurity in enterprises is improved by artificial intelligence, despite its limitations.

REFERENCES

1. Digital 2019: Global digital overview (2019). https://datareportal.com/reports/digital-2019-digital-overview.
2. V. Hajisalem, S. Babaie, A hybrid intrusion detection system based on ABC-AFS algorithm for misuse and anomaly detection, *Comput. Netw.* (2018) 136: 37–50.
3. J. Jabez, B. Muthukumar, Intrusion detection system (ids): Anomaly detection using outlier detection approach, *Procedia Comput. Sci.* (2015) 48: 338–346.
4. I. Quepons, Vulnerability and trust, *PhaenEx* (2020) 13: 1–10.
5. C.M. Research, Cyber security market by component, security type, deployment, organization and application – global industry analysis and forecast to 2022 (2017) 202.
6. P. García-Teodoro, J. Díaz-Verdejo, G. Maciá-Fernández, E. Vazquez, Anomaly-based network intrusion detection: Techniques, systems and challenges, *Comput. Secur.* (2009) 28: 18–28.
7. S. Chakrabarti, M. Chakraborty, I. Mukhopadhyay, Study of snort-based IDS. In *ICWET '10: Proceedings of the International Conference and Workshop on Emerging Trends in Technology*, 2010, pp. 43–47.
8. Z. Inayat, A. Gani, N.B. Anuar, M.K. Khan, S. Anwar, Intrusion response systems: Foundations, design, and challenges, *J. Netw. Comput. Appl.* (2016) 62: 53–74.
9. M.A. Ferrag, L. Maglaras, S. Moschoyiannis, H. Janicke, Deep learning for cyber security intrusion detection: Approaches, datasets, and comparative study, *J. Inf. Secur. Appl.* (2020) 50.
10. I. Sharafaldin, A.H. Lashkari, A.A. Ghorbani, Toward generating a new intrusion detection dataset and intrusion traffic characterization. In: *ICISSP 2018: 4th International Conference on Information Systems Security and Privacy*, 2018, pp. 108–116.

11. R. Patil, H. Dudeja, C. Modi, Designing an efficient security framework for detecting intrusions in virtual network of cloud computing, *Comput. Secur.* (2019) 85: 402–422.

12. J. Kim, Y. Shin, E. Choi, An intrusion detection model based on a convolutional neural network, *J Multimed Inf. Syst.* (2019) 6(4): 165–172.

13. V. Kanimozhi, D.T.P. Jacob, Calibration of various optimized machine learning classifiers in network intrusion detection system on the realistic cyber dataset CseCic-Ids2018 using cloud computing, *Int. J. Eng. Appl. Sci. Technol.* (2019) 4: 209–213.

14. C. Khammassi, S. Krichen, A NSGA2-LR wrapper approach for feature selection in network intrusion detection, *Comput. Netw.* (2020) 172: 107183.

15. M. Ring, S. Wunderlich, D. Scheuring, D. Landes, A. Hotho, A survey of network-based intrusion detection data sets, *Comput. Secur.* (2019) 86: 147–167.

16. V. Kanimozhi, T.P. Jacob, Artificial intelligence based network intrusion detection with hyper-parameter optimization tuning on the realistic cyber dataset CSE-CICIDS2018 using cloud computing, *ICT Express* (2019) 5(3): 211–214.

17. N. Moustafa, J. Slay, UNSW-NB15: A comprehensive data set for network intrusion detection systems (UNSW-NB15 network data set). In: *2015 Military Communications and Information Systems Conference (MilCIS)*, 2015.

18. N. Moustafa, J. Slay, The evaluation of network anomaly detection systems: Statistical analysis of the UNSW-NB15 data set and the comparison with the KDD99 data set, *Inf. Secur. J.* (2016) 25(1–3): 18–31.

19. N. Moustafa, J. Slay, G. Creech, Novel geometric area analysis technique for anomaly detection using trapezoidal area estimation on large-scale networks, *IEEE Trans. Big Data* (2019) 5(4): 481–494.

20. J. Zhang, Y. Ling, X. Fu, X. Yang, G. Xiong, R. Zhang, Model of the intrusion detection system based on the integration of spatial-temporal features, *Comput. Secur.* (2020) 89: 101681.

21. F. Gottwalt, E. Chang, T. Dillon, CorrCorr: A feature selection method for multivariate correlation network anomaly detection techniques, *Comput. Secur.* (2019) 83: 234–245.

22. C. Khammassi, S. Krichen, A GA-LR wrapper approach for feature selection in network intrusion detection, *Comput. Secur.* (2017) 70: 255–277.

23. S.M. Kasongo, Y. Sun, A deep learning method with wrapper-based feature extraction for wireless intrusion detection system, *Comput. Secur.* (2020) 92.

24. A. Rashid, M.J. Siddique, S.M. Ahmed, Machine and deep learning based comparative analysis using hybrid approaches for intrusion detection system (2020).

25. J. David, C. Thomas, Efficient DDoS flood attack detection using dynamic thresholding on flow-based network traffic, *Comput. Secur.* (2019) 82 284–295.

26. F. Ertam, I.F. Kilinçer, O. Yaman, Intrusion detection in computer networks via machine learning algorithms. In: *2017 International Artificial Intelligence and Data Processing Symposium (IDAP)*, 2017.

27. C. Kolias, G. Kambourakis, A. Stavrou, S. Gritzalis, Intrusion detection in 802.11 networks: Empirical evaluation of threats and a public dataset, *IEEE Commun. Surv. Tutor.* (2016) 18(1): 184–208.

28. A. Verma, V. Ranga, Statistical analysis of CIDDS-001 dataset for network intrusion detection systems using distance-based machine learning, *Procedia Comput. Sci.* (2018): 709–716.

29. A. Verma, V. Ranga, On evaluation of network intrusion detection systems: Statistical analysis of CIDDS-001 dataset using machine learning techniques, *Pertanika J. Sci. Technol.* (2018) 26 1307–1332.

30. Y. Xin, L. Kong, Z. Liu, Y. Chen, Y. Li, H. Zhu, M. Gao, H. Hou, C. Wang, Machine learning and deep learning methods for cybersecurity, *IEEE Access* (2018) 6 35365–35381.

31. J. Song, H. Takakura, Y. Okabe, Description of Kyoto University Benchmark Data, 2010, pp. 10–12.

32. M. Ring, S. Wunderlich, M. Ring, Technical report CIDDS-001 data set (2017) 16: 361–369.

33. M. Ring, S. Wunderlich, D. Grüdl, D. Landes, A. Hotho, Flow-based benchmark data sets for intrusion detection. In: *Proceedings of the 16th European Conference on Cyber Warfare and Security*, 2017, pp. 361–369.

34. A. Shiravi, H. Shiravi, M. Tavallaee, A.A. Ghorbani, Toward developing a systematic approach to generate benchmark datasets for intrusion detection, *Comput. Secur.* (2012): 357–374.

35. Intrusion detection evaluation dataset (CICIDS2017) (n.d.). https://www.unb,Ca/cic/datasets/ids-2017.html.

36. CSE, CIC-IDS2018 on AWS (n.d.). https://www.unb.ca/cic/datasets/ids-2018.html.

37. S. Wang, Y. Gong, G. Chen, Q. Sun, F. Yang, Service vulnerability scanning based on service-oriented architecture in web service environments, *J. Syst. Archit.* (2013).

38. A. Tantawy, S. Abdelwahed, A. Erradi, K. Shaban, Model-based risk assessment for cyber physical systems security, *Comput. Secur.* (2020).

39. C.L. Zhang, G.H. Yang, A.Y. Lu, Resilient observer-based control for cyber-physical systems under denial-of-service attacks, *Inf. Sci. (Ny).* (2021) 545: 102–117.

40. K.B. Virupakshar, M. Asundi, K. Channal, P. Shettar, S. Patil, D.G. Narayan, Distributed denial of service (DDoS) attacks detection system for openstack-based private cloud, *Procedia Comput. Sci.* (2020).

41. L. Barki, A. Shidling, N. Meti, D.G. Narayan, M.M. Mulla, Detection of distributed denial of service attacks in software defined networks. In: *International Conference on Advances in Computing, Communications and Informatics (ICACCI)*, 2016.

42. M.M. Najafabadi, T.M. Khoshgoftaar, C. Kemp, N. Seliya, R. Zuech, Machine learning for detecting brute force attacks at the network level. In: *BIBE '14: Proceedings of the 2014 IEEE International Conference on Bioinformatics and Bioengineering*, 2014.

43. D. Stiawan, M.Y. Idris, R.F. Malik, S. Nurmaini, N. Alsharif, R. Budiarto, Investigating brute force attack patterns in IoT network, *J. Electr. Comput. Eng.* (2019).

44. Exploit-db, anatomy of exploit – world of shellcode, (n.d.) 35646.

45. U.K. Singh, C. Joshi, D. Kanellopoulos, A framework for zero-day vulnerabilities detection and prioritization, *J. Inf. Secur. Appl.* (2019).

46. S.W. Boyd, A.D. Keromytis, SQLrand: Preventing SQL injection attacks, *Lect. Notes Comput. Sci.* (Including Subser. Lect. Notes Artif. Intell. Lect. Notes Bioinformatics) (2004).

47. W.G.J. Halfond, J. Viegas, A. Orso, A classification of SQL injection attacks and countermeasures (2008).

48. S. Mukkamala, G. Janoski, A. Sung, Intrusion detection using neural networks and support vector machines, *Proc. Int. Jt. Conf. Neural Netw.* (2002).

49. S. Han, M. Xie, H. Chen, Y. Ling, Intrusion detection in cyber-physical systems: Techniques and challenges, *IEEE Syst. J.* (2014) 8(4): 1052–1062.

50. N. Shone, T.N. Ngoc, V.D. Phai, Q. Shi, A deep learning approach to network intrusion detection, *IEEE Trans. Emerg. Top. Comput. Intell.* (2018) 2(1): 41–50.

51. B.M. Aslahi-Shahri, R. Rahmani, M. Chizari, A. Maralani, M. Eslami, M.J. Golkar, A. Ebrahimi, A hybrid method consisting of GA and SVM for intrusion detection system, *Neural Comput. Appl.* (2016).

52. S. Sun, Z. Ye, L. Yan, J. Su, R. Wang, Wrapper feature selection based on lightning attachment procedure optimization and support vector machine for intrusion detection. In: *Proceedings of the IEEE 4th International Symposium on Wireless Systems within the International Conferences on Intelligent Data Acquisition and Advanced Computing Systems, IDAACS-SWS*, 2018, pp. 41–46.

53. S. Mukkamala, A.H. Sung, A. Abraham, Intrusion detection using an ensemble of intelligent paradigms, *J. Netw. Comput. Appl.* (2005) 28(2): 167–182.

54. B. Dong, X. Wang, Comparison deep learning method to traditional methods using for network intrusion detection (2016).

55. A. McDole, M. Abdelsalam, M. Gupta, S. Mittal, Analyzing CNN based behavioural malware detection techniques on cloud IaaS, *Cloud Comput. Cloud* (2020) 2020: 64–79.

56. M. Gupta, J. Benson, F. Patwa, R. Sandhu, V. Secure, 2V and V2I communication in intelligent transportation using cloudlets, *IEEE Trans. Serv. Comput.* (2020) 1.

57. D. Gupta, S. Bhatt, M. Gupta, O. Kayode, A.S. Tosun, Access control model for Google cloud IoT. In: *Proceedings of the IEEE 6th International Conference on Big Data Security on Cloud (BigDataSecurity), IEEE International Conference on High Performance and Smart Computing, (HPSC) and IEEE International Conference on Intelligent Data and Security (IDS)*, 2020, pp. 198–208.

58. F. Farahnakian, J. Heikkonen, A deep auto-encoder based approach for intrusion detection system (2018).

59. Y. Mirsky, T. Doitshman, Y. Elovici, A. Shabtai, Kitsune: An ensemble of autoencoders for online network intrusion detection (2018).

60. Q. Niyaz, W. Sun, A.Y. Javaid, M. Alam, A deep learning approach for network intrusion detection system (2015).

61. T.A. Tang, L. Mhamdi, D. McLernon, S.A.R. Zaidi, M. Ghogho, Deep learning approach for network intrusion detection in software defined networking (2016).

62. L. Cao, X. Jiang, Y. Zhao, S. Wang, D. You, X. Xu, A survey of network attacks on cyberphysical systems, *IEEE Access* (2020 Mar 2) 8: 44219–44227.

63. R. Alguliyev, Y. Imamverdiyev, L. Sukhostat, Cyber-physical systems and their security issues, *Comput. Ind.* (2018 Sep 1) 100: 212–223.

64. H. Orojloo, M.A. Azgomi, A method for evaluating the consequence propagation of security attacks in cyber–physical systems, *Future Gener. Comput. Syst.* (2017 Feb 1) 67: 57–71.

65. X. Liu, M. Dong, K. Ota, L.T. Yang, A. Liu, Trace malicious source to guarantee cyber security for mass monitor critical infrastructure, *J. Comput. Syst. Sci.* (2018 Dec 1) 98: 1–26.

66. G. Li, Y. Shen, P. Zhao, X. Lu, J. Liu, Y. Liu, S.C. Hoi, Detecting cyberattacks in industrial control systems using online learning algorithms, *Neurocomputing* (2019 Oct 28) 364: 338–348.

67. H. Orojloo, M. Abdollahi Azgomi, Predicting the behavior of attackers and the consequences of attacks against cyber-physical systems, *Sec. Commun. Netw.* (2016) 9(18): 6111–6136.

68. A.E. Ibor, O.B. Okunoye, F.A. Oladeji, A. Khadeejah, C. Abdulsalam, Novel hybrid model for intrusion prediction on cyber physical systems' communication networks based on bio-inspired deep neural network structure, *J. Inf. Sec. Appl.* (2022) 65: 103107.

69. A.G. Busygin, A.S. Konoplev, D.P. Zegzhda, Providing stable operation of selforganizing cyber- physical system via adaptive topology management methods using blockchain-like directed acyclic graph, *Autom. Control Comput. Sci.* (2018) 52(8): 1080–1083.

70. I. Ko, D. Chambers, E. Barrett, Adaptable feature-selecting and threshold-moving complete autoencoder for DDoS flood attack mitigation, *J. Inf. Sec. Appl.* (2020 Dec 1) 55: 102647.

71. X. Ge, Q.L. Han, X.M. Zhang, D. Ding, F. Yang, Resilient and secure remote monitoring for a class of cyber-physical systems against attacks, *Inf. Sci.* (2020 Feb 1) 512: 1592–1605.

72. R. Mitchell, I.R. Chen, A survey of intrusion detection techniques for cyber-physical systems, *ACM Comput. Surv. (CSUR)* (2014 Mar 1) 46(4): 1–29.

73. F. Pasqualetti, F. Dörfler, F. Bullo, Attack detection and identification in cyberphysical systems, *IEEE Trans. Autom. Control* (2013 Jun 21) 58(11): 2715–2729.

74. E. Anthi, L. Williams, M. Rhode, P. Burnap, A. Wedgbury, Adversarial attacks on machine learning cybersecurity defences in Industrial Control Systems, *J. Inf. Sec. Appl.* (2021 May 1) 58: 102717.

75. M.A. Ferrag, L. Maglaras, S. Moschoyiannis, H. Janicke, Deep learning for cyber security intrusion detection: Approaches, datasets, and comparative study, *J. Inf. Sec. Appl.* (2020 Feb 1) 50: 102419.

76. G. Wu, J. Sun, J. Chen, Optimal data injection attacks in cyber-physical systems, *IEEE Trans. Cybern.* (2018 Jun 26) 48(12): 3302–3312.

77. H. Orojloo, M.A. Azgomi, A method for evaluating the consequence propagation of security attacks in cyber–physical systems, *Future Gener. Comput. Syst.* (2017 Feb 1) 67: 57–71.

78. A. Tantawy, S. Abdelwahed, A. Erradi, K. Shaban, Model-based risk assessment for cyber physical systems security, *Comput. Sec.* (2020 Sep 1) 96: 101864.

79. Y. Mo, B. Sinopoli, Integrity attacks on cyber-physical systems. In: *Proceedings of the 1st International Conference on High Confidence Networked Systems*, 2012 Apr 17, pp. 47–54.

80. C.M. Chen, H.W. Hsiao, P.Y. Yang, Y.H. Ou, Defending malicious attacks in cyber physical systems. In: *2013 IEEE 1st International Conference on Cyber-Physical Systems, Networks, and Applications (CPSNA)*, IEEE, 2013 Aug 19, pp. 13–18.

81. C. Kwon, W. Liu, I. Hwang, Security analysis for cyber-physical systems against stealthy deception attacks. In: *2013 American Control Conference*, IEEE, 2013 Jun 17, pp. 3344–3349.

82. F. Nizam, S. Chaki, S. Al Mamun, M.S. Kaiser, Attack detection and prevention in the cyber physical system. In: *2016 International Conference on Computer Communication and Informatics (ICCCI)*, IEEE, 2016 Jan 7, pp. 1–6.

83. A.Y. Nur, M.E. Tozal, Defending cyber-physical systems against dos attacks. In: *2016 IEEE International Conference on Smart Computing (SMARTCOMP)*, IEEE; 2016 May 18, pp. 1–3.

84. A. Hoehn, P. Zhang, Detection of covert attacks and zero dynamics attacks in cyberphysical systems. In: *2016 American Control Conference (ACC)*, IEEE, 2016 Jul 6, pp. 302–307.

85. X. Jin, W.M. Haddad, T. Yucelen, An adaptive control architecture for mitigating sensor and actuator attacks in cyber-physical systems, *IEEE Trans. Autom. Control* (2017 Jan 11) 62(11): 6058–6064.

86. A. Gumaei, M.M. Hassan, S. Huda, M.R. Hassan, D. Camacho, J. Del Ser, G. Fortino, A robust cyberattack detection approach using optimal features of SCADA power systems in smart grids, *Appl. Soft Comput.* (2020 Nov 1) 96: 106658.

87. O.A. Beg, T.T. Johnson, A. Davoudi, Detection of false-data injection attacks in cyberphysical DC microgrids, *IEEE Trans. Ind. Inform.* (2017 Jan 23) 13(5): 2693–2703.

88. S.R. Chhetri, A. Canedo, M.A. Al Faruque, Kcad: Kinetic cyber-attack detection method for cyber-physical additive manufacturing systems. In: *IEEE/ACM International Conference on Computer-Aided Design (ICCAD)*, IEEE, 2016, pp. 1–8.

89. H. Sadreazami, A. Mohammadi, A. Asif, K.N. Plataniotis, Distributed-graph-based statistical approach for intrusion detection in cyber-physical systems, *IEEE Trans. Signal Inf. Process. Netw.* (2017 Sep 7) 4(1): 137–147.

90. A. Ferdowsi, W. Saad, Generative adversarial networks for distributed intrusion detection in the internet of things. In: *2019 IEEE Global Communications Conference (GLOBECOM)*, IEEE, 2019 Dec 9, pp. 1–6.

91. Y. Hong, U. Hwang, J. Yoo, S. Yoon, How generative adversarial networks and their variants work: An overview, *ACM Comput. Surv. (CSUR)* (2019 Feb 13) 52(1): 1–43.

92. D.G. Reina, S.L. Toral, F. Barrero, N. Bessis, E. Asimakopoulou, The role of ad hoc networks in the internet of things: A case scenario for smart environments. In: *Internet of Things and Inter-Cooperative Computational Technologies for Collective Intelligence*, Springer, Berlin, Heidelberg, 2013, pp. 89–113.

93. R. Vinayakumar, S. Kp, P. Poornachandran, Applying convolutional neural network for network intrusion detection. In: *2017 International Conference on Advances in Computing, Communications and Informatics (ICACCI)*, 2017, pp. 1222–1228.

94. R. Vinayakumar, K.P. Soman, P. Poornachandran, Evaluating effectiveness of shallow and deep networks to intrusion detection system. In: *2017 International Conference on Advances in Computing, Communications and Informatics (ICACCI)*, 2017, pp. 1282–1289.

95. S. Sriram, K. Simran, R. Vinayakumar, S. Akarsh, K.P. Soman, Towards evaluating the robustness of deep intrusion detection models in adversarial environment, *Commun. Comput. Inf. Sci.* 1208 CCIS 2020:. p. 111–120.

96. D. Chamou, P. Toupas, E. Ketzaki, S. Papadopoulos, K.M. Giannoutakis, A. Drosou, D. Tzovaras, Intrusion detection system based on network traffic using deep neural networks. In: *IEEE International Workshop on Computer Aided Modeling and Design of Communication Links and Networks*, 2019, pp. 1–6.

97. P. Toupas, D. Chamou, K.M. Giannoutakis, A. Drosou, D. Tzovaras, An intrusion detection system for multi-class classification based on deep neural networks. In: *The Eighteenth International Conference on Machine Learning and Applications (ICMLA 2019)*, 2019, pp. 1253–1258.

98. I. Ullah, Q.H. Mahmoud, A two-level hybrid model for anomalous activity detection in IoT networks. In: *2019 16th IEEE Annual Consumer Communications & Networking Conference (CCNC)*, 2019, pp. 1–6.

99. L. Monostori, Cyber-physical production systems: Roots, expectations and R&D challenges, *Proc. CIRP* (2014) 17: 9–13, Variety Management in Manufacturing.

100. X. Fang, S. Misra, G. Xue, D. Yang, Smart grid — The new and improved power grid: A survey, *IEEE Commun. Surv. Tutor.* (2012) 14(4): 944–980.

101. X. Fang, S. Misra, G. Xue, D. Yang, Smart grid — The new and improved power grid: A survey, *IEEE Commun. Surv. Tutor.* (2012) 14(4): 944–980.

102. B. Neyshabur, S. Bhojanapalli, D. McAllester, N. Srebro, Exploring generalization in deep learning. In: *Proceedings of the 31st International Conference on Neural Information Processing Systems, Nips'17, Eventplace: Long Beach, California, USA.* Curran Associates Inc., 2017, pp. 5949–5958.

103. The Smart Grid Interoperability Panel–Smart Grid Cybersecurity Committee, Guidelines for smart grid cybersecurity, Tech. Rep., (NIST IR 7628r1) National Institute of Standards and Technology, 2014.

104. P.N. Bahrami, A. Dehghantanha, T. Dargahi, R.M. Parizi, K.-K.R. Choo, H.H. Javadi, Cyber kill chain-based taxonomy of advanced persistent threat actors: Analogy of tactics, techniques, and procedures, *J. Inf. Process. Syst.* (2019) 15(4) 865–889.

105. U.S.G.A. Office, Cybersecurity: Challenges in securing the electricity grid, CreateSpace independent publishing platform (2012).

106. J. Sakhnini, H. Karimipour, A. Dehghantanha, R.M. Parizi, G. Srivastava, Security aspects of internet of things aided smart grids: A bibliometric survey, internet things, 2019, p. 100111.

107. A. Tajer, S. Kar, H.V. Poor, S. Cui, Distributed joint cyber attack detection and state recovery in smart grids. In: *2011 IEEE International Conference on Smart Grid Communications, SmartGridComm*, IEEE, Brussels, Belgium, 2011, pp. 202–207.

108. Y. Shoukry, M. Chong, M. Wakaiki, P. Nuzzo, A. Sangiovanni-Vincentelli, S.A. Seshia, J.A.P. Hespanha, P. Tabuada, SMT-based observer design for cyber-physical systems under sensor attacks, *ACM Trans. Cyber Phys. Syst.* (2018) 2(1).

109. S. Yong, M.Q. Foo, E. Frazzoli, Robust and resilient estimation for cyberphysical systems under adversarial attacks. In: *2016 American Control Conference, ACC*, 2016, pp. 308–315.

110. A. Teixeira, I. Shames, H. Sandberg, K.H. Johansson, Revealing stealthy attacks in control systems. In: *2012 50th Annual Allerton Conference on Communication, Control, and Computing*, Allerton, 2012, pp. 1806–1813.

111. D. Hadžiosmanoviundefined, R. Sommer, E. Zambon, P.H. Hartel, Through the eye of the PLC: Semantic security monitoring for industrial processes. In: *Proceedings of the 30th Annual Computer Security Applications Conference, ACSAC '14*, Association for Computing Machinery, New York, 2014, pp. 126–135.

112. S. Bhatia, N. Kush, C.I. Djamaludin, A.J. Akande, E. Foo, Practical modbus flooding attack and detection. In: *AISC* 2014.

113. B. Chen, N. Pattanaik, A. Goulart, K.L. Butler-purry, D. Kundur, Implementing attacks for modbus/TCP protocol in a real-time cyber physical system test bed. In: *2015 IEEE International Workshop Technical Committee on Communications Quality and Reliability, CQR*, 2015, pp. 1–6.

114. S. Figueroa-Lorenzo, J. Añorga, S. Arrizabalaga, A role-based access control model in modbus SCADA systems: A centralized model approach, Vol. 19, MDPI, 2019.

115. E.E. Tsiropoulou, J.S. Baras, S. Papavassiliou, G. Qu, On the mitigation of interference imposed by intruders in passive RFID networks. In: Q. Zhu, T. Alpcan, E. Panaousis, M. Tambe, W. Casey (Eds.), *Decision and Game Theory for Security*, Springer International Publishing, Cham, 2016, pp. 62–80.

116. H. Bedi, S. Roy, S. Shiva, Game theory-based defense mechanisms against ddos attacks on TCP/TCP-friendly flows. In: *IEEE Symposium on Computational Intelligence in Cyber Security, CICS*, 2011, pp. 129–136.

117. J. Zhang, L. Sankar, Physical system consequences of unobservable stateand-topology cyber-physical attacks, *IEEE Trans. Smart Grid* (2016) 7(4): 2016–2025.

118. H.-M. Chung, W.-T. Li, C. Yuen, W.-H. Chung, Y. Zhang, C.-K. Wen, Local cyber-physical attack for masking line outage and topology attack in smart grid, *IEEE Trans. Smart Grid* (2019) 10(4): 4577–4588.

119. Y. Mo, T.H.-J. Kim, K. Brancik, D. Dickinson, H. Lee, A. Perrig, B. Sinopoli, Cyber–physical security of a smart grid infrastructure, *Proc. IEEE* 100(1): 195–209.

120. X.-L. Huang, X. Ma, F. Hu, Editorial: Machine learning and intelligent communications | springerlink, *Mobile Networks and Applications*, Springer International Publishing, 2018, pp. 68–70.

2 Cybercrimes in the Associated World

R. Gunavathi and K. Mani Bharathi

2.1 INTRODUCTION: WHY, WHAT, WHO

The Internet has created a major kind of revolution in human interactions. Almost four decades have passed since the beginning of the telecommunication era. Now in the 21st century, all activities we are performing are becoming digitalized. We are living in a world of digital technology where everything is being automated and flexibile – switching human life into a robotic nature. The Internet has become a technical boon to humanity. The term "hacking" has become very popular since the invention of the very first personal computer Altair 8800 in the 1970s.

In this technological world, a new strain of techno crime called cybercrime is emerging. In this chapter, we will explore "cybercrime" or "E-crime," which involves criminals using computer systems and smart devices as tools or targets. There is a myth that hacking is the only kind of E-crime that evolves. But hacking is just one part of cybercrime and it's not the whole of it.

Why are cybercrimes taking place? What does an attacker gain by doing them? Such questions arise in everyone's mind. Criminals commit these cyber attacks or impose harm to the victim's system mainly for five reasons: fame, fun or thrill, personal moral compass, money (notoriety), and revenge. The motives of the attacks will be different in different scenarios. Here we not only have the evil hackers but also the defenders and offenders to protect our valuable assets. And we call the super heroes white hat hackers or information security analysts and specialists. Professionals participating in cyber activities are referred to as the following (Figure 2.1).

These Hats will be identified based on their level of knowledge and acquired traits.

2.2 THE FIRST CYBER ATTACKS

Many people think that cyber attack is a new thing which has evolved over the last 15 to 20 years. But when we scroll back to the past, the first cyber and computer worm attacks occurred in 1971, the first Denial-of-Service attack in 1988 (Morris worm), and the very first Trojan horse attack in 1989 (AIDS Trojan Ransomware). Cybercrime assaults mark their place in history. Multiple cyber security companies and groups have started protecting valuable assets from cybercriminals or intruders, simply called "hackers".

Computer Misuse Act 1990 in the United Kingdom: The very first legislation against cybercriminals was effectively passed in the UK in the year 1990. Worms, such as ILOVEYOU, CODERED, SASSER, and MORRIS, continue to play a significant historical role. Over time, several famous hacking groups such as Anonymous, Chaos, Legion of Doom, and Hactivists have emerged.

DOI: 10.1201/9781003251781-2

| | 1 | | 2 | | 3 | | 4 | | 5 | | 6 | | 7 | |
| Script Kiddie | White Hat | Black Hat | Gray Hat | Green Hat | Red Hat | Blue Hat |

FIGURE 2.1   White hat hackers: cybercrime activities.

TABLE 2.1
Classification of Cyber Attacks

Child pornography Cyber terrorism Stock manipulation Cyber bully/ cyber stalking	Intellectual property theft Phishing	Unauthorized access Wiretapping (call record) Embezzlement (money or information) Economic crimes credit Card fraud
Creating malwares DOS attacks Identity theft Espionage (spying)	Salami slicing Scam (duplicate sites) Spamming: (unwanted mails) Spoofing: (personal information stolen)	Employee sabotage Copyright violation

2.2.1   CHARACTERISTICS AND PURPOSE OF CYBER ATTACKS

Cyber attacks are like an ocean, where plenty of new threats and attack vectors are being classified into several categories. Let us discuss some of these categories first in detail. However, the crime classification that follows does not encompass the whole of it (Table 2.1).

2.3   PHASES OF CYBER KILL CHAIN

The cyber kill chain is one of the traditional security mechanisms or models which explain the scenario of how to defend against each attack at every phase of the threat. This model explains how advanced persistent threats (APT) execute attacks, the severity of their impact, and the defense mechanisms required to protect important assets (Figure 2.2).

The main objective of this model is to understand the stages of each attack and to provide remedial measures to stop those attacks in a better way (Figure 2.3).

2.4   LEGAL CLASSIFICATION

In very simple words, cybercrime is an unlawful activity where the computer is used as a tool or a target for committing attacks or crimes. These criminal activities include theft, fraud, forgery,

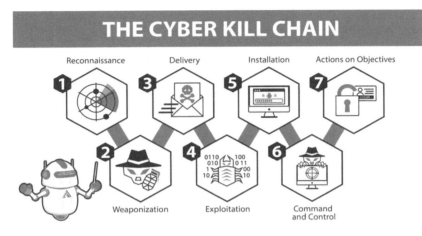

FIGURE 2.2 Phases of the cyber kill chain. Source: https://miro.medium.com/ The Computer Security Incident Response Team (CSIRT) established the traditional cyber security strategy known as the cyber death chain.

FIGURE 2.3 Classical approach of cyber security. Source: https://www.lockheedmartin.com/

defamation, and misusing digital content, and all of these crimes are subject to the Indian Penal Code (IPC) and Information Technology Act (IT Act, 2000).

We can categorize computer crimes in two ways:

- Using the computer as a target: Using a computer system as a target, the attacker performs malicious attacks on the target system (e.g. hacking, Denial-of-Service (DOS) attacks, virus/worm attacks).
- Using the computer as a weapon or tool: Instead of protecting victim computers, attackers began leveraging their own systems as a weapon or tool (e.g. cyber terrorism, credit card frauds, Intellectual Property Rights (IPR) violations, pornography, Electronic Fund Transfer (EFT) frauds).

For committing crimes using computers as a weapon, the attackers safeguard themselves using VPNs, proxy servers, and firewalls and hide their personal identities.

2.4.1 CYBERCRIME VS. CYBER ESPIONAGE

Cyber espionage is a kind of stealing of information which is not publicly available and is a part of cybercrime. Cybercrime includes the whole of illegal activities which pose a threat to a single person or a small entity (e.g. DOS and Salami Slicing)

Cyber espionage involves obtaining confidential information or resources through illegal means such as hacking, zero-day exploits, social engineering attacks, waterhole attacks, and spear phishing.

2.4.2 CYBER WAR VS. CYBER TERRORISM

Unlike cyber espionage and cybercrime, the terms "cyber war" and "cyber terrorism" refer to targeting a group of people or a society or some large community with the motive of creating a riot between them by violating the law.

Cyber terrorism includes attacks that lead to severe damage, such as body injury or sometimes even death, or major economic loss, massive explosions, and plane crashes, depending upon the impact of the violation. Cyber conflicts and terrorism often involve using parties, faiths, castes, and languages to distribute harsh, nasty, and unpleasant terminology to the public or opposing community members.

Cyber warfare or cyber war describes cyber acts which disrupt critical infrastructure systems by subjecting them to armed attacks and by using force against the territorial integrity or political independence of any region or state.

Cyber laws are very important because they traverse all aspects of transactions and activities which are carried out through the Internet and digital devices. And these cyber laws vary according to the country and sometimes the state and based on the crime rate. The working policy and the governing body of the investigation agency differ for each country.

2.5 MALWARE BREAKDOWN

    a. **Family: Stealth virus, polymorphic virus, dropper, adware, macro virus, etc.**
    b. **Top ten malware: Zeus, Kovter, Coin miner, Mirai, Ursnif, RAT, etc.**

Malware is a software package embedded with malicious packets or scripts. And the forms of malware are of different perspectives. We can classify the malware into 14 major variations (Table 2.2).

These 14 variations are termed as "malware family" or "malware breakdown" and each one of them is unique. The major malware real world examples are DarkHotel, Stuxnet, Echobot, Zeus,

TABLE 2.2
Classification of Malwares

Adware	Spyware
Worms	Trojans
Rootkits	Keyloggers
Fileless malware	Polymorphic virus
Botnets	Stealth virus
Macro virus	Droppers
Logic bombs	Ransomwares

Kovter, Coinminer, Mirai, Ursnif, and RAT, which have created a huge impact in the digital world by affecting plenty of valuable resources and servers and have enabled remote control to the hackers of victims' devices.

2.5.1 MALWARE

Malware is a Malicious Software (by means of appending scripts or packets or payload injection).

2.5.2 ADWARE

It is a piece of malicious software which comes in the form of pop-ups, unwanted advertisements, etc. by tracking the user's browsing activities. The only difference between adware and spyware is adware never captures keystrokes; instead, it will capture only information about the sites visited. Facebook's application explicitly states that it monitors users' activity after they log off to maintain them in the application for extended periods of time.

2.5.3 SPYWARE

It is a piece of malicious software which collects the information of the user who is operating the system without their knowledge by spying on their activities using some scripts and payload injections. Spyware consists of unstructured messages, payment kinds of information, passwords, and some important confidential credentials.

2.5.4 VIRUSES

One of the myths about the concept of a virus is that it will self replicate on its own. But the truth is, "Virus is a replicating one, not self-replicating", which means the replication is not done on its own as in the case of worms. A virus copies software and waits for the user to activate it. Once the software is activated or installed, the virus copies itself to the next file.

2.5.5 WORMS

Worms are self-replicating ones. They will create their own copies to all the files in the system and will spread through the networks easily to affect the interconnected system or nodes. Stuxnet is one of the major and remarkable worms that have spread across the digital world.

2.5.6 Trojans

It derived its name from the Rome story character the Trojan horse, and this kind of malicious software simply hides itself or protects itself with a shield first before inducing the attack vector. A trojan may hide in user applications, downloadable games, and sometimes even in patch management software.

2.5.6.1 Virus vs. Trojan vs. Worms

A virus needs an infected application to replicate its own copy to affect the system files.

Trojans only need a user or a victim to download their malicious copies from the Internet, and to provide a virtual space for them in the system.

Worms never need any of the above-mentioned scenarios. It neither requires an infected application nor user intervention. Rather a single copy or installation into the system starts its work automatically, like how the Robot named Chitti creates its own army in the movie *Enthiran*.

Stuxnet adeptly performs the roles of viruses, worms, and rootkit files.

2.5.7 Rootkits

It is a software which provides remote access to the user's/victim's system or node and with complete privilege rights so the attacker can customize any system settings for his needs. It will affect the kernels, firmware versions, and root rights, which is downright scary.

2.5.8 Keyloggers

Keyloggers come in the form of both hardware and software and the noticeable one is where the attacker hides the traces of running info in the background so the legitimate user or victim is unable to find out whether any loggers are running in the system without performing some unique analysis methods. These keyloggers will simply monitor and store the keystrokes and try them later on to gain system access. The concept of money laundering has gained popularity in ATM facilities.

This has widely spread with the attack vectors of phishing, whaling, and social engineering mechanisms.

2.5.9 Bots

Bots or botnets simply gain access to your (victim's) system and perform attacks by using the system as a tool to target someone else. Using this botnets concept, an attacker can target or induce attacks against IoT devices, cloud storage devices, high end networks, sophisticated servers, and supply chains simply by inducing or activating Distributed Denial of Service (DDOS) attacks.

2.5.10 Ransomware

Malware that encrypts files or folders and prevents access until the attacker decrypts them. The attacker will demand a bribe for decryption, known as a ransom. Until the ransom is released, the files will remain encrypted. This ransomware attack has a unique feature that doubles the ransom value if not decrypted within the specified time frame. There is no proof of trust after paying the ransom to the perpetrator. Creating backups of our periodicals is always a good idea.

2.6   WHAT IS THE PROPER WAY TO MAKE BACKUPS?

Data is one of the wealthiest assets in the digital world. How well we can segregate our data through different means of a database medium defines how secure our data is. Here we suggest some of the mechanisms we have to follow to create a good backup model. These six models seem to be effective:

1. Backup all your data with a secondary storage USB drive .
2. Backup all your data with an external Harddrive.
3. Backup all your data with a cron scheduling of applications .
4. Backup all your data with network devices.
5. Backup all your data with virtual cloud storage.
6. Backup all your data with hardcopies (print outs).

While taking backup, we should focus on management and recovery planning. This is the first step to analyzing where and how we are going to store and safeguard our data. This planning should include the following:

• Incidence response planning (IRP)
• Disaster recovery planning (DRP)

IRP and DRP should be maintained with a minimum of three copies, one within the organization for easier and regular access. One should be maintained in the branch offices within the city limit (if possible), or we can maintain hard copies of confidential information with high security. And the last one should be maintained abroad or in a virtual cloud platform with a well maintained server policy.

2.7   TRENDY CYBERCRIME ACTIVITIES

Cybercrime activities are conducted not only for the sake of money but also for stealing your valuable (confidential) information, even your network time, by means of DDOS attacks. Here we have listed a few trendy cybercrime activities according to level and severity of impact.

2.7.1   CITRIX BREACH

Breach is simply a violation or the breaking of some rules, policies, and frameworks. The Citrix Breach occurred when an attacker sent a document file with a .PDF extension to Citrix workers, interns, and customers using the network. The breach impacted many professionals in a very wide manner because it included highly confidential information such as PII – personally identifiable information, customer data, passport numbers, insurance, and payment information, etc.
    Remedial Action: Use real-time analysis and monitoring tools.

2.7.2   EQUIFAX

Equifax is a credit card scores reporting company that deals with handling plenty of credit card details like card numbers, CIBIL scores, loan accounts, and interconnected accounts. Leakage of such huge confidential data has highly affected the customers.
    Remedial Action: Check credit reports regularly, and freeze or block your credit information if you find something has gone wrong.

2.7.3 I LOVE YOU

The I LOVE YOU virus, also referred to as the LOVE BUG, usually comes in the form of a visual basic script (.VBS) appended with (.TXT) files by hiding the latter extension file. Take, for example, CYBERCRIMES IN ASSOCIATED WORLD.TXT.VBS, which acts as a script file and has the ability to modify the system settings. Like a worm it appends to multiple different extension files such as Mp3 and Mpeg and later it enables the attacker complete access to the system.

Remedial Action: While downloading any unknown file from the Internet or while copying from secondary storage devices, make sure of the extension name or else use a toolset like VIRUSTOTAL to check file legitimacy.

2.7.4 CODE RED AND SASSER WORM

Code Red and Sasser are computer worms that emerged in the year 2001. They became a trendy one because of their spreading mechanism and operational position. They initially capture and alter the log files and server configuration. Both appear to be extremely sensitive.

C:\win.log   C:\win2.log   C:\WINDOWS\avserv.com

2.8 21ST CENTURY HEIST

In today's data-driven world the digital transformation of all paper work makes the complexity of security a challenging task for the security professional. Most work carried out now in digital form increasingly poses a serious security threat to all our confidential information. We will discuss some of the latest serious threats along with their mitigation and handling measures (Table 2.3).

2.8.1 ADVANCED CHANNELS AND DATA EXFILTRATION

Data exfiltration is the act of moving sensitive information without proper rights from the hierarchy level of management. Breakage of perimeter security is the vital source of conducting this incident. And this can be done by means of hacking, insider threats, lack of user knowledge, and workspace management. The usage of confidential information in an illegal manner by modifying the contents makes a huge impact. And for performing these actions using covert (advanced) channels as a medium of transport to transmit vital sensitive information. Covert channel modes for processing data exfiltration techniques are discussed below.

2.8.1.1 Payload Delivery

Payload delivery is meant for the transmission of information in the form of data packets. Payload delivery differs from target to target as it targets different operating systems (Windows, Linux, Solaris, Mac, etc.); frameworks (vbs, PowerShell, HTA, MSI, Jar, JavaScript, Python, Perl, and Ruby); software (MS Office, MS Paint, Adobe); malicious links, website contents, scripting (Vbscript, JSscript, PHP), and exploits (Figure 2.4).

TABLE 2.3
21st Century Threats

Locky (2016)	BadRabbit (2017)	WannaCry (2017)
Ryuk Ransomware (2018)	REvil Ransomware (2019)	CryptoLocker (2020)
Quora – 100 million users affected (2017)	Facebook – 30 million users affected (2019)	Yahoo – 3 billion users affected (2018)

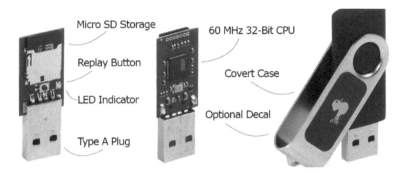

FIGURE 2.4 Payload delivery model. Source: micro.medium.com

2.8.1.2 Organizational Politics

Policies, frameworks, patch management, security training modules, internship activities, workplace management, password management policy, secure configuration of networks and cloud, and servers are the major areas on which companies (organizations) are focusing in order to leverage security skills and periodically arrange kinds of meetings that would improvise their employee knowledge on insider threats because lack of such knowledge is a cause for many possible cyber attacks. Fixing of Honeypots and Honeynets also plays a vital role in this.

2.8.2 Is Antivirus a Profession?

The role of antivirus software is to thwart possible security threats that target the victim's system either in the inbound or the outbound mode. This antivirus platform works on two modules: signature based and anomaly based. **Signature Based Detection:** With the known dataset of attack vectors, the signature of each communication will be matched and legitimate actions will be passed through.

Anomaly Based Detection: Unmatched signatures will monitor in a trial and error manner the performance and behavior of the communication that has been passed over the network by analyzing the packet consumption and the right gaining capacity.

2.9 CRYPTO CURRENCY SCAMS, SCAM WEBSITES, FAKE APPS

Coinminers (Cryptocurrency miners) are programs designed to deal with bitcoins, Ethereum, monero, dogecoins, litecoins, etc. These programs use the concept called mining, which takes control or gains advantage of system resources like CPU, GPU, RAM, and power without the user's knowledge. Many of the users fall for fake websites duplicated by means of phishing scams. Because of poor knowledge, victims are easily attacked by these kinds of mining software and websites. They come in the form of .exe files, .coinhive files, and .JSCoinminer files.

2.10 BAD TWEETS AND SCAMMING EMAILS

Mining traps even occur by means of spam emails, illicit tweets, and pokes. By clicking on them unknowingly, the users or victims are easily trapped. To get rid of these kinds of activities, check the following indications:

High CPU and GPU usage overheating.
Slow response times crashes or frequent restarts.
Unusual network activity (connections to mining-related websites or IP addresses).

2.11 HONEYPOTS AND HONEYNET TRACES

Honeypots are traps fixed or placed to attract or lure attackers to fall for them and to secure our network by identifying incoming packets and network activities. This is a lot similar to sandboxing. A sandbox is a testing environment for software development, including web development, automation, and revision control. It isolates untested changes and experimental results from production environments or repositories. A Honeynet protects an organization's perimeter and ensures the secrecy of information within its facilities (Figure 2.5).

2.12 PREVENTION/MITIGATION MEASURES

Cybercrime activities play a vital role as all communication and processing are now happening in the digital mode. We have to take care of our information as no one will do for us. We'll discuss some best practices to follow:

2.12.1 WHAT TO DO

Always use a strong password. Go through the password policy once (for more information, check the site howsecureismypassword.net)

Ensure email security and identify the compromisation (for more information, check the site haveibeenpwned.com)

Keep all your software updated.

Make sure patch management is completed on schedule. Identify vulnerabilities in your network and perimeter security.

Manage your social media accounts, including their settings.

Take a regular look at security breaches and antivirus news updates.

Learn in advance about mitigation measures in case you are attacked by any cyber threats.

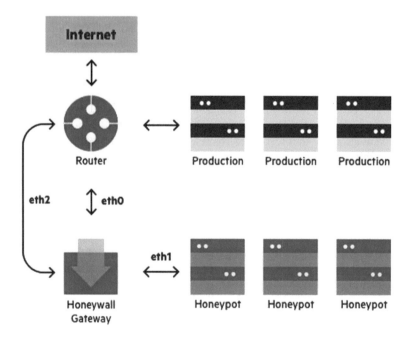

FIGURE 2.5   Honeypots and Honeynet traces.

2.12.2 WHAT NOT TO DO

Don't reveal your confidential information like passwords, credit/debit card details, PIN configurations, project proposals, billing statements, PII, health records, insurance, and budget proposals anywhere, in the workplace or on easily available platforms.

Don't trust any third party easily while surfing through social media or through the Internet.

Never save your credit or debit card information as a cache or cookies in ecommerce platforms such as Amazon, Flipkart, and eBay.

Don't accept all cookies when you are surfing any new sites without knowing what exactly the cookies are meant for.

Don't go for pirated software or freeware without checking its legitimacy and usage rights.

Never use a password hint and never use the same password for multiple accounts. Especially, use different credentials for system logins and social media accounts.

2.13 CYBERCRIME PREVENTION AGAINST WOMEN AND CHILDREN

Using the digital medium as a tool for crime, many harassment activities are threatening women and children in a wide manner. To avoid these kinds of activities, law enforcement agencies, authorized boards, and the police have taken remediation measures and have framed laws with severe punishments for such criminals. A special scheme has been proposed by the Ministry of Home Affairs (MHA), termed the Cybercrime Prevention against Women and Children (CCPWC) scheme.

2.14 LAWS AGAINST CYBERCRIMES

Section 66 – Attempting hacking activities.
Section 67A – Attempting vulgarity against girls.
Section 67B – Attempting vulgarity against minor girls (severe punishment).

Sentence: Minimum 5–7 years of imprisonment

Section 71 – Producing the wrong identity.
Section 66E – Releasing pornography images without the victim's knowledge.

Sentence: 1 lakh rupee fine, 2–5 years imprisonment

Section 502A – video voyeurism; Arms and Ammunition Act – online sales of arms; Narcotic Drugs and Psychotropic Substances Act – online sales of drugs.

Sentence: 2 years imprisonment

2.15 HOW TO REPORT CYBERCRIMES IN INDIA

To file a complaint of criminal activities against women and children, use the site https://cybercrime.gov.in/Webform/Crime_ReportAnonymously.aspx. To file a complaint against other related crime activities, use the site https://cybercrime.gov.in/Webform/Crime_AuthoLogin.aspx.

2.16 CONCLUSION

As cybercrime activities are at their peak, we have to protect ourselves by becoming digital savvies in today's modernized world. And it's also our duty to safeguard others from cyber attacks by providing good knowledge of the best practices of what to follow and what not to. We are growing a lot technology wise and security wise. But, at the same time, focusing on new trendy attack vectors, possible threats, and their mitigation measures is a must. It's advised to go through daily cyber news for at least one hour.

3 Recent Developments in Threat Intelligence and Challenges

S. Kannadhasan, R. Nagarajan,
R. Prabhu, and K. Chandramohan

3.1 INTRODUCTION

A crucial component of this research is cyber threat intelligence. This chapter outlines a few of the mission's outcomes that the mission team was able to achieve. The central claim of artificial intelligence (AI) is that a person's brain—their inherent ability to draw conclusions from data given to them—can be precisely characterized and machine-simulated. Thanks to decades of study, AI is now able to deal with problems that are more complex and interconnected than simple lookups or movement planning. Artificial intelligence (AI) refers to the representation of the brain by computers and/or software (AI). You may discover more about the aim of the development of intelligence in this chapter.

Through management, tuning, configuration, diagnosis, and healing. Self-sufficient laptop systems are made possible by AI. Artificial intelligence (AI) seems to be a particularly promising field of research that focuses on improving cyberspace safety measures when it comes to the future of information security. Artificial intelligence (AI) seems to be a viable answer to the issue of managing the expanding number of network threats, given its rapid pace of development and the requirement for increasingly powerful defenses. Artificial intelligence (AI) applications are extensively used in today's cutting-edge information culture. In order to build, simulate, and construct network penetration patterns and features, computer specialists and community engineers work together.

Operational cyber intelligence eventually strives to lower risk to an organization's vital missions and assets by describing the operational environment, outlining its impact, analyzing the opponent, and finding reliable information. Operational cyber intelligence establishes a relationship between the possibility and effect of a cyber-attack and its strategic degree of repercussions by providing a standard methodology for analysis and prioritization of potential threats and vulnerabilities. The foundation of all operational intelligence is the Active Defense Doctrine. Rather looking for evidence of a specific attack on the organization, it concentrates on all the attacks [1–5].

The attack and operation scenarios, weapon configurations, and battle tactics of the opponents are used to analyze threat intelligence. With this tactic, the organization's focus is shifted to its ability to react to an assault and stop its effects from spreading to its immediate environment. Our key hypothesis was that the Operational CTI could be mechanized using the predicted opponent's behavioral model. Since the Operational CTI is a relatively new field for which no thorough literature sources are available, it is important to note that the usage of artificial brain techniques is required. Only four companies – Exabeam (USA), Darktrace (UK), CyberX, and Interset (USA) – have provided feedback on the use of behavioral assessment based on computing device research. The TU-Sofia team arrived at the conclusion that the simulation and outgoing traffic in the opponent's network were the most relevant sources of data for developing his behavioral model. I'm reminded of the non-invasive brain–computer interface which enables the comparison

DOI: 10.1201/9781003251781-3

of physiological indicators of human intelligence with human emotional states (such EEGs). RFC 1757 Remote Network Monitoring methods may be used to collect streams of measured parameters instead of utilizing EEG with n-number of channels.

Recent malware assaults on vital infrastructure have given businesses and other stakeholders a fresh perspective on the risks posed by the internet. A cyber threat intelligence system must include alert, warning, and notification mechanisms that are intelligence based. Security analysts can comprehend the assault plan and quickly react to it with the aid of the cyber threat intelligence report. A majority of conventional models, according to the literature review, are unable to evaluate the effectiveness of CTI feeds. As a result, a stronger threat intelligence architecture is required. In this study, we provide an enhanced three-layer architecture for layered cyber threat intelligence. Data from both online and offline sources are included in Layer 1, which is the input layer. The data is pre-processed, categorized, and filtered in Layer 2. Layer 3 produces a thorough report for security analysts to work with using the ELK stack.

Identifying the bases and assault trajectories of the opposition is a component of strategic level intelligence. This matrix represents the social, political, technological, economic, and cultural motivations of the attacker. Trends and patterns discovered from tactical data as well as geopolitical open source models may be used to give this insight. When building a CTI model, strategic information is a crucial feature to take into account since although attackers' tactics change, their goal never changes. This data is often within the control of CISOs and IT administrators. Threat indicators that reflect context, traits, and domain are found via the tactical model. This often entails IOC-based profiling of the attack process and actors. Tactical intelligence will thus also include the entry of data into strategic intelligence, Security, Monitoring, and Event Management (SIEM) [6–10]. Cyber-profiling and some amount of interpretation from the analyst will be used to generate it. Such problems are handled by a network operations center (NOC) or a security operations center in an organization. Getting the most recent knowledge about the assault is what is meant by "operational level intelligence". The system looks for more breaches of this kind and reports them all at once. The Security, Incident Team, and Fraud Team are in charge of such information since the problem necessitates technological action.

Throughout history, long-lasting nations needed to grasp their rivals' identities, capabilities, intents, locations, reasons, and means of action. Of course, the opponents may be other countries, gangs of foes, or even the residents of the nation itself. The attacks, which were carried out by some kind of secret agency, were for a long time the exclusive purview of national governments. Thanks to the development of the Internet and an ever-increasing dependence on information technology, businesses in the late twentieth century, and particularly in the twenty-first century, found themselves in a dilemma similar to that which nation governments had faced for millennia. As a result, businesses began to attempt to understand more about their dangers and started to carry out duties usually designated for secret services in order to discover more about their threats, or the 5Ws. Companies, on the other hand, lacked the resources and were not legally allowed to carry out the entire spectrum of secret service gathering operations. Additionally, the cybersphere differed from the locations where secret services were active. As a result, the two domains were combined to form a new field of intelligence known as cyber threat intelligence (CTI).

This chapter's objective is to examine some research areas that the authors believe have some similarities to cyber threat intelligence (CTI) but are more established in terms of application, experience, and research than CTI. It is the notion that information acquired via study in other areas may be used in some manner to CTI. We wish to provide some suggestions for generating cyber threat information more quickly by repurposing theories, approaches, practical expertise, and other elements from earlier academic fields. We anticipate that by connecting CTI to much better established neighboring areas, the chapter's core goal of developing CTI research pathways will be achieved. Cyber threat intelligence has gained a lot of attention lately and has been praised as a solution to handle the complexity and increasing frequency of security incidents. Numerous businesses have made the decision to subscribe to different threat intelligence collections, both open-source and paid. The issue is that too much data is being used when not enough data is available. Overload of information will be a problem as a result. In order to handle cyber threat data and turn it into usable information that can be shared with other technologies and be utilized to aid in incident response, the Threat Intelligence Sharing Platform (TISP) has been developed. Threat intelligence feeds and systems that may assist with cyber threat response are being made accessible by information security firms to the general public as TISP solutions.

A majority of information security firms have also created their own definitions of cyber threat intelligence in order to achieve their marketing and commercial objectives. This uncertainty is exacerbated by the scarcity of scholarly literature on CTI as well as a lack of understanding of the standard, procedure, and idea of CTI among the general public. By describing the concept, state of affairs, and challenge, this chapter will act as a guide for understanding CTI.

Every organization is related to a variety of technology, work cultures, and procedures in the modern digital world. Because of this, cybercriminals have free rein in the workplace. Any organization will experience a constant stream of attacks and intrusions. They are aimed at both large and small businesses in the public and private sectors. As a result, cybersecurity defensive technologies, methods, and algorithms are used to identify cyber-assailants and threat scenarios. A group of strategies and techniques for defending nodes, networks, and data against damage, assaults, and unauthorized access are collectively referred to as "cyber security". Petabytes of data, including the most sensitive and important information, are held by large organizations, making it essential to safeguard the data against attacks and unauthorized access. Common attacks (manipulating known flaws), advanced assaults (taking advantage of detailed problems), and developing attacks are all covered by cyber security approaches (new attacks vulnerabilities). A few of the industries where the information system has been integrated include management, operations, and manufacturing [11–15]. Reliable data security methods and systems are required as a result of these developments. Employee awareness, prompt detection of intrusions, and research into unexpected emergent threat circumstances that have never happened in the system are all examples of cyber security techniques. The goal of cyber security is to decrease the number of vulnerability situations that are both false positive and false negative.

3.2 CYBER SECURITY

Despite using several security measures like antivirus, encryption, and firewalls, businesses continue to see an increase in intrusions. Commercial banks, cardholders, the telecommunications industry, and other challenging sectors need threat detection [8]. Here are some of the most typical risks: the use of disruptive information technology by terrorists to further their political objectives by gaining unauthorized access to confidential data without the owner's consent. The intrusion exposes vital communication systems and medical data in addition to seriously disrupting the e-commerce industry. Due to the enormous volume of data being produced, a threat intelligence system is required to detect trends of illegal or anonymous behavior. It is crucial to recognize cybercrime trends since cyberattacks are often unanticipated, making it possible to react to new patterns as they appear. By identifying a cyberattack as soon as it occurs, an organization's cyber security risks may be reduced.

Protecting systems and data from harmful online attacks is the main goal of cyber security. Cyber hazards may manifest themselves in a multitude of businesses and methods, and some examples include viruses, malware, data harvesting, and application breakouts. The surge in cybersecurity threats over the last several years has necessitated the use of automated threat assessments at all organizational levels. Cybersecurity is essential since the majority of organizations depend on data devices, which act as entry points for cybercriminals. The government has decided to invest more time and money in developing strategies to counter various threats as cyberattacks are becoming more organized and widespread. The financial sector plays a crucial role in the economy of our nation.

In order to solve the problems outlined in the previous part, the field of cyber threat intelligence, which is expanding, conducts research on the application of artificial intelligence and machine learning approaches. In order to provide security specialists a way to recognize cyber threat indications, researchers have recently looked at a number of artificial intelligence technologies. Machine learning (ML) and data mining technologies are becoming more widely used as a consequence of their proven effectiveness in malware analysis as network anomaly detection. Other strategies, such the deployment of honey pots, might be used to fool attackers in addition to the techniques that cyber defenders may utilize to prevent or detect cyber assaults. Security experts use such strategies to entice attackers by providing false information or resources that seem to be real, all the while keeping an eye on the attackers' behavior and anticipatorily spotting the assault. To provide security practitioners and analysts with up-to-date knowledge, a mix of these tactics would be necessary.

To lessen the susceptibility brought on by antagonistic disturbance, several detection and preventative techniques have been developed. For instance, it has been shown that network distillation increases neural network resilience while reducing network sensitivity. Its initial purpose was to reduce a large network's amount of information into a smaller one. By including adversarial photos into training data, adversarial training boosts resilience against recognized hostile pictures. However, it has been shown that certain image processing methods are useful for spotting hostile pictures. By way of illustration, B. Liang et al. [9] have demonstrated how noise reduction techniques like scalar quantization and spatial smoothing filters may be purposefully used to reduce the impact of adversarial disruption. It is possible to identify the disturbance by comparing the label of a picture before and after the alteration. The method works well in identifying hostile pictures with both low and high entropy. Similar to this, W. Xu et al. have demonstrated that local/non-local spatial smoothing and color bit compression may be effective methods for separating hostile pictures. Recent studies have shown that several of these protection and detection measures may be easily avoided by making minor adjustments to the initial assaults. Other black-box attacks have been developed, such as gradients, which do not need insider information about the target systems. To our knowledge, N. Narodytska et al.'s [10] paper is the only one to mention the use of one-pixel alteration to alter class labels in works done before ours. However, in contrast to our work, they just used it as a starting point to construct a more semi-black-box strategy that requires more pixels to be modified (e.g., around 30 out of 1024), without taking the possibility of a one-pixel assault into account. Furthermore, they haven't provided quantifiable data for an assessment of the attack's efficacy or undertaken a full investigation of it. There is also a need for a more thorough analysis of the one-pixel attack's implications and a geometrical analysis of it.

John McCarthy coined the term "artificial intelligence" in 1956, defining it as the science and engineering of generating intelligent automata, particularly intelligent computer applications. It entails teaching computers to function, learn, and act intelligently in the same manner as people. Despite the widespread usage of AI, human oversight of its operations is still required because of the risk of it being misused to do harm. Through internet hacking, cybercrime is on the rise and now poses a daily danger to governments, banks, and international corporations. Due to their flexibility and agility, AI systems may be able to assist in overcoming the shortcomings of conventional cyber security measures. Despite the fact that artificial intelligence is already helping to enhance cyber security, there are a few considerations. Some individuals think that mankind is in danger from artificial intelligence. Scientists and legal professionals are concerned about the rising importance of self-contained AI programmers in cyberspace as well as their moral justification. Applications with security weaknesses, such as network monitoring systems, financial systems, and self-driving cars, may become vulnerable to hacking, bypassing, and deception by AI systems. Therefore, it's essential to use techniques and practices that are both secure and long lasting. Up until now, artificial intelligence has been used to strengthen cyber security barriers. AI can be used to appropriately, reliably, and quickly analyze enormous volumes of data because of its excellent automation and data analysis capabilities. Even if the attack technique changes, an artificial intelligence system may identify similar attempts in the future based on its expertise and comprehension of earlier threats.

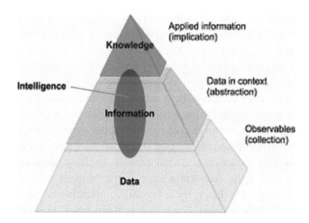

FIGURE 3.1 Cyber security threat.

Among other benefits, AI systems can process vast amounts of data quickly, identify distinctive and nuanced changes in attack changeability, and learn to forecast danger based on application behavior and the activity of the whole network. Since AI techniques are designed to learn and adapt to new scenarios, they excel at detecting even the smallest changes in network settings and allow response to anonymous threats [16–21]. They can thus analyze rare types of cyber-attacks quicker than humans can, which makes them more efficient overall as shown in Figure 3.1.

Data and information may be protected against unauthorized access by maintaining confidentiality. To put it another way, we must use some sort of protection for the data we wish to keep secure, with encryption being the most popular. The end objective is to ensure that only those who need access to the data may access it when it is shared between computers and devices. In the CIA Triad, maintaining data correctness and consistency is referred to as having integrity. Changes to data must be made in a safe setting. Data may be altered as a result of reckless use or flaws in security measures. The storage and transmission stages of data remain unaltered when integrity is implemented correctly. Availability, the third and final element of the triangle, is sometimes disregarded. The process of making data available at the appropriate time and location is referred to as "availability". System flaws are a common source of unavailability. In certain situations, having access to information is essential, and problems in this area may be difficult to resolve and result in terrible repercussions.

Threat intelligence data is a collection of labels produced by independent antivirus scanners that are not under the attacker's direct control (Figure 3.2). Label-flipping would need hostile control over the labeling process; hence, the clean-label backdoor method becomes necessary in practice. The goal of the attacker is to create backdoored, innocuous binaries and distribute them over these labeling platforms in order to contaminate the training sets for future malware classifiers. The adversary simply adds the identical watermark to the malicious binaries before releasing them and after setting up the models, guaranteeing that the new malware campaign will not be picked up by the backdoored classifiers.

3.3 THREAT INTELLIGENCE

The White House claims that a number of federal agencies, as well as businesses and sectors, have already deployed AI technology. By quickly skimming through standardized data and thoroughly analyzing and investigating unstructured data, statistics, voice patterns, and words, AI may help save resources and time. In fact, artificial intelligence (AI) has the power to protect both public funds and sensitive information. A few things are also missing. By taking advantage of vulnerabilities that we are ignorant of, hackers try to enter systems. Before a corporation learns about a data breach, years may pass. By then, the hacker would have vanished along with all of the crucial

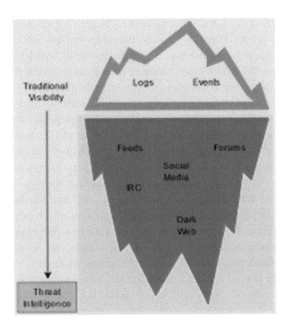

FIGURE 3.2 Framework of threat intelligence.

information. AI, on the other hand, must wait for a hacker to create trouble while passively collecting data. Starting off, AI looks for behaviors that are typical of hackers, including when a password is entered or when someone checks in. The hacker gang may be stopped in their tracks since AI is able to detect minute signals that would otherwise go unnoticed. Varughese noted that any technology may be misused. In the never-ending cybersecurity chess game, human hackers will continuously look for vulnerabilities in any system, even AI.

Artificial intelligence may still be toppled since it is directed by humans. Although AI is remarkably good at connecting and analyzing data, it can only work in the way that it is designed. Programmers will need to include additional security safeguards as hackers adapt their tactics to target AI systems. AI makes a positive contribution to the fight against data theft, but the cat-and-mouse game will still exist. Google developed a way for graphical data learning for Tensor Flow machine learning search. A neural graph learning system called Neural Structured Learning (NSL), which uses data sets and data structures to train neural networks, is a Tensor Flow-based machine learning platform that may be used by experts and novices in the field. NSL is capable of displaying information from interactive databases, including medical records and graphs, creating machine vision models, comprehending plain English, and more.

According to a blog post by Tensor Flow experts today, developers may provide superior prediction performance even with a very limited amount of data points by using structured signals during training. Structured signals are also used to test theories so that more reliable models may be built. The model's performance in Google has been greatly enhanced by the application of these techniques, such as learning semantic image implanting. In some situations, NSL may provide representations that employ visual cues to regularize development from monitored, semi-supervised, or unsupervised data in less than ten lines of code. The original system also included data structure tools and APIs for quickly producing instances of vector quantization. To supplement Auto ML Tables, Google Cloud offered more structured data techniques in 21st century, such as linked sheets in Big Query. Other advancements in AI include the publication of the GPT2 for Open AI by Google AI (formerly Google Research) and the open-source release of SM3, a compiler for powerful voice recognition systems like Google's BERT. Artificial intelligence powers Google's search engine, Facebook's face recognition tools, and voice recognition applications like Siri.

It improves an organization's digital management strategies for thwarting cybercrime and safeguarding clients' and enterprises' security. On the other side, artificial intelligence has the potential to use a lot of resources. It's conceivable that no implementation will be able to do this. Actually, it might be a deadly tool in the armory of computer thieves as it uses technology to speed up and amplify cyber-attacks. Information security wise, the talk about artificial intelligence was nothing out of the ordinary. After all, the core of contemporary cyber security advancements is information.

The topic of artificial intelligence (AI) is quickly gaining popularity in the field of computer security. We'll examine the development of AI security tools as well as how they impact businesses, online crimes, and end users and see what we can accomplish. Why do automated data protection approaches outperform human data protection strategies in terms of improving internet security? If your business is like many others, you have layers of protection in place for your border, network, edge, device, and computer storage. Network security systems and hardware or software firewall rules may be used to monitor connected devices and determine which ones should be allowed and which ones should be avoided. Malicious software and antivirus programs will be under hackers' control if they manage to get past these defenses. IDS/IPS and other security measures could then be used to combat them. But what happens when cybercrime surpasses certain security measures? When information security is solely dependent on human-based monitoring capabilities, you have a problem. After that, your cyber security deficiency should not always follow a predictable pattern, much as criminal activity does. Regardless of holidays, vacation time, or employee absences, IT workers should be able and prepared to respond quickly. Artificial intelligence-driven information security solutions are created with the goal of defending you around the clock, seven days a week. Artificial intelligence may be able to spot cyberthreats in a fraction of a second as opposed to the minutes, hours, days, months, or even years that people may need. The threat component of risk is addressed through intelligence-driven computer network defense, which entails a review of potential adversaries' capabilities, goals, doctrines, and constraints. This has to be a continual process where more new activities will be detected and discovered by more indicators. It calls for a different way of looking at intrusions, one that sees them as a chain of incidents rather than a single one.

The most apparent situations in which nations could elect to apply algorithms to allow automatic reactions include automated air defense systems and collisions involving unmanned aerial or undersea vehicles. States may create these systems using machine learning tools so that an unmanned underwater vehicle, for example, can recognize the object it is facing, comprehend and respond almost instantly to a missile fired from that foreign platform. Due to the fact that they operate in intricate dynamic environments, these systems differ from static automated self-defense systems like the Phalanx Close-In Weapons System. Programmers may also be able to link various systems to enable automated counteroffensive operations or incorporate the concept of imminent danger, allowing automatic anticipatory self-defense. A "human upon the loop" may be maintained in both cyber and autonomous vehicle scenarios, but the researchers point out that "the success of such algorithms hinges on their power to launch swift answers". The effectiveness of an AI system that can anticipate an attack depends on how fast it can respond. As a consequence, there will be significant incentives to just use the algorithm to make decisions.

The main problem that first hindered AI development was how the human behavior component was included. The first method included building a decision-making stack up of multiple if-then expressions. Rule-based systems, like expert systems, function well in a constrained setting like chess and other games, and in the 1990s, a computer easily beat the World Chess Champion. The next stage for AI was to develop the capacity to process outside input, learn from it, and adjust to a changing operating environment. The examples from the 1960s and 1970s do not really represent artificial intelligence as we know it now since the aforementioned term basically defines it as we use it today. Since the turn of the century, artificial intelligence has advanced significantly, and the developments in neural networks and deep learning have accelerated this development even further. Since they are essential to the AI solutions proposed in this study, these two ideas will be examined further in this book. One of the foundational pieces of AI technology was created in

2015 when Google created AlphaGo, a computer program designed to play the game of Go. Using the computational power of machine learning and neural networks, AlphaGo vanquished the best Go players in the world, and it is still recognized as one of the most complicated AI programs. The entire potential of AI technology has not yet been realized, and recent breakthroughs in the area include speech and face recognition, advertising algorithms, and smart speakers. Obtaining vast quantities of labeled binaries from third-party threat intelligence services is often the first step in the normal training pipeline for a machine learning (ML)-based malware classifier. Through these services, users—including attackers—can submit samples for modern antivirus (AV) engines to tag on binary files. Companies may then use the platforms to obtain the labeled data. The enormous volume of data involved, however, as well as the operation's inherent complexity, which necessitates the use of specialized staff and equipment, make the incoming flow screening process highly difficult. A labeled training data set may be made using this outsourced data together with small collections of exclusive, validated binary files. In the training strategy, the ML algorithm is trained after a feature extraction stage (in this instance, static analysis of PE files). Following their release into the world, the trained malware classifiers are used to evaluate the risk (malware) or benign (non-malware) character of new binary files.

3.4 CONCLUSION

This chapter has introduced the incursion death chain model, a tool for analyzing invasions and planning defenses. CND that is intelligence driven produces a more durable security posture. By definition, APT attackers undertake intrusion after incursion while adapting their strategies based on the results of each effort. Every repetition made by the attacker in a kill chain paradigm creates a weakness that the defenders must identify and take advantage of since only one mitigation may stop the chain and stop the enemy. The costs incurred by an adversary to accomplish their goals increase as defenders develop countermeasures quicker than attackers adjust. Contrary to popular belief, this model demonstrates that attackers do not always have an edge over defenders.

REFERENCES

1. The national cybersecurity authority Website. Retrieved from https://nca.gov.sa/pages/about.html.
2. Rania (2017 October 20). Saudi Arabia is more than Middle Eastern countries vulnerable to cyber-attacks. Retrieved from https://www.aleqt.com/2017/10/19/article_1269641.html.
3. Tounsi, W., and Rais, H. (2018). A survey on technical threat intelligence in the age of sophisticated cyber-attacks. *Computers and Security*, 72, 212–233. K. Elissa. Title of paper if known ‖ unpublished.
4. Kim, D., and Kang Kim, H. (2019). Automated dataset generation system for collaborative research of cyber threat analysis. *Security and Communication Networks*, 2019.
5. Mavroeidis, V., and Bromander, S. (2017). Cyber threat intelligence model: An evaluation of taxonomies, sharing standards, and ontologies within cyber threat intelligence. In *2017 European Intelligence and Security Informatics Conference (EISIC)*. IEEE.
6. Bromiley, M. (2016). Threat intelligence: What it is, and how to use it effectively. *SANS Institute InfoSec Reading Room*, 15, 172.
7. Chismon, D., and Ruks, M. (2015). *Threat Intelligence: Collecting, Analysing, Evaluating*. MWR InfoSecurity Ltd.
8. Shackleford, D. (2017). *Cyber Threat Intelligence Uses, Successes and Failures: The Sans 2017 Cti Survey*. SANS Institute.
9. B, Liang, H Li, M Su, X Li, W Shi, X Wang. (2018). Detecting adversarial image examples in deep neural networks with adaptive noise reduction, *IEEE Transactions on Dependable and Secure Computing*.
10. N. Narodytska, SP Kasiviswanathan. (2016). Simple black-box adversarial perturbations for deep networks, arXiv.
11. Burger, E. W., Goodman, M. D., Kampanakis, P., and Zhu, K. A. (2014). Taxonomy model for cyber threat intelligence information exchange technologies. In *Proceedings of the 2014 ACM Workshop on Information Sharing & Collaborative Security* (pp. 51–60). Academic Medicine.

12. Wang, A. J. A. (2005, March 18–20). Information security models and metrics. In *Proceedings of the 43rd Annual Southeast Regional Conference,(ACM-SE 43)* (pp. 178–184).
13. Hosseini, R., Qanadli, S. D., Barman, S., Mazinani, M., Ellis, T., and Dehmeshki, J. (2012). An automatic approach for learning and tuning gaussian interval type-2 fuzzy membership functions applied to lung CAD classification system. *IEEE Transactions on Fuzzy Systems*, 20(2), 224–234. https://doi.org/10.1109/TFUZZ.2011.2172616.
14. Sillaber, C., Sauerwein, C., Mussmann, A., and Breu, R. (2016). Data quality challenges and future research directions in threat intelligence sharing practice. In *WISCS '16: Proceedings of the 2016 ACM on Workshop on Information Sharing and Collaborative Security* (pp. 65–70).
15. Kotenko, I., and Ulanov, A. (2007). Multi-agent framework for simulation of adaptive cooperative defense against internet attacks. *Lecture Notes in Computer Science (Including Subseries Lecture Notes in Artificial Intelligence and Lecture Notes in Bioinformatics)*, 4476 *LNAI*, 212–228. https://doi.org/10.1007/978-3-540-72839-9_18.
16. Kotenko, I. V., Konovalov, A., and Shorov, A. (2010). Agend-based modeling and simulation of botnets and botnet defense. In *Conference on Cyber Conflict* (pp. 21–44). http://ccdcoe.org/229.html.
17. Jagpal, N., Dingle, E., Gravel, J.-P., Mavrommatis, P., Provos, N., Rajab, M. A., and Thomas, K. (2015). Trends and lessons from three years fighting malicious extensions. In *USENIX Security Symposium*.
18. Jung, J., and Sit, E. (2004). An empirical study of spam traffic and the use of dns black lists. In: *Proceedings of the ACM Conference on Internet Measurement*.
19. Kapravelos, A., Grier, C., Chachra, N., Kruegel, C., Vigna, G., and Paxson, V. (2014). Hulk: Eliciting malicious behavior in browser extensions. In: *USENIX Security Symposium*.
20. Kührer, M., Rossow, C., and Holz, T. (2014). Paint it black: Evaluating the effectiveness of malware blacklists. In: *International Workshop on Recent Advances in Intrusion Detection*. Springer.
21. Levchenko, K., Pitsillidis, A., Chachra, N., Enright, B., Félegyházi, M., Grier, C., Halvorson, T., Kanich, C., Kreibich, C., Liu, H., Mccoy, D., Weaver, N., Paxson, V., Voelker, G. M., and Savage, S. (2011). Click trajectories: End-to-end analysis of the spam value chain. In: *Proceedings of the IEEE Symposium and Security and Privacy*.

4 AI in Forensics
A Data Analytics Perspective

Lija Jacob, K.T. Thomas and M. Savithri

4.1 INTRODUCTION

The field of Artificial Intelligence, popularly known as AI, is an expanse of the current digital world which is well established besides being effective at solving computationally complex or massive problems quickly. Forensic science is a burgeoning field of computation that requires extensive cognitive examination of highly complex data. There exist some major issues in utmost situations such as the exponential increase in single-user storage capacity, the storage devices (hard discs, USB sticks, and optical media). Distributed systems are growing more advanced, resulting in novel sorts of assaults. The sophistication of these attacks is increasing, and opponents now have greater technological competence. Furthermore, the tools that are now accessible appear to be ineffective in dealing with sophisticated threats. Consequently, AI appears to be an excellent tool for handling many of the current challenges in forensics.

As part of criminal investigations, it is very important to be able to examine a large amount of data promptly during computer forensic examinations. Time and resource constraints, both computational and human, have a negative impact on the outcomes. Thus, the existing capabilities of existing forensic tools need to be enhanced, as well as better use of available resources.

An artificial intelligence approach to computer forensics is described by developing intelligent automation using learning algorithms. The technology analyses and correlates the evidence gathered in an investigation, and then displays the most compelling evidence to the human examiner, thus reducing the amount of data that must be manually examined. Correlation functions aid in discovering relationships between evidence that a human expert could overlook, particularly when a large amount of data is involved.

The chapter begins with a high-level overview of artificial intelligence and its use in forensics. The chapter discusses the viewpoint on AI and its components, as well as an outline of forensic science. The impact of artificial intelligence on forensic science is discussed, as well as the role of machine learning and deep learning in the area. The chapter also discusses the advantages and disadvantages of AI in the forensic field.

4.2 OVERVIEW OF ARTIFICIAL INTELLIGENCE

Since its emergence, the ability of computers or machines to perform numerous tasks has expanded exponentially. Computer systems have grown in power as humans have expanded their working domains, improved their speed, and reduced their size over time. One of the most significant technological advances was the invention of AI.

AI is a division of computational science whose goal line is for developing computers or machines that are as intelligent as humans. The goals of AI can be focused on creating expert systems, which can understand, illustrate, clarify, and assist their users, as well as incorporating human intelligence into machines by creating systems that comprehend, analyze, gain knowledge, and respond like people. As a result, AI has proven to be a versatile tool that can be utilized across industries to improve decision-making, increase productivity, and eliminate repetitive tasks.

DOI: 10.1201/9781003251781-4

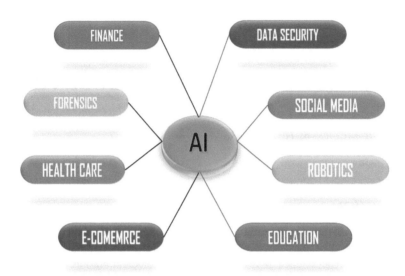

FIGURE 4.1 Domains in which artificial intelligence contributes.

The real-world applications of AI are not limited to Astronomy, Finance, Gaming, Healthcare, Data Security, social media, Travel and Transport, Automotive Industry, Robotics Agriculture, E-commerce, Education.

The Figure 4.1 shows various domains where AI is contributing to the current tech world.

4.3   ARTIFICIAL INTELLIGENCE, MACHINE LEARNING, AND DEEP LEARNING: WHAT IS THE RELATIONSHIP?

Technology providers all over the biosphere are discussing adopting artificial intelligence (AI), machine learning (ML), and deep learning (DL) in the current technological era. In the field of technology, all of these abbreviations are regularly used. It is crucial to note that all of these terminologies fall under the AI umbrella.

The relationship between these three tech buzzwords is introduced in the following section.

4.3.1   ARTIFICIAL INTELLIGENCE (AI)

Since the dawn of technological development, humans have been enamored with automation. AI enables machines to think independently of humans. It's a major topic in computational science. There are three types of AI systems. Artificial narrow intelligence (ANI) can be considered a subset of artificial intelligence, is goal-centric, and is designed to complete a specific job. Artificial general intelligence (AGI) is a technology that permits computing machines to learn, comprehend, and work in ways that are vague to normal human vision and thoughts, in a given context. Artificial Super Intelligence (ASI) is a theoretical AI in which machines can outperform even the sharpest humans in terms of intelligence.

4.3.2   MACHINE LEARNING (ML)

ML is a subfield of AI which can build embedded technologies using statistical learning algorithms.

Without being explicitly programmed, machine learning systems can learn and improve on their own. ML is used in music and video streaming services to make recommendations.

There are three types of machine learning algorithms: supervised, unsupervised, and reinforcement learning.

In supervised learning algorithms, a large set of units with known labels, referred to as a training set, is used. The algorithms "learn" how the input variables/features relate to the labels from this training set, or, to put it in different words, generates an approximation of the function f(X) that defines the relationship between attributes X and the output variable Y. The concept is, after training the algorithm, or given an estimate f, it can be utilized in the prediction of output variable for previously unknown entities. Unsupervised learning algorithms, on the other hand, do not depend on the availability of labeled training dataset. A collection of measurements or attributes X is detected on a large number of units, but not the matching response or label. Rather, the algorithm selects the best set of characteristics to describe a class and improve the chances of accurately labeling a new unit [1].

4.3.3 DEEP LEARNING (DL)

This subfield of artificial intelligence is a method that tries to mimic how the human brain filters data. In fact, it follows the philosophy of learning from the mistakes of others. In order to perform forecasting and classification of data, DL systems help a computational model's capability for filtering input data through layers. Deep learning works in a similar way to the human brain when it comes to processing information. It's employed in technologies like self-driving cars. Convolutional Neural Networks, Recurrent Neural Networks, and Recursive Neural Networks are the three types of DL network designs.

The Figure 4.2 shows the relationship with AI, ML, and DL

4.4 OUTLINE OF FORENSIC SCIENCE

The application of a wide range of sciences to solve difficulties in the legal system can be referred to as forensic science. This could be in areas such as criminal law, civil law, or regulatory law. It could also refer to non-contentious issues. The popular abbreviation for the term "forensic science" is "Forensics". Forensics can be considered as the application of natural science concepts and physical science technologies to support the investigations of criminal and civil cases.

Forensic science can be used not only in the investigation and prosecution of crimes such as rape, murder, and drug smuggling, but also in cases where a crime has not been committed but a civil wrong has been done, such as intentional pollution of the air or water or affecting industrial concussions. The instruments of science and the logic of scientific inquiry are used in forensic science to reconstruct the who, what, where, when, and how of occurrences of the events under observation.

Chemistry, Biology, Physics, Anthropology, Engineering, Toxicology, Psychiatry, Entomology, Odontology, Computer/Digital Studies, and Pathology are all used in forensic science [2].

Forensic science is a broad term that encompasses a variety of disciplines. The section below depicts a high-level overview of the various fields of forensic science.

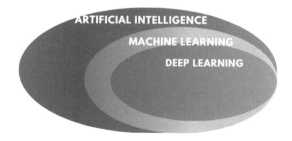

FIGURE 4.2 Relationship with AI, ML, and DL.

Trace Evidence Analysis: Trace evidence analysis provides essential ties to the culprit. Anything that is transported during the commission of a crime, such as human/animal hair, rope, soil, fabric fibers, feathers, building materials, and so on, is considered trace evidence.

Trace evidence analysis entails recovering such evidence and forensically examining it in order to gather information that can be utilized in court to support a case or to answer any other legal question.

Forensic Toxicology: Forensic toxicology is the study of the presence of harmful substances inside a person's body and their effects. It includes tools and processes from a variety of disciplines, including analytical and clinical chemistry, as well as pharmacology, to assist in the medical and legal investigation of deaths caused by poisoning or drugs.

In cases of car accidents, poisoning, and sexual violence, this section of forensic science is critical.

Forensic Podiatry: Forensic podiatry involves the application of specific podiatric expertise, such as an awareness of anomalies and disorders of the ankle, feet, and lower body, as well as lower limb anatomy and musculoskeletal functions. This is especially useful in the case of a criminal inquiry using foot-based data.

Forensic Pathology: Forensic pathology is the branch of pathology that deals with the study of a corpse to identify the cause of death. It entails collecting and analyzing medical samples in order to derive facts that are admissible as evidence. A forensic pathologist, for example, can study a wound to determine the weapon that caused it. As a result, forensic pathology aids in the determination of whether a death is legal, unlawful, or incidental [3].

Some other common branches in forensic sciences are as follows [4, 5].

Computational Forensics: It is the study of the use of computers to solve crimes. To research and solve problems in numerous domains of forensic science, computational science is used.

Forensic Accounting: It is a type of accounting that is used in court cases. It investigates and evaluates evidence in the field of accounting.

Forensic Anthropology: It is a branch of forensic anthropology that deals with the study of skeletal remains. It refers to the use of anthropology and osteology to determine information about a human body in a state of advanced decomposition.

Forensic Archaeology: It is the study of forensic artifacts. Archaeological approaches are used in this discipline of forensic science.

Astronomy for Forensic Purposes: The use of celestial constellations to address legal concerns is relatively uncommon. It's most frequently utilized to solve historical issues.

Forensic Document Examination: Examining forensic documents. It involves investigating, analyzing, and determining the facts around documents that are in issue in court.

Forensic Analysis: DNA testing for forensic purposes. This branch is concerned with the gathering and analysis of DNA evidence that can be used in court.

Forensic Entomology: Entomology for forensic purposes. It involves investigating insects found on the scene of a crime or on the body of a victim and is especially useful in pinpointing the time and place of the victim's death.

Forensic Geology: Geology for forensic purposes. It entails the use of geological variables such as soil and minerals to obtain evidence in connection with a crime [4].

4.5 FORENSIC SCIENCE – A HISTORICAL PERSPECTIVE

The meaning of the word "forensic" could be much broader than we assume currently. It's worth noting that C.F. Daniel's 1784 bibliography and C.F.L Wildbert's 1819 bibliography both have a great number of entries about it. Perhaps we're using it in the same way we've been using the term for years, but with significantly multiple interpretations. The history of forensic science can be traced back to Archimedes in the 17th century, when he used the concept of density and buoyancy to determine the fraudulence of a counterfeit golden crown. With a scientific approach, it developed more popular in the 19th and 20th centuries.

Sir Arthur Conan Doyle was one of the people who pioneered the practical application of scientific or forensic methods in criminal investigations. He popularized the scientific approach of inquiry through his fictional character Sherlock Holmes. Humankind continued to receive contributions on forensics from many great researchers. Some of their names and their major contributing areas are listed below.

Mathieu Orfila (1757–1853) wrote a book on the effects of poisons on animals and methods for detecting them. His book contributed much in establishing Toxicology as a respectable field of science. He was acknowledged as the Father of Toxicology. Alphonse Bertillon (1813–1914) came up with the scientific technique of personal identification. He began to establish empirical anthropometry, which is a method of systematically measuring a set of body measures to distinguish one person from another. He was known as "Father of criminal investigation" [5].

Francis Galton (1822–1911) invented a system for classifying fingerprints. Credit goes to him for the current fingerprint identification system. He also established the groundwork for the adoption of fingerprints as evidence in legal proceedings at courts of law. Later Henry Faulds introduced a classification system for fingerprints which is still used by many police departments [6].

Hans Grossis was a criminologist (1847–1915) whose research around the early 1900s contributed to the development of forensics in principles of evidence transmission from criminal to victim. He is now known as Father of Criminology [7].

Edmond Locard (1877–1966) discovered the Locard's exchange principle, which states, "Every interaction leaves a trace". Leone Lates (1887–1954), Father of Bloodstain Identification, discovered a straightforward method for detecting blood type from a drop of blood or a speck of dried bloodstain, which is still in use today [8].

Later, towards the end of 20th century, as computers became a great tool for forensic activities as well as a tool for crime, the novel branch of digital forensics started to grow and is still growing. Off late, digital forensics backed by the power of artificial intelligence has earned popularity in identifying, guessing, or classifying objects.

Crime by Computer, a book authored by Donn Parker, published in 1976, discusses the use of electronic material to correctly investigate crimes done with the support of software. During the 1970s, system administrators used to do system audits. I opine that it could be proper to consider this audit as a comprehensive and integrated approach to digital security for the first time, and some wrong doings were caught using the data collected during these audits.

Many organizations, including the Department of Defense, the Internal Revenue Service (IRS), and the Federal Bureau of Investigation (FBI), during the 1970s, started small groups of agents to be trained to assist regular investigators in collecting knowledge from mainframe machines, other local storage, and comprehensive archives.

What is currently known as digital forensics was formerly known as "computer forensics" until the late 1990s. Law enforcement personnel who were also computer aficionados were the very first computer forensic investigators. In the United States during 1984, the Federal Bureau of Investigation started planning for a team to investigate computer crimes and by 1991 a team officially known as "Computer Analysis and Response Team" (CART) was formed. During 1985 The Metropolitan Police in the United Kingdom established a computer crime division [9].

At the start of the 1990s, a significant shift occurred. Investigators and technical support operators from UK police departments and other supporting agencies, as well as independent investigators, recognized that digital forensics (like other professions) needed uniform methodologies, standards, and procedures. These formalisms did not exist apart from informal recommendations and were urgently needed to be established. In 1994 and 1995, the Serious Fraud Office and the Inland Revenue held a series of seminars at the Police Staff College in Bramshill, during which the contemporary "British digital forensic approach" was formed.

The idea of early digital forensics was first noticed in the 1990s. Criminal investigation departments and the police, on the other hand, were not willing to engage in digital forensics. While researching the cause of a tiny variation in utilization between two accounting systems, Stoll, a system administrator, discovered that hackers had accessed a vast number of computers, along with a few super sensitive systems. He experimented and created his own software to track the destructive activities of hackers. Perhaps this is the first automated cyber forensics tool.

During 1985 to 1995, with the advent of the IBM PC, many hobbyists, including some law enforcement officers, began writing computer code to gain access to the operating systems and hardware's internals. Many of the aforementioned hobbyists became members of the International Association of Computer Investigative Specialists (IACIS). European and Asian law enforcement officers quickly followed suit.

In 1993, the FBI Academy in Quantico, Virginia, convened the 1st International Conference on Computer Evidence, with delegates from 26 different countries in attendance. The International Organization on Computer Evidence (IOCE) was created in 1995 at the 2nd conference, which was hosted by Baltimore. From today's perspective, the instances examined by these innovators were quite simple. The recovery of information from solitary PCs received a lot of attention. Because storage was expensive, users often destroyed data and re-formatted media, data recovery was a serious concern. Although the Internet was not widely used at the time, fraudsters exploited dial-up connections to infiltrate computers. Computer crime investigations have focused on traditional offenders who used computers to aid their operations, as well as youth who exploited their tech skills to illegitimately get digital access and applications. A few tools were available which were being used in command lines, like IRS utilities, Marsware, IACIS utilities, and RCMP utilities. These tools were mostly distributed among law enforcement officers [10].

Various groups and agencies have issued recommendations for digital forensics since 2000 in response to the demand for uniformity. The Scientific Working Group on Digital Evidence (SWGDE) published "Best Practices for Computer Forensics" in 2002, and an ISO standard (ISO 17025), in 2005, which comprises of the General Requirements for Testing and Calibration Laboratories were published. This decade saw a lot of AI advancements in cyber forensics, more so in finance related crimes [34].

Currently on a routine basis, the field of computer forensics is establishing, especially with the support of artificial intelligence, machine learning, etc., huge forensic agencies, and private detectives are all learning things and information in this area. Software companies continue to develop better and more robust forensic software solutions. Furthermore, law enforcement and the military are continuing to identify and educate more of their personnel in the fight against technology-related crimes.

4.6   FORENSIC SCIENCE: METHODOLOGY

In any forensic science case, the stages should be followed systematically. Observe the instances to determine the broad characteristics of the evidence and to investigate the specific features. In most cases, there will be proof linking the crime to the solution.

In a broader sense, the scientific approach involved in a forensic methodology:

- Collect objective data after observing the situation or questioning the proof.
- Create a hypothesis or a possible solution based on your findings.
- Make a work plan using inductive reasoning, experience, and imagination.
- Examine, test, and analyze the hypothesis to prove or disprove it.
- Using a deductive approach, determine the importance of the evidence.
- When analyzing and confirming evidence, keep in mind its validity, dependability, uniformity, and precision.
- Write a report based on your findings.

The diagram in Figure 4.3 shows the flow of the process.

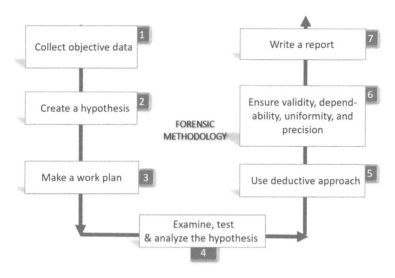

FIGURE 4.3 Forensic methodology.

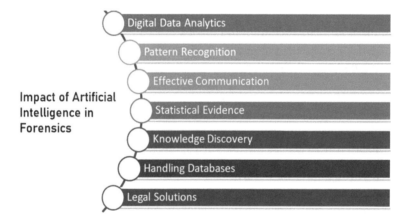

FIGURE 4.4 AI in forensic science.

4.7 IMPACT OF AI IN FORENSICS

The forensic industry has benefited from recent breakthroughs in machine learning and artificial intelligence (AI). AI can assist forensic teams with tasks such as digital data analysis, pattern recognition, legal solutions, and encouraging communication among all members of the forensic team, creating repositories and compiling statistics data, and finding out fresh information. This section goes through some of the most fascinating tasks where AI has an impact on forensics. The graph (Figure 4.4) depicts some of the influences of AI in forensics.

4.7.1 Data Analysis and Data Analytics in Forensics

AI can be used to pool meta-data from various sources and do a meta-analysis on it to simplify complex data. This is useful in converting the data to a simplified and understandable format in a reasonably brief measure of time. In the forensics world, data analytics is the procedure of gathering, analyzing, and filtering large amounts of data from a system. Such approaches aid in the improvement of system efficacy, including resource allocation optimization and risk evaluations. Visualization tools can be used to quickly discover trends and abnormalities that demand additional scrutiny, improving accuracy. Datamining, trend analysis, and outlier detection are some of the other processes done in the field of forensics. Based on historical data, statistical and machine learning algorithms can be used to model, forecast, and quantify risk. Patterns that indicate fraud can be recognized using such algorithms, which can assist businesses in detecting fraud in the early stages itself.

Using forensic data analytics, users can make more knowledgeable and targeted decisions about the internal control systems, which can help anyone to overcome fraud risks. Data analytics will assist any company in doing the assigned objectives by examining and processing big data sets [11].

Trend analysis, internal control system optimization, policy revision and reinforcement increased productivity and profitability, and increased efficiency and effectiveness are some of the activities involved in forensic data analytics.

4.7.1.1   Trend Analysis

Data analytics allows for a comprehensive analysis of trends depending on currently available data and historical data.

This enables a company to assess if it is improving, keeping the same, or deteriorating. By analyzing this data, professionals can focus their attention on areas that are regarded to be becoming worse. This aids in determining whether or not there is any possibility for fraud or abuse within the business.

4.7.1.2   Amendment and Enhancement in Policies

Forensic data analytics may be used to uncover policies that need to be amended. These insights can also help the organization discover areas where its employees may require additional training.

4.7.1.3   Review and Analysis of Internal Controls

Funds can be reviewed using data analytics social ties. This enables a company to determine whether its internal controls are functioning properly. Outlier trends can also reveal potential weaknesses. This data can help businesses enhance their internal controls and reduce vulnerabilities.

4.7.1.4   Boosted Throughput and Returns

Organizations are constantly on the lookout for new and cutting-edge ways to save money. The notion of "doing more with less" is one method used by businesses to reduce total costs. Using data analytics, several companies have been able to broaden the possibility of their core investigations/audits without needing to hire more people.

4.7.1.5   Improved Efficacies and Effectiveness

Businesses by means of data analytics in their interior audits can review far bigger capacities of data in much less time. This enables organizations to use technology to perform more comprehensive testing, potentially reducing human error.

Data analytics allows these massive data sets to be assessed as a whole instead of depending on data sampling as more organizations deal with an elevated amount of transactions. In addition, data analytics helps to reduce sample error and the identification of abnormalities with greater precision. The detection of these anomalies may lessen the likelihood of suspicious transactions getting unnoticed.

Forensic data analytics can thus be an aid in the detection of a variety of fraud schemes that may be taking place within an organization. The following are some examples of detectable fraud schemes:

- Unauthorized alterations to the master vendor file
- Fabricated salary and/or work hours
- Inventory policies

- Substantiate tampering
- Unendorsed wage adjustments
- Schemes of corruption
- Employees who don't exist or ghost employees
- Disingenuous financial statements
- Commission structures or schemes
- Deceitful expense reimbursements
- Robbery of cash receipts

4.7.2 PATTERN RECOGNITION IN FORENSICS

The study of any item where a mark or an impression formed during criminal behavior to link the mark with the instrument or technique that made it, is known as marks evidence/impression evidence. It includes a broad range of fields such as fingerprint recognition and gunshot detection, and analyses of cartridge cases, tool markings, footprints, gashes, and even traces of handwriting and signatures can be used as marks evidence.

Pattern recognition is the foundation of the mark examination system. To connect a criminal suspect or tool to a crime, patterned evidence is reviewed and matched. Unique qualities within a piece of patterned evidence, such as scars or nicks, provide for more accurate matching. When comparing patterned evidence from a specimen from the crime scene with a known sample from the suspect, a skilled expert must look for distinguishing characteristics and determine whether the samples were from the very same source. Handwriting, footprints, trace evidence, ballistics, traces of blood, and other impressions such as shoe prints or tire markings are examples of patterned evidence. The pattern of ridges in a fingerprint, or the pattern of striation lines in tool marks or ballistics exams, provides strong evidence that can be used to link a crime scene mark to a person, a weapon, or a piece of equipment [12].

In forensic investigations, pattern recognition can be used to determine a person's gender, which is one of the most important stages in creating identity. Other traditional sex determination methods have worse accuracy than DNA-based sex determination analyses [13].

Health and forensic education and investigations rely heavily on structural sciences. For proper investigation, teamwork between anatomical scientists and forensic experts is required. Biometrics is an anatomical discipline that employs pattern recognition to identify or recognize objects. Dermal impressions left on surfaces (fingerprints, palm patterns, tracks, ear prints, and lip prints). Forensics experts can retrieve some patterns from a crime scene which can be then used to aid in criminal investigations. The patterns are viewed, gathered, examined, appraised, and analyzed with recorded data in biometric technology, and a precise crossmatch with suspects aids in correctly identifying the perpetrator. The physical/anatomical features (fingerprints, face, hand/finger geometry, iris, retina, ear, etc.) and behavioral characteristics (signature, keyboard usage pattern, gait, odor, etc.) are done by robots to create information that helps the direct identification of the suspect. Biometric features should be looked up on as a physical and behavioral feature or an anatomical feature. As a result, a biometric system can be defined as a pattern-matching technology that captures physical or behavioral data from a person, extracts a significant feature set from the available data, contrasts these features and functionality to a database's feature set, and generates the output of the analysis.

4.7.3 EFFECTIVE COMMUNICATION

In order to conduct a forensic investigation, forensic statisticians, advocates, criminal detectives, and others must communicate. Miscommunication among these stakeholders might result in flawed conclusions or data misapprehension, resulting in delayed or incorrect justice. AI aids in bridging the communication gap between many stakeholders in this industry. AI can improve operational effectiveness through automation and augmentation as a set of technologies that replicate human features such as knowledge, reasoning, problem-solving, perception, learning, and planning on a large set of data. They complement the human experience and produce faster and better solutions when used together. Humans can contextualize data insights and decision-making with intuition and experience, whereas AI can discover patterns that are not visible to the human eye. Through the use of visualization tools, AI aids in the effective transmission of data insights, allowing for proper analysis and decision-making.

The automation of data-intensive processing tasks, such as visual inspections of public spaces and the interpretation of security camera footage, can aid in resource management. This frees up scarce human capacity for higher-value work and more complicated problem-solving, enhancing productivity and engagement in the workplace.

Machine self-learning has predictive and prescriptive applications. By quickly generating insights through deeper data analysis and presenting them using visualization tools, AI opens up new ways to make sense of the forensic world.

4.7.4 STATISTICAL EVIDENCE

In forensic science, significant statistical proof is required to support arguments and narrations. These judgments can be reinforced with the use of AI, which can create pictorial frameworks to aid in the creation of scenarios and case studies. It can also assist in the creation of graphical model situations which could be utilized to verify or refute arguments, allowing judges to reach a better decision.

In general, AI technologies can improve statistics by improving the understanding of the statistics behind a study. This is performed by offering mathematical and computational tools that aid in the construction of statistically meaningful evidence. Technology developments such as artificial intelligence (AI) will undoubtedly affect the law and forensic accountants as expert witnesses. Any expert, including a forensic accountant, is vital to the prosecution of a case. It is common for forensic accountants to sift through large amounts of data to determine the good from the bad, which is both time-consuming and expensive. AI may streamline that task. As a result, judges, practitioners, and forensic experts must adjust to new technology and comprehend how juries utilize it to make decisions based on a thin layer of evidence [14]. In forensic science, significant statistical evidence is used to back up the narrative and reasoning. AI can create graphical frameworks to aid in the creation of scenarios and case studies. It can also assist in the creation of information visualization scenarios that can be utilized as a proof or for refuting arguments, allowing judges to reach superior decisions. Artificial intelligence (AI) provides software technology which could assist in the development of statistically meaningful and substantial evidence. All of this will help to eliminate errors and increase understanding of a study's statistics.

4.7.5 KNOWLEDGE MANAGEMENT AND DISCOVERY – A STRATEGIC APPROACH FOR FORENSICS

In Digital Forensic Investigation (DFI), the detectives employ specific skills and knowledge to acquire, manage, and analyze massive volumes of structured and unstructured evidence data and information. Such information is used to support legal actions during civil or criminal proceedings in the court of law.

As the nature of data and DFI process is changing, new skills and knowledge may sometimes be needed to handle an incident at hand and make quick and accurate results.

This is because each DFI approach is distinctive and might even differ significantly from prior DFI processes, necessitating the acquisition of new information and skills. Such research in knowledge discovery and data mining requires artificial intelligence which combines statistical analysis and probability to create solutions even for large problems.

Almost all of the unique knowledge gained during each DFI procedure is not explicitly documented in the current circumstances, which makes external assessments and training of other digital forensic investigators difficult. As a manner of facilitating knowledge exchange and re use among digital forensic investigators and law enforcement organizations, previous experience may and should be used to train new digital forensic personnel.

Such activities will, in the long run, expose any newly created ideas and insights to quality review by the digital forensic community and other third parties.

Thus, in digital forensic investigations, knowledge management and knowledge discovery can be used as a strategic asset to support legal activities in court and civil processes [15].

Figures 4.5 and 4.6) show the flow, reuse, and enhancement of knowledge from knowledge capturing to development during a forensic investigation process.

4.7.6 Handling Database

It was simple for anyone to analyze or derive intellectual data from prior decades' data, when there were no large storage devices and when maximal storage could only be done via hard discs in computers. Later, as technology advanced, there was an exponential increase in data storage, spanning from portable sources like USB sticks and SD cards to scattered sources like Cloud Services, resulting in the term Big Data. Big Data could be defined as a significant mass of data, which could be either structured or it could be even un-structured, stored in zettabytes/petabytes on diverse storage mechanisms [16]. This section on handling database can be described in two views. The first can be how to use the database to handle the forensic investigation [17].

A forensic analyst will better serve if he can be assisted with the ability to automatically detect patterns in massive data sets. For example, keeping the specifics of emails sent by well- known authors. Another example is the recording of computer network activity by personnel in different roles within a company in order to spot irregularities.

There are also examples of enterprise databases that have been used for forensic purposes.

In the case of family DNA, this is one example. The family link can be traced back, especially through family members and criminal DNA. The accuracy of this method can be improved by combining other facts about the crime, such as geographic location.

The second can be how big data can be handled in digital forensics [17, 18]. Suitable investigation of structured, semi-structured, and unstructured data can be utilized to improve the user's

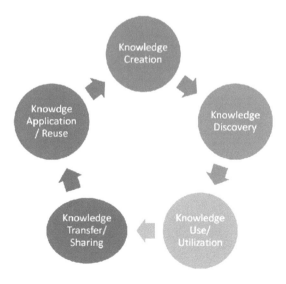

FIGURE 4.5 Knowledge flow and management in an investigation process.

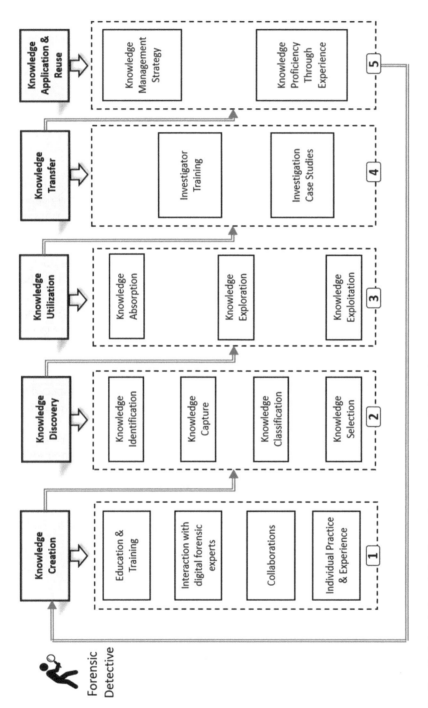

FIGURE 4.6 Detailed view in knowledge flow and management in an investigation process.

experience, forecast valuable behaviors, and possibly aid in making smart business decisions. As a result, to make efficient use of large data, it must be correctly handled.

The application of big data analytics is underappreciated, although it is increasingly being used in digital and mobile forensics. Most of the time data could be frequently found in the semi-structured form on seized or studied artifacts, typically in application databases. The information gathered by investigators from storage chipsets of mobile phones, personal computers, and other digital storage devices can also be characterized as unstructured information. Following successful extraction, the data is transferred to processors that perform minimal intelligent computing.

In terms of digital forensics, the four major pillars of big data could be rephrased as follows:

1. "Volume" is frequently employed to refer to the quantity of data extracted from a single seized device or a number of them.
2. "Variety" refers to the various file formats or data that can be found on the storage. Data allocated from recognized file systems and unallocated information from volume and file slack areas are examples of such data.
3. "Velocity" refers to the chunk of time required for processing obtained data, and the time needed to gather the information in the first place.
4. "Value" is the worth of true intelligence derived from properly processed data, not the resale value.

Analyzing data on these big data dimensions – volume, variety, and velocity – has become very complicated, posing a unique challenge for digital forensics. There's no disputing how difficult it is to analyze massive amounts of data at a high velocity without knowing which device or source it originated from.

Furthermore, it would be even more difficult to extract intricate correlations and frameworks from this data, resulting in an increase in crime and making digital forensic investigators' jobs more difficult.

Structured data is a type of data that is frequently used in investigations and recorded in database files, which has a specified structure. Numbers, dates, word groups, and strings are examples of the structured data. Such data can be processed with tools that can parse user data from apps, execute data decoding and encoding, and present recorded data in a usable way, all while focusing on the database file format and recognized structures.

Amorphous data is described as information that lacks a predetermined data model or that cannot be organized logically (like in rows and columns format as used in databases). Unstructured data includes text in all formats, e-mails, movies, voice recordings, internet pages, and social network platforms. To make sense of unstructured data, to retrieve and show all of the data in a more logical fashion, sophisticated queries are typically utilized. An examiner will be able to find material in the same context as the inquiry using the search queries.

Another mechanism to handle such data is the metadata. Metadata, sometimes known as data on data, can be utilized to help with data volume issues. Metadata is divided into two categories: descriptive and structural. What if a database existed that contained information about a photograph, such as where it was taken, when it was taken, and what the photograph was about? The descriptive metadata for this photo is the same for all images, but the structured metadata fills in the specifics, such as the location of New Delhi, the time 12 o' clock, and the image of Qutub Minar, which is unique to each image. As a result, attempting to deal with massive quantities of data can be simplified by first using explanatory metadata and then creating an architecture metadata database from it.

4.7.6.1 Prediction of Intelligence from Big Data

To develop concrete information from vast data, an organized and controlled intelligence extraction technique is employed to analyze the data and to provide the examiner with an actionable dataset.

The actions taken are usually carried out in stages. The major goal of these phases is to transform organized, unstructured, and semi-structured data into a tangible representation that closely resembles the evidence under investigation. Many law enforcement agencies are reported to not evaluate their stored data for authentic intelligence that can be utilized in behavioral analysis, the likelihood of committing a crime, or digitally monitoring in the future. As a result, forensic investigators can benefit greatly from big data analytics, especially when the content is properly processed.

To deal with specific objects within emails or search history, the examiner would often use advanced search capabilities incorporated into the software. When an examiner searches for names, email IDs, telephone numbers, or data strings, the acquisition program incorporates these and other strategies to provide rapid results. Adding to it, during the data retention and extraction of certain datasets, forensic experts are underutilizing the intelligence analysis' potential. The techniques help law enforcement officials predict behavioral trends and, in some situations, identify the involvement of a subject in other types of crimes or that has ties to other people known to the agency.

4.6.7.2 AI and Data Science Can Be Incorporated?

Digital forensics can be enhanced with artificial intelligence and data science to counter big data, since analyzing a vast amount of content is near impossible for a human to do. Data sources include past resolved cases, evidence, and databases. Based on the analysis of the given data, one can formulate suitable algorithms using the derived data. To avoid making mistakes during the initial test phase, the ultimate choice should be done manually.

Predictive policing is one such technique, which involves the use of quantitative and predictive analytics, as well as other analytical tools, by police force to detect possible illegal activities. It is among the most innovative ideas since it may help to prevent crime from happening in the first place. It does, however, have the downside of discriminating in contradiction of a certain group of people and usually reaching wrong results.

There are several tools, such as MapReduce, available in digital forensics for handling large amounts of data. Apache Hadoop, a cluster of open-source packages, uses the MapReduce software design model to handle huge data.

The massive amount of data from the source is split among several machines called nodes, which are linked together to shorten the time taken to store the data. The data is subsequently replicated by the nodes based on the application. Numerous top-tier businesses, as an example, Netflix, rely on Hadoop and Big Data analytics.

Neural networks are another tool that is used. Neural networks are interconnected networks of neurons that make judgments based on mathematical processing. Deep learning algorithms can be developed to eliminate repeatability, obtain reliable data assessment and analysis, and evaluate all tools and methods utilized in specific challenges, as well as make future forecasts. Studies show that the total data volume on Earth is expected to reach 163 zettabytes by 2025. Big data analytics and data science can be used by businesses to power their economies more effectively than ever before, but this will also pose a challenge for digital forensics, as existing systems cannot handle such a huge amount of information. Hence it is recommended that, in order to accomplish investigative objectives with big data, data science and AI, digital forensics has to expand its current principles and investigate new tools and technologies [19].

4.6.7.3 Legal Solutions in Forensics

Artificial intelligence continues to revolutionize many industries, including legal services. Specialists in the field of law enforcement are unified in their prediction of AI's explosive increase as core technologies for bringing new-fangled tools and applications to strengthen legal support and gaining justice.

According to research, legal tech solution benefactors will almost certainly acclimate and incorporate prevailing AI technologies, transforming them into instruments that will assist in growing legal businesses. With AI-powered intelligent juries, AI robot lawyers, and automation tools, this trend will continue to find its way into the day-to-day work of lawyers and change the judicial sector [20].

Richard Susskind [21] anticipated that notaries and customers would interact via email in the future. Though it seemed unacceptably inconvenient at the time, reality has proven that e-mail communication has become a fairly common means of communication. The paper delves into the difficulties of adapting the traditionally conservative legal system to the front-line corporate climate in which AI can succeed.

Susskind contends in his book *Online Courts and the Future of Justice* [22] that artificial intelligence (AI) will lead a span of transformation in the legal sector, transmuting judicial institutions. While automating our traditional ways of working plays a role, artificial intelligence and technology will also play a role in ensuring that more people have access to justice.

The world is now facing a future in which judges will receive evidence and arguments via emails or other methods of automated communication. In this state, the decision-making process could move from the court to the internet. As we move into the digital era, courts should expand beyond judge-made decisions to include some sort of analytical systems that walk people through their legal options, evidence gathering techniques, and alternate dispute resolution approaches.

Using AI technology in the future legal system could help resolve conflicts without the need for attorneys or the traditional judicial system. Using prediction analytics, the legal department will soon be able to predict the outcome of court proceedings based on previous judgments. An individual will definitely benefit from having access to an automated machine learning classification that makes a forecasted calculation about a case's probable outcome and then accepts that prediction as a binding conclusion. AI technologies can be utilized in legal services for document analysis, legal research, and practice automation, in addition to automated prediction.

Document analysis encompasses e-discovery, contract analysis, document examination, and due diligence. Contract Intelligence (COIN), a proprietary program owned by JPMorgan, is one of the number of established and emerging organizations that offer AI-powered document analyzing capabilities [23]. Legal research tools that use artificial intelligence (AI) provide a wide range of analytical and prediction capabilities [19].

Lawsuit analytical tools analyze the precedent case data and other data to support lawyers in envisaging the case outcomes, and the brief analysis tools helps to recognize relevant cases not included in an uploaded brief. The Chinese Supreme People's Court uses FaXin, an AI-based program, to assist judges in finding precedents, while Introspection uses deep learning to predict and alert users of their lawsuit risks [27].

- CourtQuant, a predictive analytics startup, has partnered with two lawsuit finance firms to use artificial intelligence to help them analyze litigation funding possibilities [24].
- IP attorneys can practice AI-based tools from companies like Trademark Now and Anaqua to conduct IP research, trademark protection, and risk assessment [25].

The application of AI technology to conduct duties extending from document automation to e-billing management is referred to as practice automation [26].

There are tools like PerfectNDA that employ the company's AI platform to automate the development of numerous litigation-related credentials such as pleadings and discovery requests, as well as tools that use AI to rationalize the procedure of generating non-disclosure agreements. WeVorce and Hello Divorce use artificial intelligence to automate divorce-related tasks [25].

Allstate employs artificial intelligence to automate the creation of claim summaries [29]. Multiple AI-powered solutions for personal injury litigation have been developed by a business named Keoghs in the United Kingdom [30]. Specifio's AI-based package robotically creates the first provisional patent from a consumer collection of claims in patent prosecution. To assist patent drafters in accurately defining the scope of their invention, CLOEM S.U.S.A. has developed alternates of input claims [31].

All these tools help to develop a cost saving and highly efficient legal solution. Additionally, this type of technology can facilitate the bridging of barriers between disciplines in multidisciplinary research in this field, allowing societal, engineering, and computer scientists to jointly work to address today's major challenges. The application of artificial intelligence (AI) to public issues can enhance outcomes and provide individuals with new methods of addressing issues that were previously not available. Although AI as a service may not solve all of the judicial system's problems or address the issue of access to justice, it can significantly improve access to justice.

4.7 ROLE OF DEEP LEARNING AND MACHINE LEARNING IN FORENSIC INVESTIGATIONS

From the last decade of the twentieth century, we are currently experiencing a world-changing digital revolution. Mobile phones, the Internet, and other forms of digital technology have all become part of our daily lives. With the onset of the Covid pandemic, it is visible how important digital technologies are in both our personal and our professional lives in this day and age. As a result, it is evident that the vast bulk of our important data will be stored digitally. Traditional crimes, particularly those involving banking and business, are constantly altering their faces as a result of technological advancements. As a result, in this age of information technology, it is necessary to update and enforce regulations.

Today's biggest challenge for law enforcement organizations is "Big digital forensic evidence".

The amount of data that must be analyzed is always increasing. Each case must be examined in order to arrive at a conclusion. Existing digital investigation techniques and practices necessitate a lot of human contacts, which slows down the process and slows down the rate at which digital crimes are committed. Machine learning (ML) and deep learning (DL) are two fields of science that regulate the subject of artificial intelligence (AI). Explicit programming is used in these advanced technologies to depict human-like behavior. At various phases of the inquiry, ML and DL paired with automation in the digital investigation process offer considerable potential to assist digital investigators [32].

4.7.1 MACHINE LEARNING APPROACHES TO FORENSICS SCIENCE

In forensics, there are two basic methods to machine learning: inductive reasoning and deductive reasoning.

Inductive reasoning as a method of learning – Inductive reasoning is based on a broad understanding of exact data. The expertise and knowledge is novel and therefore does not retain the truth. This implies that new information has the potential to invalidate previously acquired knowledge. There isn't a single theory that is well supported. There are numerous objectives in this domain, including the need to find broad perceptions from a partial range of examples. The instances are referred to as "experience". The foundation for the category is to look for comparable traits in different examples. Inductive learning is the basis of these strategies.

Deductive reasoning as a method of learning – Deductive reasoning derives knowledge from deep-rooted logic methodologies. Deductive reasoning uses well-established strategies to derive information from knowledge. The information is not novel. However, it is intrinsic in the preliminary understanding. Existing knowledge and its foundation in mathematical logic cannot be invalidated by new knowledge.

Literature survey has shown that machine learning contributed an intelligent associate for digital forensics which supported polls directed by non-IT expert and expert investigators [33].

Machine learning in forensics is based on AI and is used to process large amounts of data, analyze it for criminal activity, risk, and segment it to find criminal conduct and behavior. Forensic science via machine learning is the most recent trend in using AI's promise as a leading security solution capability.

Using behavioral analytics in medical, manufacturing, advertising, and corporate intelligence, ML is a key component of modeling, profiling, and prediction, and it has lately been employed in law enforcement. Data is collected via wireless or wired networks, as well as web or cloud computing, in order to uncover illicit behavior. As a result, ML algorithms strive to supply new information in order to enhance the solutions found over time.

ML algorithms can be used to evaluate large amounts of data in order to identify danger, segment data, and detect illegal behavior. Investigators can use machine learning algorithms to comb through huge amounts of data distributed across social and physical networks, as well as web and cloud computing. In essence, machine learning algorithms are pattern recognition software that is used to analyze large amounts of data in order to predict behavior. ML algorithms attempt to learn from past experiences in order to forecast future behavior.

Through machine learning algorithms, forensics gains the ability to discern patterns of criminal activity to predict when and where the crime will occur.

Currently, every sector is dealing with more sophisticated cybersecurity threats that are difficult to detect using typical security techniques. Attackers have developed additional efficient systems of attacking the system, which have become increasingly intricate over time. The system administrator would be unable to identify such attacks on a consistent basis. Human experience and competencies, on the other hand, have some limitations, resulting in a slow rate of occurrences, a longer delay in detecting and preventing cyber dangers, and the need for more advanced skills to remove these cyber threats. As a result, establishing more advanced machine learning models may aid in the prevention and defense against cyber threats. Nowadays, there is a plethora of automated software that can assist humans in performing complex and scientific tasks.

Karie et al. has used swerving deep learning and cognitive computing techniques into cyber forensics [34]. Forensics is a field of study that employs investigation and analysis techniques to compile and preserve evidence gathered from specific computing and electronic equipment in such a way that it can be presented in a court of law. For a rising number of crimes, computers are an important source of forensic evidence. Even traditional criminals are employing computers as part of their operations, despite the fact that cybercrime has been rapidly increasing in recent years. The basic goal of computer forensics is to investigate a well-structured issue while providing a recorded analysis sequence of evidence or proofs in order to determine what happened on an electronic device and who is guilty [28]. The capacity to accurately collect forensic data from these machines could be critical in apprehending and convicting these perpetrators. Forensic investigators follow a quality set of procedural criteria, such as physically isolating the electronic equipment in question to ensure it is not damaged by chance, investigators ensure that a digital duplicate shared copy of the electronic equipment is made. Suitable frameworks and tools of intelligent automation can also contribute to digital forensics. In brief, machine learning and deep learning forensics solutions will focus on well-defined challenges and methodologies, with sufficient data availability to enable modeling. It aids in clearly explaining the reasoning process and formally structuring the knowledge representation. Even with the integration of existing architecture, tools, and applications, automated systems using ML and DL can deliver a well-organized performance review.

4.8   OPPORTUNITIES AND CHALLENGES OF AI IN FORENSIC SCIENCES

In a forensic investigation, combining people and AI can provide a corporation more opportunities as well as advantages.

It introduces automation, which saves time and money while allowing investigators to concentrate on areas where fraud may occur. This aids businesses in detecting illicit activities from massive amounts of unstructured data, such as videos, photos, emails, and text files.

It's more dynamic than rule-based testing, which is restricted to monitoring fraud risk across a single data set. It eliminates information silos that can obstruct an analytics-assisted inquiry: this occurs when locally tailored processes prohibit integrated data sharing, resulting in investigative hurdles.

Plasma Pattern Recognition and Analysis, Crime Act Reformation, Digital Forensics, Image Processing, and, of course, Satellite Broadcasting are all areas where AI may be applied to provide more opportunities. It entails the application of effective scientific tools and methodologies to the investigation of the crime and the administration of justice to the persons concerned.

Artificial intelligence (AI) has the potential to make digital forensics more reliable, capable, and adaptable to changing conditions. It still has a long way to go, though. The sections that follow provide an overview of some of AI's shortcomings in forensics.

4.8.1 Changes in the Representation of Knowledge

To begin with, knowledge representation remains a significant barrier for analysts. Knowledge of computer forensics is largely a "closed world". If a piece of information isn't included in the ontology for any reason, it isn't taken into account during the investigation. Missing critical information is a severe problem, especially in the fast-paced world of computing, because it can lead results to be skewed and conclusions to be incorrect. The obvious solution is to acquire new information. Rebuilding the knowledge base, on the other hand, could be difficult.

4.8.2 Availability of Large Storage Capacity

Another issue confronting digital forensics is that end-users have access to ever-increasing amounts of storage capacity. There are a large number of storage devices, especially with the influx of electronic devices that are connected. Data analysts can be overwhelmed by the sheer volume of data stored, so its proliferation is a cause for concern.

4.8.3 Increase in Illegal Acts

Another issue for digital forensics is not just the rising number of cyber-attacks, but also their advancement of technologies. However, the majority of forensics analysts' techniques and methodologies are still finding it difficult to keep up with the attacks' constant development and quality. Malicious actors can design even more elegant ways in distributed networks, which increases the severity of cyberattacks.

4.9 THE FUTURE OF ARTIFICIAL INTELLIGENCE IN CRIME INVESTIGATIONS

It has been predicted that artificial intelligence will be the leading technology in almost all fields in the future because AI can achieve humanoid-like tasks such as pictorial perception, speech recognition, decision making, experiential learning, and solving multifaceted problems at a much faster and lower error rate than humans. With its rapid development, artificial intelligence can also be used to improve forensic science and the justice system. In today's criminal science and legal investigation environment, specialists face numerous encounters due to bulky volumes of facts and figures, trivial pieces of evidence in a confused and compound environment, old-style laboratory structures, and occasionally inadequate knowledge. All of these contribute to investigation failures or miscarriages of justice.

Artificial intelligence (AI) is the weapon of choice for combating these difficulties, which include machine learning and deep learning. In diverse domains of forensics, neural networks and case-based reasoning are used to produce error-free, objective, and repeatable outcomes. Pattern recognition, data analysis, computer vision, mining of data, statistical analysis and probabilistic methods, artificial olfaction, computational and mathematical approaches, graphic modeling are just some of the ways AI is assisting almost every major field of forensic science and criminal investigation.

As a result, AI is assisting forensic specialists and investigators at all levels of the investigation by constructing rational evidence, 3D reconstruction of crime scenes, handling evidence properly, and investigating it to reach rational conclusions. AI-based algorithms can detect risk in large amounts of data and are utilized for detection.

The use of AI techniques in the field of forensics will undoubtedly have favorable consequences that cannot be contested. To dispense justice in every case, AI can automate the forensic investigation process as well as collaborate with an expert.

4.10 CONCLUSION

Artificial intelligence (AI) has demonstrated its ability for human-like execution in activities such as visual observation, speech recognition, learning from experiences, and solving complicated problems at a faster rate and with fewer errors than living beings. AI is a rapidly developing field that is also being used to advance forensics and the system of justice. In today's forensic science and crime analysis environment, experts face numerous encounters as a result of big data, small pieces of evidence in a chaotic and intricate environment, outmoded laboratory structures, and occasionally poor information, both of which can lead to investigation failure or travesty of justice. Artificial intelligence (AI), which includes machine learning techniques, is the key tool for fighting these challenges. In forensics, neural networks and specific instance reasoning are utilized to create error-free, objective, and repeatable results in a variety of fields. By producing logical evidence, AI is supporting forensic specialists and investigators at all levels of investigation, according to the chapter. The chapter has also discussed the impact of AI in forensics, the function of deep learning and machine learning in forensic investigations, the opportunities and challenges of AI in forensic sciences, and the future of AI in crime investigations.

REFERENCES

1. Machine learning in forensic applications - Alicia Carriquiry, Heike Hofmann, Xiao Hui Taiand Susan VanderPlas.
2. https://advocatetanmoy.com/2020/08/12/branches-of-forensic-sciences/.
3. https://ifflab.org/branches-of-forensic-science/.
4. https://advocatetanmoy.com/2020/08/12/branches-of-forensic-sciences/.
5. World of Forensic Science. encyclopedia.com, 24-Jan-2022, Encyclopedia.com, 31-Jan-2022 [Online]. https://www.encyclopedia.com/people/social-sciences-and-law/crime-and-law-enforcement-biographies/alphonse-bertillon. Accessed: 31-Jan-2022.
6. Stigler, S.M. (1995). Galton and identification by fingerprints. *Genetics*, 140(3), 857–860.
7. Gross, H., Adam, J., Adam, J.C. & Gross, H. (1962). *Criminal Investigation a Practical Textbook for Magistrates, Police Officers and Lawyers*. Sweet & Maxwell, London.
8. https://forensicyard.com/forensic-science/.
9. https://www.fbi.gov/news/stories/piecing-together-digital-evidence.
10. Spring 2002. *International Journal of Digital Evidence*, 1(1) www.ijde.org.
11. An historical perspective of digital evidence: A forensic scientist's view. Carrie Morgan Whitcomb, Director, National Center for Forensic Science 11. Controlling Fraud with Forensic Data Analytics (eidebailly.com).
12. Marks evidence and pattern recognition in forensic science - From fingerprints to ballistic, patterned evidence - Florida forensic science.
13. The impact of chimerism in DNA-based forensic sex determination analysis - Abstract - Europe PMC] Victor N. Metallo, The impact of artificial intelligence on forensic accounting and testimony–Congress should amend "the Daubert rule" to include a new standard, 69 Emory L. J. Online 2039 (2020). https://scholarlycommons.law.emory.edu/elj-online/3.
14. Karie, N. & Kebande, V. (2018). Knowledge management as a strategic asset in digital forensic investigations. *International Journal of Cyber Security and Digital Forensics*, 7, 10–20. https://doi.org/10.17781/P002311.
15. Big data, digital forensics and data science | by Vividha Rawat | Analytics Vidhya | Medium.

16. http://www.dba-oracle.com/forensics/t_forensics_investigation.htm.
17. https://www.msab.com/blog/big-data-in-digital-forensics-the-challenges-impact-and-solutions/.
18. https://medium.com/analytics-vidhya/big-data-digital-forensics-and-data-science-fd5167f81891.
19. Kauffman, M.E. & Soares, M.N. (2020). AI in legal services: New trends in AI-enabled legal services. *SOCA*, 14, 223–226. https://doi.org/10.1007/s11761-0.
20. Susskind, R. (1996). *The Future of Law*, 1st edn. Clarendon Press, New York.
21. Susskind, R. (2019). *Online Courts and the Future of Justice*, 1st edn. Oxford University Press, Oxford.
22. Rayo, E.A. (2017, November 29). AI in law and legal practice—A comprehensive view of 35 current applications' techemergence [Online]. https://www.techemergence.com/ai-in-law-legal-practice-current-applications/. Accessed: 15-Sept-2020.
23. AI in legal services: New trends in AI-enabled legal services Marcos Eduardo Kauffman & Marcelo Negri Soares.
24. https://www.news-medical.net/life-sciences/ai-in-forensic-science.aspx.
25. PerfectNDA, neota logic. https://www.neotalogic.com/product/perfectnda/. Accessed: 13-Sept-2020.
26. Shepherd, D. & Laurence, A. (2020). How artificial intelligence could impact the future of family law, family lawyer magazine. https://familylawyermagazine.com/articles/artificial-intelligence-and-the-future-of-family-law/. Accessed: 13-Sept-2020.
27. How all state leverages technology along an "innovation continuum". *Bloomberg Law*, May 17, 2019. https://biglawbusiness.com/how-allstate-leverages-technology-along-an-innovation-continuum. Accessed: 21-Sept-2020.
28. What Lauri does. https://lauri.lawyer/what-lauri-does. Accessed: 11-Sept-2020.
29. Features, cloem. https://www.cloem.com/flat/features/. Accessed: 11-Sept-2020.
30. https://www.intechopen.com/chapters/70281.
31. Karabiyik, U. (2015). Building an intelligent assistant for digital forensics. *Forensic Science International: Synergy*, 1, 61–67. https://doi.org/10.1016/j.fsisyn.2019.03.006
32. https://www.techslang.com/ai-in-digital-forensics-prospects-problem-areas/.
33. Jadhav, E., Singh Sankhla, M. & Kumar, R. (2020). Artificial intelligence: Advancing automation in forensic science & criminal investigation. *Seybold Report*, 15, 2064–2075.
34. SWGDE [Online]. https://www.swgde.org/home. Accessed: 4-Mar-2022.

5 Big Data for Intelligence and Security

S. Vijayalakshmi, Savita, P. Durgadevi,
and A.S. Mohammed Shariff

5.1 INTRODUCTION

To put it another way, data was created through the union of technological progress and the information society. As technology progressed and became more affordable, the amount of data produced grew, and it has continued to grow ever since, to the point where we are now living in the petabyte era. The term "big data" is coined to describe the enormous amount of data that is being generated and accumulated. Everything that you need to work with large amounts of data can be found in big data analytics.

Big data is also used to store data in the same way as MYSQL, SQL, and many other methods. As compared to previous languages, it is faster and more practical and has quick and simple control over the manipulation rate. The term "big data" refers to the management (manipulation) of vast amounts of digitally stored data amassed by a wide range of businesses and organizations. With the proliferation of applications, networks, social media, and other means of data collection, big data is becoming a reality. The term "Big Data Analytics for Security and Intelligence" means the procedure for examining the massive data (petabytes, exabytes, and zettabytes) from a variety of sources such as IP addresses, emails, and information gathered from other sources. Organizations utilize big data analytics for mainly security reasons to identify abnormalities, threats, and security events, as well as to identify security alerts, to counter cyber-attacks [1].

5.2 BIG DATA ANALYTICS

When you think about a world where there is no way to store data, imagine if every detail about a person or an organization, every transaction, or every other thing that has been documented is lost right after it is used. Organizations would then lose the ability to get important information and knowledge, do detailed analyses, and offer new opportunities and advantages. Everything from customer personal information, to purchased products information, to employees hired, and so on, has become important for day-to-day continuity, so it's important to keep track of everything. In any business, data is the building block that helps it grow and succeed.

Decision-makers now have access to massive amounts of data which helps them to make better decisions very faster. It is difficult to work with traditional tools and techniques when dealing with big data, which includes datasets that are not only large but also diverse and rapidly changing. Solutions are required to study and handle this massive amount of data to extract valuable information.

When you look at lots of raw data, you can look for trends, patterns, and correlations that can help you make smarter decisions. This is called "big data analytics". Statistical analysis techniques like clustering and regression are used in these processes, but they are used with the support of newer tools. Analysis and mining of big data can yield operational and business insights on a scale and with a level of specificity never before possible. Big data analysis tools are in high demand because of the need to analyze and utilize trend data gathered by businesses [2].

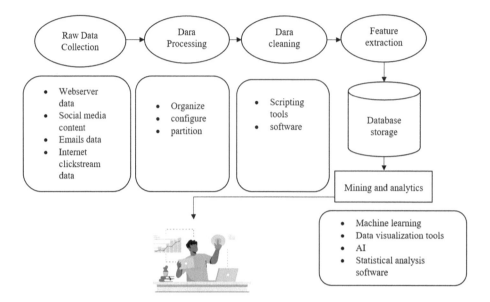

FIGURE 5.1 Data analyst's workflow.

There has been a lot of talk about "big data" since the early 2000s, when new software and hardware made it possible for businesses to deal with a lot of unstructured data. Since then, new technologies, like Amazon and smartphones, have added even more to the huge amounts of data that organizations can access. With the rise in data, early projects like Hadoop, Spark, and NoSQL databases were created to store and process big data. People in this field are always working on new ideas for integrating data from sensors and networks and transactions and smart devices and web use and more into a single picture of what's going on in the world. Big data analytics are being used with new technologies i.e., machine learning to find and grow more complex insights [3, 4]. Figure 5.1 shows how it works.

It is becoming increasingly difficult for governments to define their own cyberspace boundaries. There are many advantages to using social media, mobility and the cloud, but there are also many disadvantages, such as the risk and vulnerability that they bring. Distributed Denial of Service (DDOS) and supply chain attacks, advanced persistent and insider (APT) and social engineering attacks can all be exploited through this method.

5.3 BIG DATA LIMITATIONS

Analysis of large amounts of data is known as big data. As a result of these assumptions, designs, customer preferences, and other trends can be discovered. Data analysis, text analytics, modeling, predictive modeling, and optimization are some of the techniques used by big data analysts to discover these insights. Big data analytics has recently been touted as a business panacea. Big data is the key to unlocking the door to progress and success. Although big data analytics is a useful tool for making business decisions, it has some drawbacks that must be taken into consideration [5–7]. Figure 5.2 presents some limitations of big data.

5.3.1 RELYING HEAVILY ON CORRELATIONS

Correlation is a term used by data analysts to describe the relationship between two variables. However, not all of these correlations are significant or significant in the scientific sense of the word. If two variables are associated with each other, it doesn't mean that the two variables are directly linked.

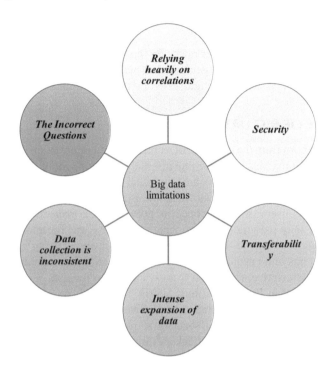

FIGURE 5.2 Limitations of big data.

5.3.2 The Incorrect Questions

Using an infinite number of questions, big data can be used to deduce correlations and insights. However, the user must determine which questionnaires are significant. If you obtain the correct answer to the incorrect question, you are performing a costly disservice to yourself, your clients, and your business.

5.3.3 Security

As is the case with a large number of technological endeavors, big data analytics is susceptible to data breaches. Security is the primary consideration for any technology. Data breaches are common with big data. Important data that is shared with a third party may be leaked to clients. Adequate encryptions should be used to secure the information.

5.3.4 Transferability

Because so much of the information that needs to be analyzed is stored under a firewall or in a private cloud, transferring it to an analytics department efficiently requires technical expertise. Additionally, it may be challenging to transfer information consistently to professionals for repetitive analysis.

5.3.5 Data Collection Is Inconsistent

The tools users use to collect large data sets can be inaccurate at times. If you're looking for something on Google, for example, you'll likely get different results depending on what you're searching for at any given time. The correlations you derive from data sets produced by Google search would be subject to change if the data points were updated frequently.

5.3.6 INTENSE EXPANSION OF DATA

The amount of data is increasing at a faster rate than the ability to process it. Past years have seen an explosion in the amount of data being generated. If we don't get some new machines, we'll be overwhelmed with data. This issue may be addressed by the use of massive data centers.

5.4 IMPORTANCE OF BIG DATA

The concept of data was born from the marriage of technology and information society. As time passed and access to technological marvels became more affordable, the amount of data produced increased, and it continues to grow to the point where we are now in the petabyte era. Big data refers to the massive amount of data generated and stacked. Big data analytics is a tool for working with big data.

As data volumes grow, users' security concerns grow as well. Protection of assets is security. Data security is not the only paradigm. The concept of security was born long before we knew it. Protecting personal data has evolved from the early days of cavemen using guard dogs to modern day home security systems and cryptography. Big data is popular because it is prescriptive, diagnostic, predictive, and descriptive, making it a good candidate for data security. The subsequent two data breaches presented in Figure 5.3 impacted the world and caused people to lose faith and confidence in data security controls implemented at the very highest levels of firms [8].

Such attacks have demonstrated that if security at some of the world's largest organizations, such as Apple, can be breached so easily, attackers targeting data at smaller organizations cannot be much more difficult.

Analytics that use a lot of data can help improve data security and context acknowledgement. Let's take a case: Big data technology can be used to look at banking records, log files, and n/w activity to look for suspicious or unusual activity, and to combine information from different sources into a single picture. Large-scale cloud infrastructures and IoT (the Internet of Things) generate huge amounts of data at a rapid pace, making traditional security and privacy measures ineffective in dealing with the onslaught of data in such a dispersed computing environment. Since big data analytics have become increasingly commonplace in business and government, security

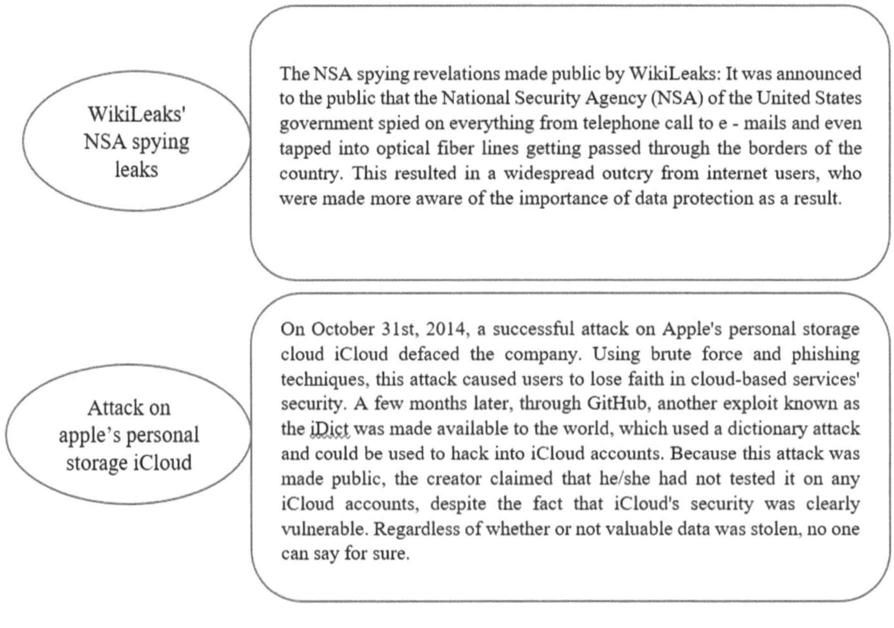

WikiLeaks' NSA spying leaks

The NSA spying revelations made public by WikiLeaks: It was announced to the public that the National Security Agency (NSA) of the United States government spied on everything from telephone call to e - mails and even tapped into optical fiber lines getting passed through the borders of the country. This resulted in a widespread outcry from internet users, who were made more aware of the importance of data protection as a result.

Attack on apple's personal storage iCloud

On October 31st, 2014, a successful attack on Apple's personal storage cloud iCloud defaced the company. Using brute force and phishing techniques, this attack caused users to lose faith in cloud-based services' security. A few months later, through GitHub, another exploit known as the iDict was made available to the world, which used a dictionary attack and could be used to hack into iCloud accounts. Because this attack was made public, the creator claimed that he/she had not tested it on any iCloud accounts, despite the fact that iCloud's security was clearly vulnerable. Regardless of whether or not valuable data was stolen, no one can say for sure.

FIGURE 5.3 List of data breaches that shook the world.

risk mitigation has become an important part of big data infrastructures. The scalability, interoperability, and adaptability of modern technologies necessitated by big data have proven too much for traditional security measures to handle.

Bank fraud identification and anomaly-based intrusion recognition systems were the first examples of data-driven information security. The most obvious application of big data analytics is in the detection of fraud. For decades, credit card companies have been detecting fraud. It was, however, prohibitively expensive to repurpose the custom-built big data mining infrastructure for other fraud detection purposes. As a result of commercial big data tools and techniques, fraud detection in healthcare and insurance is receiving more attention than ever before.

5.5   APPLICATIONS OF BIG DATA

Soon, big data will be all over the place. Big data analytics can now be used in every field of business, health, or general living standards. To put it simply, Big Data is a field that can be used in any field because so much data can be used for good. Big data can be used for a lot of different things. Here are some of them [9]. Big data analytics has spread its roots across all industries. As a result, big data is being used in a variety of industries, including financial services, medical services, education, administration, retail, industrial production, and many others. Big data analytics is being used by many industries, including Amazon, Netflix, online music websites, LinkedIn, food delivery services, and others. The banking industry makes extensive use of big data analytics. The education industry is also utilizing data analytics to improve student performance and make educational services easier for instructors. Big data assists traditional and e-commerce retailers in understanding customer behavior and recommending products based on customer involvement. This assists humans in designing innovative products, which greatly benefits the company.

5.5.1   Big Data and the Healthcare Sector

Big data has the potential to have the greatest social impact in the healthcare industry. Big data is present in every aspect of medical research, from the diagnosis of individual health risks to the development of new treatments. To keep track of and upload data, there are a variety of devices available, including Fitbits, Jawbones, and Samsung Gear Fits. Doctors will soon be able to access this data, which will help them make a more accurate diagnosis. A number of alliances have been formed, one of which is the Pittsburgh Health Data Alliance, formed by Carnegie Mellon University, the University of Pittsburgh, and the University of Pittsburgh Medical Center. "The health care industry generates enormous amounts of data every day", they write on their website. We have a responsibility and an opportunity to make this data available to medical experts and practitioners so they can put it to good use and help people. It is our goal to find ways to prevent disease, improve diagnosis, and improve the quality of care. In addition, one of the most difficult problems facing our country is the rising cost of health care. In addition, the Alliance will bring hundreds of businesses and entrepreneurs, and thousands of jobs, from around the world to Pittsburgh. A comparison of the patient's symptoms with those of other patients will be made in order to find patterns and ensure better treatment. If you want to find a cure for cancer or make medicines that are specific to each person's genetic makeup, you can use big data. Sundar Ram, the CEO of Oracle, said that big data solutions that help the industry get, organize, and analyze this data to improve resource allocation, plug inefficiencies, cut costs, enhance access to medical care, and advance medicinal investigations [10, 11].

5.5.1.1   Big Data into Healthcare Security

Healthcare organizations keep, store, and send a lot of data to help them provide efficient and correct care. However, securing all such data has been a difficult task for a long time. In addition, the healthcare industry is still one of the most vulnerable to public data breaches. As it turns out, data mining processes and techniques can be used by hackers to discover confidential material and then make it public, which leads to a data breach. Putting in security measures is still a complicated process, but the stakes keep getting higher as the ways to get around security controls get better.

As a result, it is important for businesses to use healthcare information security alternatives that will prevent important assets while also meeting healthcare regulations. Useful technologies are being put to good use. Many different technologies are used to keep healthcare data safe and private. There are a lot of different types of technology that people use [12, 13].

5.5.1.1.1   Encryption of Sensitive Information

Big data security in healthcare relies heavily on the use of data encryption. In order to protect sensitive information while it is in transit and at rest, healthcare organizations should use encryption. The data should be inaccessible to anyone but the intended recipients and authorized users. Encrypted files cannot be decrypted by cyber criminals because they lack the decryption keys. The healthcare providers have the option of selecting the encryption method that best fits their workflow. The data should be inaccessible to anyone but the intended recipients and authorized users. As long as the decryption keys aren't stolen, hackers won't be able to access any encrypted data.

Encryption schemes used by healthcare providers and organizations must be user-friendly, efficient, and easily configurable to also include new electronic medical records. The number of keys that each party has should also be kept to a minimum.

Data Encryption Standard (DES), Triple Data Encryption Algorithm, Advanced Encryption Standard (AES), Rivest–Shamir–Adleman, International Data Encryption Standard (IDEA) and Blowfish encryption algorithms are available. However, choosing an appropriate encryption algorithm to ensure safe data storage remains an ongoing challenge.

5.5.1.1.2   Authentication

Authentication is the process of establishing or verifying the subject's claims. It secures access to networks, protects user identities, and verifies customer's true identity. Authentication algorithms include digital signatures, password mechanisms, and hash functions in sensor networks. Tinysec by Kansas State University is the most widely used algorithm in sensor networks. Cryptographic protocols include endpoint identity verification to protect MITM attacks. For example, Secure Sockets Layer (SSL) and Transport Layer Security (TLS) are cryptographic protocols that secure communications over networks like the Internet. The Bull Eye algorithm can be applied to track all sensitive data in 360 degrees. Use this algorithm to ensure data security and to manage the relationship into original and reproduced data. Only authorized individuals are permitted to access the system's critical data. Every time a patient or a customer enters a healthcare facility, both their medical information and their identity should be verified.

55.1.1.3   Restriction and Tracking of Data and Application Access

Protecting patient data and applications by only letting people who need them to do their jobs results in strengthening data security and privacy in medical. If you want to be even more safe, you should also put in access controls like permissions and passcodes. Access restrictions require users to be authenticated, ensuring that only people who are supposed to have access to protected patient data can see it. Institutions can also use multi-factor verification, which requires users to verify their identity through multiple methods. Thus, by restricting and tracking access to sensitive information, security teams can quickly find unauthorized users and find out what happened to privacy in healthcare. This way, they can figure out what happened and fix it.

5.5.1.1.4   Data Masking

Masking hides sensitive data by replacing it with a value that can't be identified. This isn't really an encryption method, so the original data can't be found from the masked value. It de-identifies the data sets or hides personal identifiers like names and social security numbers. It also hides or generalizes quasi identifiers like date of birth and zip codes. So, data masking is a way to make sure that live data isn't seen. This method has the added benefit of lowering the overall cost of securing a big data deployment. Masking minimizes the need for extra safety restrictions on information while it is in the forum as it is shifted from a protected source.

5.5.2 Big Data into Sentiment Analysis

Big Data Sentiment Analysis is the most widely used application. Currently, millions of conversations are taking place on social media, which can help businesses discover new trends, prevent their company's image, and fragment their client base to increase product advertising and client experience. Several major companies are currently working on tools that can quickly and accurately analyze user sentiment. One powerful SaaS solution is IBM's Social Media Analytics. Information from social networking websites, both structured and unstructured, is gathered in order to gain a fuller picture of people's attitudes, opinions, and trends. Predictive analytics tools are then used to better understand customer behavior and enhance customer satisfaction. Using this information, a company can tailor its marketing and advertising efforts to better target its customers and increase sales [14, 15].

5.5.3 Big Data in Government Sectors

In terms of the cost, efficiency, and innovative thinking, the incorporation of big data into government processes has the potential to improve efficiency. The use of the identical large datasets throughout multiple government uses necessitates the cooperation of multiple departments. The current focus is on improving data storage and analytics. Big data enables governments to better serve their constituents by automating the processing of old paper records and building predictive systems based on the collected data [16, 17]

5.5.3.1 Public Safety

There are cameras on police officers' uniforms, on cars' dashboards, and on city infrastructure itself. As cities become more crowded, police departments are seeing an increase in the number of 9-1-1 calls they receive.

A warrant can now be obtained for information from companies like Google, Apple, or Facebook, including location data gleaned from GPS, Wi-Fi connections, and cell towers. As a result of this data, a number of recent investigations and even cold cases have come to a successful conclusion. The new data and big data techniques used to analyze it help law enforcement protect against internal threats and prevent or resolve the harm that individuals can inflict on each other.

5.5.3.2 Weather Forecasting

A wide range of sensors on land, at sea, and in space provide the National Oceanic and Atmospheric Administration with a constant stream of data. Over 20 terabytes of data are analyzed each day by NOAA using big data.

5.5.3.3 Cyber Security and Intelligence

The federal government has begun a strategy to achieve the security of US computer networks by researching and developing new ways to analyze large amounts of data. "Map of the World" is being developed by the National Geospatial-Intelligence Agency (NGIA) to gather and analyze information from different sources, including satellite and social platforms. Information from classified, unclassified, and top-secret networks is all included in this repository.

5.6 BIG DATA ANALYTICS FOR SECURITY

5.6.1 NETWORK SECURITY

Using Hadoop clusters and business intelligence tools, Zions Bancorporation has recently revealed in a case study that it can parse more data faster than with traditional SIEM tools. There is too much data and too many events for traditional SIEMs to handle alone, according to their experience. It could take up to an hour to search through a month's worth of data in their old systems. They get the same results in about a minute using Hive queries in their new Hadoop system. There is a data warehouse that helps people find useful security data from sources like firewalls and other security devices, as well as from website traffic and everyday transactions. It is one of the main promises of big data that unstructured data and different data sets can be put together into one analytical framework [18–21].

5.6.2 ADVANCED PERSISTENT THREAT IDENTIFICATION

Also called "Advanced Persistent Threat", it's a specific attack on something that's worth a lot. In contrast to malware that spreads quickly like works, the APT attackers work in a "low-and-slow" way. "Low mode" keeps a low profile in the n/w, and "slow mode" lets you run things for a long time. APT attackers mostly use stolen user personal information or exploits that haven't been seen before to avoid alerts. An APT (Advanced Persistent Threat) is one of the most serious threats to organizations today. For an APT, stealing intellectual property (IP), obtaining sensitive customer data, or obtaining data that could be applied for profit, embarrassment, or illegal insider trading are all common goals. Alternatively, APTs may seek to disrupt an organization's business. APTs are carried out by strong, well-funded and dedicated attackers who target specific organizations and start operating for months or even years. APT detection can be made easier through the use of big data analysis. Detecting APTs is difficult because of the sheer volume of data that must be sifted through in order to find anomalies. An ever-increasing variety of data sources must be audited in order to obtain the information. Due to the sheer volume of information available, finding relevant information is akin to looking for a needle in a haystack. It is becoming increasingly difficult to detect targeted attacks with traditional network perimeter defense systems because of the increasing volume of data. Because of this, a new strategy is needed. For example, firewalls, web proxies, domain administrators, intrusion detection systems, and VPN servers log information about the activities of users and hosts within the organization's network. Aside from compliance and forensic investigation, this data contains valuable information about user behavior that can be used to detect stealthy attacks [22, 23].

5.6.3 BOTNET'S IDENTIFICATION USING NETFLOW MONITORING

The word "bot" comes from the word "Robot", which is an intelligent software program that runs via worms, trojans, or other malicious programs to conduct a series of cyberattacks over the Internet. Zombie is another name for a bot. A "Botnet" is a group of connected bots under the control of a "Botmaster", a human operator who monitors and controls the bots remotely.

Many researchers are using the MapReduce paradigm to analyze huge amounts of Netflow data and find botnet members using the BotCloud research project (François, 2011 November). As a result of the massive amount of Netflow data collected for this project, MapReduce has been chosen as the data processing framework. In just 23 hours, 720 million Netflow records (77GB) have been gathered. Trying to analyze this data using conventional methods is a challenge. Analytics are greatly enhanced by big data solutions like MapReduce, which make distributed computing possible while also making it easy to deploy. BotCloud is based on BotTrack, which uses a union of PageRank and clustering methods to analyze host relationships in order to track and trace the command-and-control channels in the botnet. Botnet identification process can be divided into the different steps: creation of a dependency graph, application of the PageRank algorithm, and clustering using DBScan.

Netflow records were used to build a dependency graph that represented each IP address as a node. If at least one Netflow record has A as the source address and B as the destination address, then there is an edge between nodes A and B, assuming that P2P communications between bots have similar characteristics because they are engaged in similar activities, PageRank will discover patterns in this graph, and the clustering phase will then group together hosts with the same pattern. MapReduce only implements PageRank because it is the most resource-intensive part [24].

5.6.4 Enterprise Events Analytics

Security relevant information such as network events, software events, and people action is routinely collected by enterprises for a variety of reasons, including regulatory compliance and post-hoc forensic analysis. Data overload quickly sets in when dealing with this much information. The data can't even be stored, much less used for anything useful. To put this into perspective, a company like HP generates an estimated 1 trillion events per day, or more than 10 million events per sec. Event logging will increase as more sources are enabled, new employees are hired, and more devices are deployed and run more software. Due to the high number of false positives produced by current analytical techniques, they are rendered ineffective when applied to such a large sample size. As businesses migrate to cloud architectures and amass greater amounts of data, the problem only gets worse. Thus, the more data that is gathered, the less actionable information can be found.

A recent HP Labs research effort aims to improve analytics and actionable information with more data (Manadhata, Horne, & Rao, forthcoming). The objective is to extract admissible security intelligence from large organization data sets while minimizing false positives. In this case, more data means more value. But many hurdles must be overcome before big data analysis can truly shine. Concerns about scalable data collection, transport, storage, analysis, and visualization are among the challenges.

Many big data analytics for security problems have been successfully addressed by HP Labs. An approach using large-scale graph inference was implemented to capture malware-infected hosts and malicious domains visited by enterprise hosts. From large enterprise event data sets, a host-domain access graph was built by connecting every enterprise host to the domains visited by the host. It was necessary to use limited ground truth data from a black list and a white list to predict the likelihood that a server or domain was fraudulent in order to estimate the possibility that it was dishonest. Experiments on 2 billion HTTP requests, 1 billion DNS requests, and more than 30 billion network intrusion identification system alerts from over 850 enterprises worldwide showed high TPR and low FPR with very limited ground truth information.

A third method was used to analyze terabytes of DNS events containing billions of DNS requests and responses from an ISP. The objective was to detect botnets, malicious domains, and various suspicious attacks in a particular network by analyzing DNS information. Maliciousness-indicating features have been discovered. As an example, malicious fast-flux domains tend to expire quickly; hp.com, on the other hand, is a long-lasting domain name that resolves quickly to a wide range of IP addresses. Domain names, timestamps, and DNS response time-to-live values were all used to create a diverse set of features. After that, infected hosts and malicious domains were identified using decision tree like classification techniques. Many malicious activities in the ISP data set have already been discovered through the analysis.

5.7 BIG DATA SECURITY: CHALLENGES

The exponential growth of data creates both opportunities and challenges. While the prospect of improved analysis enables businesses to make more informed decisions, there are some drawbacks,

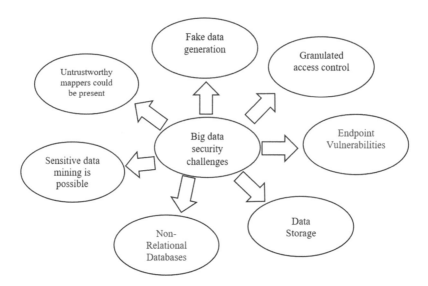

FIGURE 5.4 Challenges faced by big data in security and intelligence.

such as security concerns that could land businesses in hot water when dealing with sensitive data. The following are some of the big data security risks that businesses should avoid (Figure 5.4) [25–29].

5.7.1 Fake Data Generation

Before delving into the myriad of operational security concerns raised by big data, it's important to address the issue of fake data. Companies face a serious threat from fake data generation because it takes time away from identifying and resolving more important problems. A company's assessment of each individual data point can be a daunting task, so there is a greater opportunity to leverage inaccurate information on a large scale.

Spotting the red flags of a scam it's also possible that data can lead to unnecessary actions that could harm production or other critical business processes. The best way to avoid this is to make sure that companies are critical of the data they are working with to improve their business processes. The best strategy is to conduct periodic assessments of the data sources and test machine learning models with a variety of test datasets to identify anomalies.

A financial firm, for example, may be unable to detect fraud if false flags are generated by this fake data creation. A manufacturing company may receive a misleading temperature report, likely to result in a production slowdown and significant revenue loss.

5.7.2 Granulated Access Control

When data items are restricted, virtually no one can see the secret information they contain, such as medical records containing patients' personal information (name, email, blood sugar, etc.). Such items could theoretically be useful to users without access to the secret parts, such as medical researchers, who could theoretically benefit from some parts of such items that are not subjected to harsh restrictions. Despite this, they are unable to access any of the useful information. And it's at this point that granular access becomes an issue. Those data sets can be accessed, but only the information that they are allowed to see can be viewed. When it comes to big data, granting and controlling access is difficult due to the limitations of big data technique. A common workaround is to copy to a separate big data warehouse, the parts of required huge datasets that clients can see, and then provide the new "whole" to specific user groups as a replacement. If you're doing a medical study, for example, only the medical information is copied (no names or addresses). However, this method increases the volume of your big data even faster. System performance and upkeep can be adversely affected by more complex solutions to access issues at the granular level.

5.7.3 ENDPOINT VULNERABILITIES

The information on endpoint devices can be manipulated by cybercriminals and transmitted to data lakes. Authentication is required for security solutions that analyze endpoint logs. Manufacturing systems with sensors, for example, are vulnerable to intrusion by hackers. In order to fool the sensors, hackers first gain access to them. Fraud detection technologies are commonly used to address issues like this.

5.7.4 UNTRUSTWORTHY MAPPERS COULD BE PRESENT

After the collection of your big data, it is processed in parallel. The MapReduce paradigm is one of the techniques used here. When data is partitioned into multiple bulks, a mapper processes each one and assigns them to specific storage alternatives. If outsiders gain access to the code for your mappers, they can modify the existing mappers' settings or add "alien" mappers. This way, cyber-criminals can effectively sabotage your data processing by causing mappers to generate insufficient lists of value pairs. As a result, the MapReduce process's output will contain errors. Additionally, sensitive information can be accessed by outsiders.

The problem is that it would be easy to get access to this information because big data techniques don't usually add an extra layer of security to keep information safe. They often use perimeter security devices. However, if those aren't correct, your big data is easy to find.

5.7.5 DATA STORAGE

Cloud data storage is being adopted by businesses in order to move their data more quickly. When it comes to security, the dangers are multiplied exponentially. Even the tiniest error in data access control can open the door to a treasure trove of sensitive information. In order to achieve both security and flexibility, large technology companies are turning to both on-premise and cloud-based data storage.

On-premise data sources can be used to store project data, but for the sake of accessibility, less sensitive information is stored in the system. Security policies can be implemented in on-premise databases, but this requires the expertise of cyber security professionals. Data management in on-premise databases is more expensive, but businesses can't assume that storing all data in the cloud is safe.

5.7.6 NON-RELATIONAL DATABASES

There are rows and columns in traditional database systems. As a result, they are unable to deal with large amounts of data due to the sheer volume and variety of formats. As an alternative to relational databases, non-relational databases, also known as NoSQL databases, were created.

Instead of rows and columns, non-relational database systems make use of a hierarchical structure. NoSQL databases, on the other hand, tailor their storage models to the type of data they store. The flexibility and scalability of NoSQL databases make them more attractive to businesses than relational databases. Performance and scalability are more important to NoSQL databases than security. An additional layer of security is required for NoSQL databases to be implemented by organizations.

5.7.7 SENSITIVE DATA MINING IS POSSIBLE

Big data security is frequently based on perimeter defenses. Secured areas of entry or exit are referred to in this context. However, it is still a mystery as to what IT experts do within your system. It is possible for your IT staff or your competitors to mine unsecured data and sell it for profit if you lack control over your big data solution. With regard to your company's finances, new product/service launches, or user personal information, such information could cost you a lot of money.

Additional parameters can be added to protect data more effectively. Anonymization may also improve the safety of your system. Your users' personal information can be accessed without their names, addresses, or phone numbers, so they can do little harm.

5.8 SECURITY SYSTEM MODELS: BIG DATA

To combat cybercrime on a broad scale, we require effective threat identification and enquiry services. A perfect security personnel needs a system that is flexible enough to gather information from a variety of security-related domains. This allows the system to detect security threats and risks and warn experts in seconds, promptly allowing them to solve the problem. Some models have a lot of extra attributes, like an integrated security system, including the following:-

5.8.1 RSA SECURITY ANALYTICS

RSA detects and examines security issues using big data. Increasingly, organizations are looking to incorporate big data tools and technologies into their security services in order to better detect and investigate cyber threats. Traditional security protocols that only monitor and analyze a small portion of an organizational field are no longer sufficient for today's organizations. Organizations can't rely on perimeter or signature-based devices to stop today's more sophisticated attackers. All network-connected assets, as well as external threat intelligence data, must be able to be monitored and detected for suspicious activity by an organization's security teams.

It is RSA's security analytics that is leading the charge in big data's promise to collect and analyze a broader range of security data. In order to better detect, investigate, and understand threats, security analysts can now capture and analyze in near real time enterprise-wide network traffic and log event data, as well as the most current threat intelligence.

One of EMC2's most popular products is RSA security analytics, a software solution that has changed security management from a log-centric framework to one that has exceptional workflow ethics and thus stands out from other solutions [30–32].

5.8.1.1 Visibility of Infrastructure

Security-related data can be gathered from a wide range of sources using this system. A single, consolidated source of information on security, threats, and malicious activity can now be made available to analysts. In addition to real-time analytics, the architecture also allows for historical data queries. A real-time threat adjustment, investigation analysis, as well as data archiving are all possible with this architecture.

5.8.1.2 Analytics That Is Iterative

This security system gives analysts with quick investigation tools as well as intuitive tools for quick analysis that aid in the detailed analysis of a data set, allowing for better decision-making. This is based on how many people are linked to the infrastructure. It uses signature-free analytics to look for unauthorized attackers and events. Other features let you replay and relive events in their default state.

5.8.1.3 Improved Incident Management

It is possible to monitor the status of open processes by using workflow systems, which can be used to initiate responses just before threats are noticed. The platform provides functionalities that allow security teams to access and monitor threats. An industry-leading provider to help security teams maintain and acknowledge security incidents, this includes third-party tools and the RSA platform. When incidents occur, the responses improve and the learning gained from each experience is greater, resulting in better reactions in the future.

5.8.2 Beehive Model

Advanced Persistent Threats refer to attacks on intellectual property or physical systems of high value (APT). Slow and low-level APT attackers, unlike trojans, viruses, and worms, are more difficult to detect and contain. Slow mode refers to an application's ability to persist for an extended period of time despite its low visibility in networks.

Attackers use APT to acquire financial benefits, embarrass customers, contaminate data, or engage in illegal insider trading activity, all of which can lead to the devastation of a company's reputation. There are many different types of advanced persistent threats (APTs) out there, and they're all achieved by highly professional hacktivists. However, a big data approach can handle these threats superbly.

Beehive is an APT behavior profiling technology developed by RSA laboratories. According to RSA laboratories, a suspect's actions are not subtle; when an attacker intends to take sensitive information, he accommodates his activities and detracts from the standard. There are many stages to an advanced persistent threat (APT) attack, and each one allows the attacker to gain insight into how a system's users are changing their behavior, making it possible to uncover evidence of the attacker's stealthy and intrusive tactics.

Beehive uses anomaly sensors to detect behavioral anomalies. Each sensor monitors a specific user activity in the enterprise network. An anomalous access pattern can be detected by counting the number of machines a user logs into. A sensor can also monitor a user's regular working hours to flag both normal and abnormal activity and search for unauthorized sinks between public and private sites.

Activating just a single sensor indicates the appearance of a single anomalous task, while activating multiple sensors at one time indicates the appearance of multiple anomalous tasks. Thus, an investigation and a response plan are developed in accordance with the attacker's working ethics as a result of this. This is a simulation of a real-life beehive with many sensitive elements (sensors) working together to attain a common purpose [33, 34].

5.8.3 IBM QRadar SIP

As the name implies, IBM QRadar is a product that the company has created on its own. With the help of big data capabilities, it is able to predict and prevent attacks before they can occur. Analytical methods that reduce security incidents to a manageable number of high-priority incidents are used to find previously unknown connections in enormous amounts of security data. These next-generation systems can deliver benefits by increasing visibility into network and application activity and providing actionable intelligence on security breaches within an organization. This security intelligence platform was designed from scratch to do just that!

QRadar has a number of features that make it an ideal method for dealing with advanced threats [35–37]:

5.8.3.1 Capabilities for Spotting Anomalies

If there are any deviations from the standard in the recent activities, this solution can be used to identify them. It is capable of defining which deviations are significant in order to find a certain short breach.

5.8.3.2 Interoperability

It enables the creation of a unified architecture capable of collecting, storing, analyzing, and querying logs, threats, vulnerabilities, and risk-related information. It also includes a custom database that allows for reliability and flexibility tuning by scanning lots of records in seconds.

5.8.3.3 Forensic Skills

Security and network personnel benefit from QRadar's console view of all enterprise data, which makes it easier for them to quickly determine where and how a breach occurred.

5.8.3.4 Reduced False Positives

Deprioritizing innocuous events helps analysts focus on more serious threats, allowing them to spend less time on non-compliance detection and analysis.

5.9 CONCLUSION

Despite the fact that big data has been around for a while, it has now reached a critical mass as more and more people digitize their daily lives. When it comes to human adaptation in space, "people are walking sensors", says project manager Nicholas Skytland of NASA's Human Adaptation and Countermeasures Division.

According to prime big data trade analysts and research organizations, about 25% of IT organizations will migrate to cloud service platforms, and the service market is expeted to grow by more than 55% in the next decade.

In this chapter, we tried to summarize the security and privacy related concerns that are to be addressed in order to build a more secure big amount of data processing and computing structure. In today's world, the amount of data that has security concerns is enormous. Big data security analysis tools aren't secure when we pass over some of the information or can't properly analyze it. Real-time actionable intelligence is the goal of big data in security. There are various obstacles that must be overcome in advance so that the full potential of data analytics can be realized. There are a variety of security protocols for big data analytics. Each algorithm has its own set of advantages and disadvantages, and each algorithm behaves differently in a variety of circumstances. A specific protocol should be used in light of the security concerns and the application. Analyses of big data security point out some of the key differences between them and more traditional forms of analysis, as well as some of the potential research challenges they may present. Security intelligence of big data is a major focus of research in the field of computer science and emerging applications in industry at this time, with the goal of creating a safe and secure environment against unauthorized access.

REFERENCES

1. Gandomi, A., & Haider, M. (2015). Beyond the hype: Big data concepts, methods, and analytics. *International Journal of Information Management*, 35(2), 137–144.
2. Al-Shiakhli, S. (2019) Big data analytics: A literature review perspective.
3. Russom, P. (2011). Big data analytics. *TDWI Best Practices Report, Fourth Quarter*, 19(4), 1–34.
4. Kambatla, K., Kollias, G., Kumar, V., & Grama, A. (2014). Trends in big data analytics. *Journal of Parallel and Distributed Computing*, 74(7), 2561–2573.
5. Suresh, C., &Siddardha, K. (2018). Big data analytics: Challenges, tools and limitations.
6. Wilson, A., Watson, C., Thompson, T. L., Drew, V., & Doyle, S. (2017). Learning analytics: Challenges and limitations. *Teaching in Higher Education*, 22(8), 991–1007.
7. https://www.ciklum.com/blog/limitations-of-big-data-analytics.
8. Prabhu, C., Neogi, O., Shrivastava, K., & Katre, N. (2015, November). Review paper on security intelligence with big data analytics. *International Journal of Advanced Research in Computer and Communication Engineering*, 4(11), 453–458.
9. Rodríguez-Mazahua, L., Rodríguez-Enríquez, C. A., Sánchez-Cervantes, J. L., Cervantes, J., García-Alcaraz, J. L., & Alor-Hernández, G. (2016). A general perspective of big data: Applications, tools, challenges and trends. *The Journal of Supercomputing*, 72(8), 3073–3113.
10. Abouelmehdi, K., Beni-Hssane, A., Khaloufi, H., & Saadi, M. (2017). Big data security and privacy in healthcare: A review. *Procedia Computer Science*, 113, 73–80.
11. Manogaran, G., Thota, C., Lopez, D., & Sundarasekar, R. (2017). Big data security intelligence for healthcare industry 4.0. In *Cybersecurity for Industry 4.0* (pp. 103–126). Cham: Springer.

12. Patil, H. K., & Seshadri, R. (2014, June). Big data security and privacy issues in healthcare. In *2014 IEEE International Congress on Big Data* (pp. 762–765). IEEE.
13. Abouelmehdi, K., Beni-Hssane, A., Khaloufi, H., & Saadi, M. (2017). Big data security and privacy in healthcare: A review. *Procedia Computer Science, 113,* 73–80.
14. Shayaa, S., Jaafar, N. I., Bahri, S., Sulaiman, A., Wai, P. S., Chung, Y. W., … Al-Garadi, M. A. (2018). Sentiment analysis of big data: Methods, applications, and open challenges. *IEEE Access, 6,* 37807–37827.
15. Sharef, N. M., Zin, H. M., &Nadali, S. (2016). Overview and future opportunities of sentiment analysis approaches for big data. *Journal of Computer Science, 12*(3), 153–168.
16. Kim, G. H., Trimi, S., & Chung, J. H. (2014). Big-data applications in the government sector. *Communications of the ACM, 57*(3), 78–85.
17. Fredriksson, C., Mubarak, F., Tuohimaa, M., & Zhan, M. (2017). Big data in the public sector: A systematic literature review. *Scandinavian Journal of Public Administration, 21*(3), 39–62.
18. Cardenas, A. A., Manadhata, P. K., & Rajan, S. P. (2013). Big data analytics for security. *IEEE Security and Privacy, 11*(6), 74–76.
19. http://www.darkreading.com/monitoring/a-case-study-in-security-big-data-analys/232602339.
20. http://www.darkreading.com/security-monitoring/167901086/security/news/232602339/a-case-study-in-security-big-data-analysis.html.
21. http://www.businesswire.com/news/home/20110802005827/en/Zettaset%E2%80%99s-Security-Data-Warehouse-Enables-Big-Data.
22. Curry, S. et al. (2011). RSA security brief: Mobilizing intelligent security operations for advanced persistent threats. Retrieved July 15, 2013, from http://www.rsa.com/innovation/docs/11313_APT_BRF_0211.pdf.
23. Verizon Inc. (2010). 2010 data breach investigation report. Retrieved July 15th, 2013, from http://www.verizonenterprise.com/resources/reports/rp_2010-data-breach-report_en_xg.pdf.
24. Amini, P., Azmi, R., & Araghizadeh, M. (2014). Botnet detection using NetFlow and clustering. *Advances in Computer Science: An International Journal, 3*(2), 139–149.
25. Benjelloun, F. Z., & Lahcen, A. A. (2019). Big data security: Challenges, recommendations and solutions. In *Web Services: Concepts, Methodologies, Tools, and Applications* (pp. 25–38). IGI Global.
26. Venkatraman, S., & Venkatraman, R. (2019). Big data security challenges and strategies. *AIMS Mathematics, 4*(3), 860–879.
27. Toshniwal, R., Dastidar, K. G., & Nath, A. (2015). Big data security issues and challenges. *International Journal of Innovative Research in Advanced Engineering (IJIRAE), 2*(2).
28. Moura, J., &Serrão, C. (2015). Security and privacy issues of big data. In *Handbook of Research on Trends and Future Directions in Big Data and Web Intelligence* (pp. 20–52). IGI Global.
29. Singh, J. (2014). Real time BIG data analytic: Security concern and challenges with machine learning algorithm. In *Conference on IT in Business, Industry and Government (CSIBIG) 2014* (pp. 1–4). https://doi.org/10.1109/CSIBIG.2014.7056985.
30. Cardenas, A. A., Manadhata, P. K., & Rajan, S. P. (2015, February). Big data analytics for security. In *IEEE Security and Privacy Magazine.*
31. A case study in big data analytics. http://darkreading.com.
32. Curry, S., Kirda, E., Shwartz, A., Stwart, W. H. and Yoran, A. (2013, January). Big data fuels intelligence-driven security.
33. Yen, T.-F., Oprea, A., Onarlioglu, K., Leetham, T., Robertson, W., Juels, A. and Kirda, E. Beehive: Large-scale log analysis for detecting suspicious activity in enterprise networks.
34. R cloud security alliance big data analytics for security intelligence. http://cloudsecurityalliance.org/research/bigdata.
35. IBM security intelligence with big data. http://www-03.ibm.com/security/solution/intelligence-big-data/.
36. Security intelligence and analytics. http://www-03.ibm.com/software/products/en/category/security-intelligence.
37. IBM big data and information management. http://www-01.ibm.com/software/data/bigdata/enterprise.html.

6 Deep Learning Decision Support Model for Police Investigation

Arun Mozhi Devan, V. Raghul, Urvashi Dhasmana, Asutosh Rath and Lija Jacob

6.1 INTRODUCTION

Criminal activities have risen abruptly in recent years. Such a sudden rise can be challenging to be handled by traditional policing methods. Police can address these challenges by using dedicated technologies like artificial intelligence (AI), cyber analytics, IoT, big data, and augmented reality to analyze and predict more accurate solutions. These new reliable technologies in policing will make crime-scene investigation and criminal analysis much more manageable when compared to the traditional methods. Likewise, doctors can use AI algorithms to analyze radiological pictures in the medical field, which might have significant ramifications for the illicit integrity system and pathologist communities when determining the fatal cases. The criminal justice and law enforcement assemblies utilize video and image analysis to acquire information about persons, objects, and behaviors to aid criminal investigations. Traditional software algorithms are confined to fixed eye shape, eye color, the distance between eyes, or demographic information for pattern analysis for facial identification. AI image and video algorithms learn complex tasks to determine and develop independent, complex facial recognition features/parameters (Strengthen Science. Advance Justice., n.d.). These algorithms could match faces, recognize weapons and other items, and detect challenging criminal occurrences [in progress or after the fact]Many organizations are working on the technology development of AI policing and continual learning of crime analysis techniques (Khan et al., 2019).

The emergence of neural networks (NN), a subset of artificial intelligence, has reshaped the standard approaches to machine learning (ML) models. Researchers are developing neural network models to predict specific types of crime using location and time information. They can predict the location of a crime based on the incident and time of day, demonstrating the use of neural networks in police decision-making (Walczak, 2021).

According to one of the research projects conducted by the University of South Florida researchers, the artificial neural network crime prediction models currently functional utilize geospatial data to furnish primary data on offenses to enhance law enforcement decision-making. Neural networks are shown to correctly foreshadow a distinctive type of crime cluster 16.4% of the time over 27 criminality groups, or 27.1% of the time if the numeral of collections is reduced to 7 to concentrate on the most common offenses (Khan et al., 2019). This prediction accuracy is much higher than simply guessing at random, which would yield a prediction accuracy of 14.3% with a p 0.001 value (standard Z-Test) (Walczak, 2021).

6.2 BACKGROUND OF CRIME ANALYSIS

Under certain circumstances, crime might be summarized as the nucleus of the circumstances in which one is compelled to live. Conversely, it can be defined as an implication of intentional pain to

DOI: 10.1201/9781003251781-6

serve the biologically selfish wants of human nature. There ought to be a suitable junction between crime's effect on society. It is unintelligent to conclude that crime can, to the point, be predicted to an extent where it can be prevented altogether. However, identifying the multi-component nature of the integrated phenomenon can be developed based on policing policies adopted by subsequent governments in crime-prone countries and can be evolved through unbiased learning.

The components of crime and the lack of crime are not the same; the causational effects are drawn differently due to the facts. For example, the developing world observes more blue-collar crimes than the developed countries. The functions of crime are too vast for the scope of this introduction. Given that the homogeneity of crime is hazy, the predictive analytical methods cannot be applied in their current form.

We ought to depend on the difference between the symptomatic and the truly malicious crimes, which would clean the criminal data obtained following thorough research.

The advancement in crime and policing strategies has dramatically publicized the role of intellect in the system, increasing crime analysis units in police organizations. Crime investigation has lured investigators from all domains to give their valuable contributions to make impressive models and methodologies. Moreover, this bridges a gap between unlawful spying and scientific understanding.

Ribaux and Margot (Baechler et al., 2012) developed a substructure for crime analysis, primarily focusing on forensic data. However, a query was raised on Ribaux and Margot's development with suggestions for a better structure for the model.

1. A structured memory stands for knowledge

The framework of organized and systematic approach to use diverse data types for analysis contributes a lot to building up an understanding between forensic sciences and crime analysis. The interpretation of new circumstances is based on prior knowledge and orientation of proficiency stemming from these different and unknown circumstances. The concept of policing will be recalled and popularized in the analysis concept.

Krishnan, Sarguru, and Sheela (Krishnan et al., 2018) discussed the predictive analysis of crime data and the model that can prevent suicide attacks from historical data. Cybercrimes considerably impact a person's mental health, and more such models are needed. They followed Deep Learning methodologies to form an artificial neural network to analyze data and predict outcomes to avoid such circumstances. These theories can help spread awareness in regions based on their criminal records. This approach is also applicable to real-time data, making it more resourceful.

6.3 THE DARK SIDE OF DEEP LEARNING

The downside of using artificial intelligence (AI) is that sometimes minor errors can fool the system. We are in the era of self-driving cars. For instance, a self-driving vehicle accelerates into a busy intersection instead of slowing down when approaching a stop sign. The report says that someone had stuck small rectangles to the face of the stop sign. The small rectangles on the face of the stop sign interfered with the system and fooled the onboard system with some other sign compared to the original sign. This, one of the potentials for sabotaging AI, is genuine which researchers do (Artificial Intelligence, n.d.).

It shows that it is easy to distract the onboard system by carefully positioning stickers into misreading a stop sign. Researchers have also shown this by adding some random noise to the media file (Crew, 2020). These are examples of how one can fool AI technology. Almost everyone might have heard of neural networks (NN), interconnected nodes similar to neurons (information messengers) in our brain. Researchers use several algorithms to find correlations in raw data, recognize hidden patterns, and classify them – a continual learning process to improve over time. Neural networks (NN) can organize all kinds of input, including images, audio, and text documents. Artificial intelligence (AI) has been part of our daily lives, from finding a phone call spam to user recommendations on streaming services like Netflix and Amazon (Gaikwad & Kolhe, 2015). Even tiny alterations to inputs are so minor that the changes are almost invisible to the naked eye, which may also fool the robust, sophisticated systems.

As mentioned, adding some random noise to the media file is an example of how one can fool AI technology.? These are examples of how one can fool AI technology. Everyone might have heard of the neural networks (NN), interconnected nodes similar to neurons (information messengers) in our brain. Several algorithms seek to find correlations in raw data, recognize hidden patterns, and classify them, continuously learning and improving over time. Neural networks (NN) can organize all input, including images, audio, and text documents. Artificial intelligence (AI) has been part of our daily life, from finding a phone call spam call to recommendations systems on media services.

Tiny bots can help surveil the house and can capture information and send to theburglars about the subject's premises. In most cases, these bots could even fetch the resident's keys.

Research scholars at University College London identified that bot burglars are one of 20 ways in which burglars or thieves could use AI to facilitate crime over the next 15 years The next concern is "deep fake" videos and images that thieves can use to exploit and terrorize victims.

For data poisoning, the algorithm can train in two ways. One method introduces data into the system, causing inaccurate classifications to be returned. On the surface, poisoning the algorithm appears to be a simple task. Artificial Intelligence and machine learning can only learn from humans and what they train them to be. Assume someone is developing an algorithm to recognize images of heep. Researchers could feed hundreds of photographs of brown sheep into the system to train models simultaneously. If he wants to educate his model to recognize cows, he can feed them by providing hundreds of black-and-white photographs of cows to the system. However, when a brown cow joins the data set, there might be a chance that the system could label it as a sheep. According to the algorithm, the white animal is a sheep according to the model we built. A human would tell which is which just by seeing, but they need to be trained (Security Intelligence – Cybersecurity Analysis & Insight, 2021).

Deep fakes are a type of data poisoning method many believe will be the next big thing in cybercrime. Attackers can create realistic-looking images by editing videos, photos, and audio recordings. These realistic-looking images are ripe for blackmail or disgrace because they can be mistaken for actual pictures or movies by numerous eyes. Data poisoning also includes fake news. Social media algorithms are tainted, allowing false material to surge to the top of a user's news feed, displacing legitimate news sources..

Along with the advancements, there is growing worry among the public about the potential for these hypothetical AI systems to be lethal. Humans have shown themselves to be quite skilled in murder, but there is a growing concern that these legendary machines may go rogue and humans will lose control. Commentators, researchers, and potential producers are all concerned about this. The Laws of Armed Conflict might be programmed into its software (International Committee of the Red Cross Unit for Relations and Armed Security Forces, 2002).

Conflicts in cities may overwhelm most people, and it is unlikely that a computer with such a limited vision of the world could traverse it, let alone fight and win without making severe mistakes. While "killer robots" do not exist yet, they continue to be a concern for many, and ethical standards are currently being developed for the same. Is it possible for a robot warrior to comprehend and implement the Laws of Armed Conflict? Could it know the difference between friend and adversary, and if so, how would it react?

Militias, troops from different sides utilizing comparable equipment, fighters who do not usually wear an identifying uniform, and non-combatants are all examples of this. Human Rights Watch has called for banning entirely autonomous AI units capable of making fatal judgments, similar to the prohibitions for mines, chemical and biological weapons, and other weapons. Another major fear is that there is a big chance that a hacker can compromise a computer in ways that someone cannot compromise an individual. It may fight beside one minute before turning against someone else the next.

Human troops have already mutinied and switched allegiances, but turning one's whole army or fleet against them with a single keystroke is a horrifying prospect for military planners. Furthermore, the software can fail. The phrase "sorry, the system is down" is common in modern civilian life; imagine it applied to armed robots engaged in combat.

The malicious application of AI malware is maybe the most alarming. The world's most renowned cyber-weapon, Stuxnet, attempted to infiltrate the software controlling the spinning of centrifuges purifying uranium in Iran more than ten years ago. It could conceal and disguise its traces while searching for a specific section of code to target to cause the centrifuges to spin out of control and destroy the target. Although incredibly advanced at the time, it pales compared to what is available now and what may be used in a conflict.

6.4 AI-AUTHORED FAKE NEWS DETECTION

AI software is improving and media literacy becomes more challenging to differentiate between what is real and what is fake. Humans need to detect and understand the strategies employed by AI to manufacture news and generate to fulfill what we may consider the desires of intense social and political players. AI software might be dangerous for society, especially for the feeble. We did not write the previous two paragraphs. We employed an AI algorithm to construct the following text using Machine Learning and Natural Language Processing to generate writing.

Artificial intelligence and machine learning-assisted writing have progressed considerably in quality and acquisition over several years. A robot-generated essay is currently being employed in newsrooms worldwide and by businesses eager to create content fast and cheap. The disadvantage of this technology is that individuals use these technologies to spread false information.

Let us say we have a program, as the AI appears to be saying, "pose a threat to society?" We believe it does. Honesty and trustworthiness are associated with the modern world, but both lack robots and AI-generated literature, demonstrating the need for significantly more media literacy. It may, for example, convert raw data into concise, well-written articles for print and digital media. Others have utilized the technology to create brochures and web pages with marketing content. Although automated text-based journalism might be beneficial, experts caution that it can perpetuate prejudice and mislead readers. The creators of Google's Generative Pre-Trained Transformer 3 artificial intelligence platform have cautioned that propagandists and disinformation spreaders might abuse the technology.

Some bad people who rely on AI capabilities will pose severe difficulties to internet platforms, governments, and news consumers. "Confusion," "fatigue," and "doubt" are fertile ground for authoritarian and illiberal leaders,fueling the desire for divisiveness, scapegoating, and simple solutions to capitalize on the project. Technology enablers and developers will likely build tools to detect Artificial Intelligence-generated content (Marr, 2021). However, this cannot be the only solution; it is hard to see fake writing, and AI will probably stay one step ahead. Factuaand beneficial information must be prioritized on social media platforms while pushing misinformation to the background. The information landscape will only become more difficult even with the most assertive policies and processes in place. Institute must teach critical thinking and media literacy skills to individuals. The United States must promote a liberal arts education that prepares pupils to think critically.

6.5 SNAKE OIL

During the nineteenth century, salesmen would roam around towns/cities and sell an elixir – a cure to all diseases. This elixir is called "snake oil." However, most of these elixirs and lotions had little therapeutic value and did not contain snake oil. This deception was so widespread that the word "snake oil" came to mean "fake items" and "false promises."

Let us fast forward to the twenty-first century. Over time, snake oil items have changed, making their way into current technologies. Today's tech business is rife with software snake oil. Vaporware and future ware, as well as over-egged claims of functionality, are all examples. The crown gem of tech snake oil, on the other hand is artificial intelligence (Haynes, 2021).

6.5.1 THE STUDY EXPOSING THE SNAKE OIL

A recent poll conducted by MMC, a London-based venture capital firm, sheds light on the size of the AI snake oil problem. Analysis by various sources shows that nearly 40% of European start-ups labeled as "AI firms" (1,250 out of 2,830) do not employ AI. There is no proof or application of AI's "material to their value proposition."

The survey also discovered that when organizations use AI technology, the results are frequently predictable and dull. Fraud detection and chatbots were the most popular. Business process automation and rule-based systems are commonly conflated with AI, adding to the AI snake oil problem.

So, 40% of the so-called AI firms are peddling AI snake oil right from the gate. Nevertheless, it is not simply the lack of AI that is a concern, but also how the technology could be portrayed in the market.

The different flavors of AI snake oil, then, is an issue that comes in a variety of flavors.

- Misclassification of a firm: As noted in the study, consumers sometimes believe that a company employs AI in its products and operations when it does not. As a result, the products or services these businesses sell may include a side of AI snake oil.
- Pseudo-AI: A few recent cases of significant AI snake oil have been exposed. The disclosure of humans behaving as artificial intelligence. Pseudo AI is frequently unknown to the business's investors and customers, and this is a more active illusion known as the "Wizard of Oz technique." Customers are being deceived intentionally by companies.
- When a corporation advertises a non-AI product or functions as artificial intelligence, this is the last sort of AI snake oil, when non-AI applications are marketed as AI or used as a selling factor, hence addressed as AI snake oil.

6.5.2 HYPE AND IGNORANCE

So, why are there so many businesses peddling AI snake oil?

The first reason is that they are taking advantage of the publicity. Start-ups classified as "AI" receive 15–50% more investment. As AI becomes more of a buzzword, investors are keen to jump on board early (Editor's Choice, 2020).

Data are dubbed "the new oil" by many people. The million(multi?) dollar question is whether it is the fuel that builds your business or snake oil that does nothing but burn a hole in your purse.

Over time, data can transform the accompanying technical maturity and transformation. However, the assumption suggests that corporate data must be standardized or equivalent somehow. The current market has compelled enterprises to invest heavily in finding, gathering, transporting, storing, and optimizing data before others realize the value, resulting in inefficiencies and redundancies.

According to an IBM Smarter Business Review, 2.5 quintillion data bytes are generated on a daily basis, and the rate of increase will continue to accelerate as new devices, sensors, and technologies emerge (Pérez, 2020). Although the statement is accurate, it conveniently avoids that 95% of data are utterly useless. The reality remains that data quality is more important than quantity. The quality of a product is buried by its abundance. More does not always imply superiority. Technology and tool vendors promote the misguided belief that more data are always better.

Companies that provide tools for collecting, analyzing, and responding to data-driven triggers are getting fat on the revenues of burying us in statistics and diverting our attention away from the customer to the spreadsheet while bombarding us with too much data and buzz phrases.

We are sinking into a world of data-driven clichés and catchphrases. In general, the more knowledgeable the users are, the more informed their selections will be. However, there comes the point where information overload sets in. The proliferation of data has also had a significant impact on the changeover.

The goal is not to scare the users or convince them that using technology to assist data-driven choices is a bad idea. That is not to suggest that Big Data is automatically inferior to old-fashioned human expertise. The reverse is true. Any technology that accelerates the organization's innate knowledge and supports decision-making with the correct interventions presented in the right way has the potential to supercharge the way the business runs (Wright, 2012).

The users should be cautious while using an indefinite approach towards a business/ technical problem.

Machine Learning is both natural and effective, but understand how these techniques apply to businesses outside of finance.

The future of "big data" is pre-packaged algorithmic solutions. However, we currently lack imagination, which goes beyond having better instruments. The industry arose from the electronification of paper and had only recently progressed beyond basic data processing.

Microsoft Excel considered being a bogeyman. Even if we ignore Excel's immense power, it is a false analogy that perpetuates the notion that "this technology will cure all your troubles."

This argument's lynchpin is machine learning. While it is true that Excel is not the best tool for Machine Learning, the most critical question is whether or not ML adds value to the current situation. Is it possible to bring a new perspective to a situation when traditional statistical approaches have previously been deployed and successfully used?

As a corporation, operations must become actively involved in identifying data gaps, collaborating with the proper specialists, and implementing solutions to fill those gaps.

Essentially, it entails asking appropriate questions. Furthermore, only someone who knows everything there is to know about the company can achieve this. The perfect questions are those whose answers are straightforward, accurate, and convey a wealth of knowledge about the topic at hand. These inquiries lead to identifying appropriate use cases, which can subsequently aid in selecting valuable data to collect, process, and analyze.

The good news is that making better sense of data is a gradual process. The benefit is that users can let go of false hopes that an extensive tool adoption can completely revolutionize the company's data relationship.

6.6 FACIAL RECOGNITION

Facial recognition is everywhere, and the key to this is the meager cost of detecting and recognizing faces; even cheap low-cost microcontrollers like ESP camera are capable of facial detection and recognition. It means it takes less than five dollars to start creating applications that change the behavior depending on whom it sees. Because of how vital facial recognition is to our future society, it must not miss identifying people and ensuring that it works well for those who want to hide from facial recognition. However, it is a lot harder than it seems to hide from this sort of surveillance.

The average person in the world will use it for sales and automatic identification. It is one of those situations where there is nothing to hide. It does not matter if someone is a wanted person because no one knows how data will get used. A mobile app named "facer" attracts kids, automatically ages the picture, and flips the gender.

For example, China uses facial detection systems to identify homeless people stealing toilet rolls in public bathrooms. When someone looks at the camera in public restrooms, it scans the face, identifies the person, allocates the person X sheets of toilet paper, and gets X amount every half hour. Cameras were fixed there that automatically detected people jaywalking. For example, some Chinese female celebrity got a ticket for jaywalking because their face was pasted on the side of a bus to advertise their new movie. The jaywalking cameras picked it up, and they automatically got the ticket.

It is an extraneous and extreme case, but it just demonstrates the weird ways in which it could be used. It would not occur to people that they have to scan their face to get a toilet roll. Still, there could be the future. So generally, the human face has a lot of light and dark regions and is visible in eigenfaces. In general, the cheeks, forehead, the bridge of the nose, chin, mouth are bright and similarly, noses, eyes, eyebrows are dark, and based on this, it can mess with the camera systems. This happens when messing with the light and dark balances of the face. Because these regions tend to be relatively light and if it is suddenly made dark; for example, if someone is wearing a pair of black gloves and that person scratches their face. When this happens they are making the whole region dark which should have originally been light. So that can cause the system to no longer detect a look. It is a technique that is quite interesting. It is imaginable to go through a checkpoint where facial recognition technology automatically scans people's features, providing the impression that one's face is being gently stretched.. They are attempting to thwart the system while avoiding other really useful items in the front. It is questionable as to why this area is advantageous for designs, thus for some reason it is the eye between the eyes at the bridge of the nose. If someone covers this, then this causes many issues in the systems. Glasses do not count as a criterion, but factors like hairstyles defeat facial detection and recognition systems. They often have a bit of hair that comes down the middle to cover this region, or if makeup is being used, they usually have a dark patch or just something that will disrupt, like the outline of that shape, which can cause issues for these systems.

All networks have decided to put so much weight on here, but NN are like "black magic" because it is unknown what is going on all the time.

So, things like Adam Harvey's CV dazzle techniques are exciting, and seem pretty successful. He has designed a set of hair and make-up techniques that generally mess with the light and dark balances of the face, so having black lines asymmetrical haircuts because a lot of the systems rely on the fact that there is some symmetry in the face. Generally, the styles he goes for are the opposite of traditional make-up. In traditional make-up, people darken their lips by applying dark red lipstick, darken the eyes by applying eyeliner on and mascara. Many other people also use dazzling-based techniques such as glasses with a bit of reflective plastic on them at an angle. The overhead lights are then reflected into the camera system to dazzle the camera. There is some success with that. Some people have little infrared rays on LEDs around their glasses because many camera systems use infrared. After all, it gives a bit more depth perception and works better in low-light conditions. Dazzling the camera system is quite effective, some people have also done work on diming these infrared lights onto their faces to try and appear as a different person, and they have had some success with what they discovered in the trials.

There are two different types of facial recognition, one using an open-source Python library on a computer and the second running entirely on a microcontroller. The one running on a microcontroller trip quickly, but a Python-based script might present a more significant challenge in this Python script. There are two main libraries, OpenCV, a computer vision lab, and face, a modern Python library for facial recognition. There is an SP camera. What this script does is that each takes the feed from the camera and each frame from the camera. It then tries to see if there is a face in it and if there is one it tries to compare it to a bunch of images, and if it finds a match, it identifies it and says, "hey, here is someone's friend."

6.7   DNA ANALYSIS

Forensics is one of the advantageous sectors during a crime scene investigation that breaks the central part of the mystery of the case. Forensic experts believe biometrics is the vital lead for many unsolved cases. Even police officials of Avon and Somerset state solved one of the most challenging cases in the United States of America after 32 years with the help of forensic records, especially with the help of fingerprints and DNA data (Hayhurst, 2016). The semen traces found on the victim's belongings matched the assailant's DNA records and the fingerprints found at the crime scene. The test was re-run several times to get accurate results for contemplating the criminal to justice. Many people have an assumption that the generation of DNA is only possible with fingerprints and blood trials. Still, the reality is that there are a lot of other options and chances of retrieval from samples of the oral cavity, urine, saliva, palm prints, footprints, semen and skin. However, analyzing these samples with traditional methods (Manual Analysis) is a time-consuming task to get an efficient output. Hence, many new techniques like Short Tandem Repeat analysis, SingleNucleotide Polymorphisms and even whole genomes implement to retrieve data to help the crime analyst break the case.

On the other hand, these processes automate with the help of some software like Powerseq from Promega (Corporation, n.d.). The Promeg's Powerseq system uses its algorithms to automate the short tandem repeat analysis and single nucleotide polymorphisms techniques. These data are stored in libraries to map with the international and national forensic data hubs like Combined DNA Index System (CODIS; Figure 6.1) and National Institute of Criminology and Forensic Science (NICFS). Now the compared data are transformed into clusters, or we may say that there are different sets generated to compare the intensity of the level of significance of the match. Clusters are sequenced; the sample DNA obtained from the crime scene is deduced to the DNA in the database. Precisely, the structure of DNA is made up of four significant blocks: adenine, cytosine, guanine, and thymine. These sequences vary from person to person, making them unique for analysis (S Collins, n.d.). These analyses can help the police officials conclude the A1 (in criminology A1 is used to address the primary accused) and can lead to more information. Furthermore, the developers improve these technologies by implementing AI to outstand the purpose of creation. This advancement makes the system autonomous to have self-paced learning and work or automate the whole process with high accuracy.

6.8   CYBERCRIME AND THREAT INTELLIGENCE

Cybersecurity is a vast field that seeks development every second as the rate of cyber threats increases regularly. Even though there are anti-cyber associations in every country with advanced tools to overcome the situation, it is challenging to believe that the rate of cyberattacks and the method of carrying it out is becoming very complicated to crack or break the algorithms. The defenders get powerful, and the attackers are doubling their efforts to manipulate data and hack all the systems in possible ways. However, cybercrime includes not only hacking but also sex trafficking, counterfeiting, money laundering, portfolio manipulation, and other phishing activities. In a recent *The Hindu* newspaper report, a rise of 11.8% in cyber threats in 2020 was recorded (Figure 6.2), which is approximately 578 incidents (Hindu, 2021).

Many analyses from organizations like the FBI cyber division, Central Cyber Unit, cyber peace foundation, and others reveal that the number of cases and percentage of cybercrime would increase by two times the existing data.. Even though there are anti-cyber associations in every country with advanced tools to overcome the situation, it is challenging to believe that the rate of cyberattacks and the method of carrying it out is becoming very complicated to crack or break the algorithms. The defenders get powerful, and the attackers are doubling their efforts to manipulate data and hack all the systems in all possible ways.

6.9   ARTIFICIAL INTELLIGENCE: LIMITATIONS AND CHALLENGES

The problems faced in the development of AI are more centered on individual case scenarios. However, the general issues faced are faster computation of real-world issues and the ability to solve a wide range of problems by a single machine. For example, the robots developed by Boston Dynamics can obtain the minimized path from point A to point B and provide oversight in places where a human cannot access it. For this reason, they are currently being tested and deployed at a

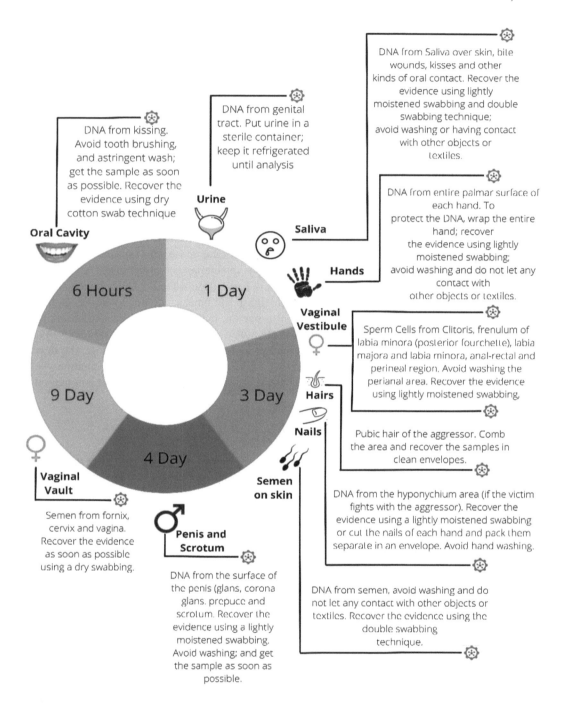

FIGURE 6.1   Forensic evidence to solve a case. (Redrawn: Combined DNA Index System)

pumped storage plant in Western Austria by Energy Robotics to provide oversight to the various operations of the plant since the area is not easily accessible in severe weather. However, if any problem arises, it becomes necessary for a human to resolve it manually. This is the area where further research is ongoing, wherein it is impossible to monitor the plant just by using AI wholly and entirely automating the systems. It still requires human oversight for brute force solutions and manual system repairs.

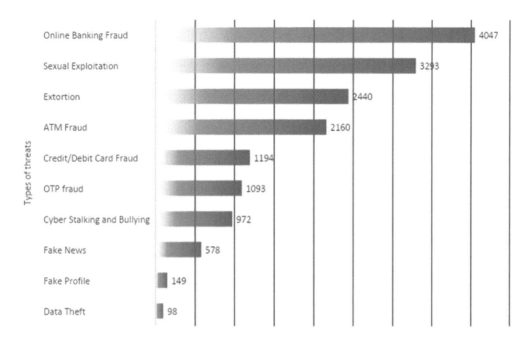

FIGURE 6.2 Types of cybercrime and their ratio in percentage from 2019 to 2020 (Redrawn: The Hindu)

This is one of many cases where AI systems cannot entirely solve all the problems. The technology is not far along enough to simply be self-sustainable. Web-searching algorithms have become extremely fast and reliant, something we see daily in our Google searches. However, there are still cases where the keywords do not return the correct index or show incorrect results. This leads us to another AI problem and application: computation power. Most web-searching algorithms and engines require incredibly high computation power, causing supercomputers to solve large algorithms and equations. Google can provide the correct index and spit out the results so quickly because of this reason (giving them a chance to boast about their search speed on top of the results). However, having sizable computational power is not possible in all cases, mainly if AI is used in small businesses for their operations.

Training algorithms need to get more advanced, causing severe problems where correct results are significant. This is prominently seen repeatedly in healthcare, wherein a false positive or a false negative can allow cases to seep through the system. Better edge detection techniques primarily employed to detect certain tumors and cancers are required, which currently pose a serious challenge. The systems deployed for various experiments in astrophysics, space research, and other branches of science sometimes miss the outliers, which are a part of meaningful results provided by the scientific instruments. This is another area where the betterment of the training algorithms and simulation runs are lacking in the forefront to further research.

The lack of understanding of the voice recognition system in the present day is baffling, especially looking at big players like Apple, Google, and every other smartphone company having their line of voice assistants. This is another area of research where the AI algorithms lack understanding of human speech and perform the assigned tasks.

One of the more nuanced challenges is philosophy, particularly ethics. The idea that as we move closer to the objective of a single device able to replicate commands and solve complex problems, the lines between intelligence and "human intelligence" continue to blur. This brings an ethical problem of AI having too much power at its disposal. Every other year as we progress in the development of AI, it is another aspect of the challenge before humanity that will someday require a discussion for its resolution.

6.10 MARKET BOMBING

Nasdaq Inc. is the parent company of the Nasdaq Stock Market, the world's biggest stock exchange in terms of stock volume. And also, this business runs independently without the intervention of any other organization. The business goal is to provide a cost-effective stock listing and exchange of stocks daily. One of the most crucial parts this business lacks is controlling fraudulent behavior without explicitly monitoring its customer. They admit the need to encourage an ethical exchange of stock between their customers. This business is increasingly focusing on technological ideas to improve market safety and effectiveness.

This technologically focused business has recently adopted AI tools to monitor fraudulent behaviors and traders exploiting stocks. The AI tools incorporate complex ML algorithms driven by data to counter stock exploitation. This integrated AI tool uses complex ML algorithms to detect unusual behavior within the system, which also alerts the concerned team. The unit may examine and terminate deceitful behaviors.

The AI tools also have deep neural networking algorithms to differentiate criminal stock frauds from the millions of regular daily orders. The authorities confirm that the AI tools correctly recognize outliers and fraudulent trades, paving the way for autonomous volatility identification and correction in the future. Also, the business maintains derivatives and fixed-income exchanges, and clearinghouses.

However, there are still considerable barriers to stock exchanges using AI algorithms. While deep learning algorithms in the equities market profit from billions of daily data, data gathering procedures and set size are lacking in relatively illiquid markets. Furthermore, the ethical dilemma of disrupting automation persists: algorithmic security procedures may eventually replace existing human market manipulation divisions. Despite the possible difficulties of implementing AI exchange monitoring, Nasdaq's investment in the field demonstrates future financial AI research (The Nasdaq Exchange Embraces AI: Market Manipulation Mitigation Built for the Future, n.d.).

Furthermore, the business authorities stress the need for human analysts to maintain the efficacy of market manipulation prevention. As a result, complementing AI systems can help us detect and mitigate equities stock fraud. The AI tools deployment indicates that AI algorithms in financial system security may only be the beginning.

6.11 MARKET OUTLOOK OF AI

Technology is not the only driving factor for innovation. Still, one of the significant factors contributing to innovation and development is the financial sector or the investments in the particular domain. According to the Homeland Security Research Corporation (Ltd, n.d.), the forecast for 2020–2025 is observed to be a $59.9 billion (~$60 billion) market for modernizing law enforcement and current policing techniques, which includes predictive policing, criminal analysis, crime scene analysis and forecast, IoT & Intelligent Video Surveillance, gunshot detectors, cybercrime, cyberterrorism, and private sector security. This growth can increase or decrease depending on various markets; for instance, if there is a growth in the AI market, ultimately it influences some of the concepts of AI policing, which leads to a steep increase and vice versa. On that note, when we compare the individual development of AI components to that of AI Policing and Law Enforcement, we can see a tremendous market value for individual members. According to the analysis carried out by market and markets (Figure 6.3), we observe a growth of market size by 39.3% of compound annual growth from 2021 to 2026, where the equivalent was $58.3 billion in 2021 and $309.6 billion in 2026 (Artificial Intelligence Market, n.d.). The individual growth of technologies like ML, NLP, computer vision, NN, and many more subfields of AI is the main consideration for the CAGR of 39.7%. Overall, we can conclude that the growth of AI Policing and Law Enforcement depends on other influencing factors, as mentioned previously.

58.3 USD BILLION 2021 - e

309.6 USD BILLION 2026 - p

The global market is expected to be worth USD 309.6 billion by 2026, growing at a CAGR of 39.7%

The increasing need to new use cases for business such as decision support, interactive games, and real-time retail recommendation engines to drive the market growth

The growth of this market can be attributed to the rapid surge of cybersecurity incidents and ransomeware attacks across the globe during the COVID-19 pandemic

The growing demand to access historical datasets to predict is expected to drive AI market growth

FIGURE 6.3 Artificial intelligence market forecast for the year 2021 – 2026 and the reasons for the compound annual growth. (Redrawn: Market and Markets)

6.12 FUTURE OF AI IN POLICE INVESTIGATION

AI policing refers to the ability to predict where crimes will occur, the people who will commit crimes, the types of crime that will be committed, and who the victims will be or could be, and the "criminology of place," a forecast on the occurrence of the place of crime. We have seen such deployment in movies like *Minority Report*, *Iron Man*, and *Avengers*. However, carrying out this process is very tedious, and is still a long way to become commonplace. Many companies and police departments from various countries have started AI-driven predictive policing systems to predict the crimes, analyze them for future deployments, and ideally help prevent crimes. This has opened a new industry and an optimal market for research and investments.

One of the essential parts of AI is facial recognition and image processing. These attributes of AI can be beneficial for intensive criminal analysis over a region. Also, the migration of a victim from one province to another could be quickly and efficiently detected using facial recognition. Such efficiency is because machines can employ various parameters to identify faces beyond the traditional way of identifying a victim (i.e., Human Detection) (2021). Not only violent crimes, but AI is adept in spotting anomalies in the pattern, which lends itself well to discovering non-violent crimes like money laundering and fraud. Analyzing images will pick out counterfeit bills and goods with high accuracy.

AI application in illicit integrity paves the path to succeeding possibilities to predict and oblige crime detection and the criminal justice system that eventually increases or improves the safety of the public. People are generating billions of data per second through various sources such as social media, online transactions, camera recording, and internet surfing. These kinds of data are more than enough to carry out some activity detection or predictive crime analysis on oneself, which could prevent the rate of crimes.

An interesting recent intel publication states the efficiency and importance of AI policing or AI crime detection using a real-time deployment by one non-profit organization (The Future of AI in Law Enforcement, n.d.). We see a lot of missing cases every day, and mostly those are children.

This non-profit organization called National Centre for Missing & Exploited Children (NCMEC) uses the concepts of ML, data analytics, and AI to find leads for the missing cases (International Missing Children, 2021). The NCMEC uses a unique centralized reporting system for online child exploitation called cyber tipline. Entries from various sources are collected regularly and analyzed within the time scheduled. These processed data might include numerous photos, videos, voice calls, recording, video calls, social media posts, comments, tweets, and real-time surveillance video, which are subjected to various analytic tests to train a model which can provide valuable and impactful deliverables that could save the lives of children (CyberTipline, 2017). However, the reports of the NCMEC state that this technological handling may increase the rate of recovery, which eventually decreases the rate of child trafficking and exploitation.

The advancement of AI in crime investigation, policing and criminal justice is an undeniable fact for argument. The future improvement may be a time-consuming process, but there could be many piloted versions from different organizations to upper hand the deployments for AI models and algorithms. One of the vital needs for all sorts of analysis is data. Continuous research and developments can outsource a vast volume of data to create an enormously large database consisting of historical, real-time, and predictive data packs for results. This sort of data converts or upgrades the databases even more potent than the existing one. All the current data are being merged with the new data acquired regularly. Ultimately this database integration could dramatically increase the accuracy and fairness of the crime scene analysis or predictive forecasts (Berk, 2021).

6.13 CONCLUSION

AI- and ML-assisted writing have progressed considerably in quality and adoption over several years. Experts warn that it can perpetuate prejudice and mislead readers. Honesty and trustworthiness are associated with the modern world, but both lack AI-generated literature. Today's tech business is rife with software snake oil. The crown gem of tech snake oil, on the other hand, is AI. Nearly 40% of European start-ups labeled as "AI firms" (1,250 out of 2,830) do not employ AI. Fraud detection and chatbots were the most popular. AI snake oil comes in various forms, from misclassification to pseudoscience. Consumers are being deceived intentionally by businesses. It takes less than five dollars to start creating applications that change the behavior depending on whom it sees. The key to this is the meager cost of detecting and recognizing faces.

The number of cases and percentage of cybercrime would increase by two times the existing data. Analyzing images will pick out counterfeit bills and goods with high accuracy. People generate billions of data per second through various sources such as social media, online transactions, camera recording, and internet surfing. The evolution of technology is an everlasting task required to run our day-to-day lives.

Nevertheless, humankind has to use it wisely for a better future and pass it to the next generations for further advancement that can serve the purpose of creation. The situation is that technology is used for both design and destruction, creating a chaotic scene to control. Even in police investigations, hi-tech and new technologies fade the pieces of evidence. On the other hand, the same technology is used to recreate a whole crime scene using data and high-level AI techniques that pose a deep learning search for getting the evidence back for analysis.

REFERENCES

Artificial Intelligence. (n.d.). Futurism. Retrieved November 18, 2021, from https://futurism.com/categories/ai-artificial-intelligence

Artificial Intelligence Market. (n.d.). Market and markets. Retrieved November 9, 2021, from https://www.marketsandmarkets.com/Market-Reports/artificial-intelligence-market-74851580.html?gclid=Cj0KCQiAsqOMBhDFARIsAFBTN3foNbQSYV3vHKqAPQ48eG1N6Whsgyc9vkxp5zTSGonQ4cDQAbZvx8UaAgrxEALw_wcB

Austin, P. (n.d.). *Deoxyribonucleic Acid (DNA)*. Genome.Gov. Retrieved September 23, 2021, from https://www.genome.gov/genetics-glossary/Deoxyribonucleic-Acid

Baechler, S., Ribaux, O., & Margot, P. (2012). 2012 student paper: Toward a novel forensic intelligence model: Systematic profiling of false identity documents. *Forensic Science Policy and Management: An International Journal*, *3*(2), 70–84. https://doi.org/10.1080/19409044.2012.744120

Berk, R. A. (2021). Artificial intelligence, predictive policing, and risk assessment for law enforcement. *Annual Review of Criminology*, *4*(1), 209–237

Boudette, N. E., & Chokshi, N. (2021, October 21). Tesla autopilot faces U.S. inquiry after series of crashes. *The New York Times*. https://www.nytimes.com/2021/08/16/business/tesla-autopilot-nhtsa.html

Brundage, M. (2018, February 20). *The Malicious Use of Artificial Intelligence: Forecasting, . . .* arXiv.Org. https://arxiv.org/abs/1802.07228

Crew, B. (2020, December 9). *Artificial-Intelligence Research Escalates amid Calls for Caution. Nature.* Retrieved August 20, 2021, from https://www.nature.com/collections/hchdibjchj/?error=cookies_not_supported&code=efe34700-c076-4160-9124-303163b88335

Editor's Choice. (2020, March 10). *AI: The Snake Oil of the 21st Century*. Information Age. https://www.information-age.com/ai-snake-oil-123481418/

Exploring How Artificial Intelligence Technologies Could Be Leveraged to Combat Fake News. (n.d.). Fake News Challenge. Retrieved September 27, 2021, from http://www.fakenewschallenge.org

Gaikwad, R., & Kolhe, K. R. (2015). Review paper on next generation collaborative filtering of data based on typicality method. *International Journal of Science and Research (IJSR)*, *4*(12), 1850–1852. https://doi.org/10.21275/v4i12.22121501

Golmohammadi, K., Zaiane, O. R., & Diaz, D. (2014). Detecting stock market manipulation using supervised learning algorithms. *2014 International Conference on Data Science and Advanced Analytics (DSAA)*. https://doi.org/10.1109/dsaa.2014.7058109

Hayhurst, C. (2016, May 10). *Melanie Road Murder: How DNA Collected in 1984 Solved the 32-Year-Old Case*. The Independent. https://www.independent.co.uk/news/uk/crime/melanie-road-murder-how-dna-collected-in-1984-solved-the-32yearold-case-with-christopher-hampton-a7022056.html

Haynes, A. (2021, February 12). *The History of Snake Oil*. The Pharmaceutical Journal. https://pharmaceutical-journal.com/article/opinion/the-history-of-snake-oil

How Artificial Intelligence Can Stop Market Manipulation | FIA. (n.d.). Fiamarket Voice. Retrieved September 27, 2021, from https://www.fia.org/marketvoice/articles/how-artificial-intelligence-can-stop-market-manipulation

International Committee of the Red Cross Unit for Relations and Armed Security Forces. (2002, June). *The Law of Armed Conflicts (No. 24–7)*. ICRC.

International Missing Children. (2021, May 24). *More than 1 Million Children Are Reported Missing Every Year*. International Centre for Missing & Exploited Children. https://www.icmec.org/global-missing-childrens-center/imcd/

Khan, J. R., Siddiqui, F. A., Mahmood, N., Saeed, M., & Ul Arifeen, Q. (2019). Predictive policing: A machine learning approach to predict and control crimes in metropolitan cities. *University of Sindh Journal of Information and Communication Technology (USJICT)*, *3*(1), 17–26. http://www.sujo2.usindh.edu.pk/index.php/USJICT/

Krishnan, A., Sarguru, A., & Sheela, A. C. S. (2018). Prediciitve analysis of crime data using deep learning. *International Journal of Pure and Applied Mathematics*, *118*(20), 23–31. http://www.acadpubl.eu/hub/2018-118-21/articles/21e/36.pdf

Marr, B. (2021, January 25). Fake news is rampant, here is how artificial intelligence can help. *Forbes*. Retrieved October 12, 2021, from https://www.forbes.com/sites/bernardmarr/2021/01/25/fake-news-is-rampant-here-is-how-artificial-intelligence-can-help/?sh=76f2b49448e4

Pérez, E. A. (2020, May 29). *How to Manage Complexity and Realize the Value of Big Data*. Smarter Business Review. https://www.ibm.com/blogs/services/2020/05/28/how-to-manage-complexity-and-realize-the-value-of-big-data/

Promega Corporation. (n.d.). *PowerSeq® 46GY System*. www.promega.com. Retrieved September 24, 2021, from https://nld.promega.com/products/forensic-dna-analysis-mps/target-amplification-and-library-prep/powerseq-46gy-system/?catNum=PS4600

S Collins, F. (n.d.). *Double Helix*. Genome.Gov. Retrieved October 21, 2021, from https://www.genome.gov/genetics-glossary/Double-Helix

Security Intelligence – Cybersecurity Analysis & Insight. (2021, December 13). Security Intelligence. Retrieved October 23, 2021, from https://securityintelligence.com

Strengthen Science. Advance Justice. (n.d.). National Institute of Justice. Retrieved May 5, 2021, from https://nij.ojp.gov

The Future of AI in Law Enforcement. (n.d.). Intel. Retrieved November 5, 2021, from https://www.intel.in/content/www/in/en/analytics/artificial-intelligence/article/ai-helps-find-kids.html

The Hindu. (2021, September 15). *India Reported 11.8% Rise in Cyber Crime in 2020; 578 Incidents of "Fake News on Social Media": Data.* The Hindu. Retrieved November 21, 2021, from https://www.thehindu.com/news/national/india-reported-118-rise-in-cyber-crime-in-2020-578-incidents-of-fake-news-on-social-media-data/article36480525.ece

Walczak, S. (2021). Predicting crime and other uses of neural networks in police decision making. *Frontiers in Psychology, 12.* https://doi.org/10.3389/fpsyg.2021.587943

Wright, E. O. (2012). Transforming capitalism through Real Utopias. *American Sociological Review, 78*(1), 1–25. https://doi.org/10.1177/0003122412468882

Cybertipline 2017, https://www.missingkids.org/gethelpnow/cybertipline

7 Big Data Paradigm in Cybercrime Investigation

*Rohan Harchandani, Palak Bansal, Shreyans Jain,
Jasleen Kaur Sondhi, and Lija Jacob*

7.1 INTRODUCTION

Big Data offers a variety of methods for analyzing and locating data as well as hidden patterns. Additionally, it aids in the management of extensive and complicated data collections. Having access to a substantial dataset can be advantageous in some circumstances, but it can also make digital forensics investigations more difficult. Traditional methods and infrastructures fall short of the anticipated reaction time when analyzing a large dataset. Big Data can assist with criminal investigations in a variety of ways, including through early warnings or predictions, proper decision-making, crime analysis, and more. This chapter provides an overview of criminal investigations, including diverse methodologies and the role that Big Data plays.

7.2 CYBERCRIME INVESTIGATION IN THE CURRENT ERA

7.2.1 CYBERCRIME

Crime entails the use of computers or information technology to engage in illicit actions such as fraud, hacking, breaking cyber security, and so on.

"Cybercrime" means any criminal or other offense that is facilitated by or involves the use of electronic communications or information systems, including any device or the internet or any one or more of them (Electronic Communications and Transactions Amendment Bill, 2012 South Africa).

7.2.2 Cybercrime Investigation

It is the process of locating, analyzing, and examining critical data from servers or networks engaged in a crime.

7.2.3 DIGITAL EVIDENCE AND HANDLING OF EVIDENCE FROM SOURCES

(i) Digital Evidence
Digital evidence is recorded information or the value of data communicated by an electronic device in binary forms, such as text messages, e-mails, media files, and browser activity history, and is admissible in court as proof. Table 7.1 presents the list of electronic devices and their potential pieces of evidences/ use cases or functions.

DOI: 10.1201/9781003251781-7

TABLE 7.1
List of Electronic Devices and Their Functions

S.No	Electronic Devices	Potential Evidence
1	Digital Cameras	Images
		Videos
		Sounds
		Time and date stamps
2	Display Monitors	Graphics and files
		Captured in media files
3	Answering machine	Voice messages
		Time and date of messages
		Caller identification
		Name and number
4	Smart cards, dongles, modems, and routers	Level of access
		Configurations and permissions
		User identification
		IP address
5	Smartphones	Calendars
		Documents
		Email and passwords
		Social media
		Address books etc.
6	Desktop cabinet	Files and folders
		Deleted files and folders
		Activity history
		Media files
7	Hard drives	Stores all the information
8	Local Area Network (LAN) or Network Interface Card (NIC)	Media Access Control (MAC) address
9	Servers	Last logins
		Exchanged emails
		Downloads
		Accessed pages
10	Network cables and connectors	Tracing of the respective computers
		Identifying types of devices connected to the computers
11	Printers	History of the number of prints
		Usage logs
		Time and date information
		Network identity information
		Sometimes fingerprints
12	Telephones	Store names
		Messages (text and voice)
		Phone numbers
		Caller identity identification
		Voice recorders
13	Global Positioning Systems	Travel logs
		Home location
		Previous destinations
		Point coordinates
		Waypoint names
14	Credit card skimmers	Card expiration date
		User's address
		Credit card numbers
		User's name
15	Keyboard and mouse	Fingerprints
16	Copiers	Documents both physical and electronic
		User usage logos
		Time and date stamps
17	CD and DVD drives	Stores files/data

7.2.4 Handling of Sources' Digital Proof

(i) Mobile Devices

Cellular and wireless capabilities are available on mobile devices. There are several techniques for retrieving information from the device, depending on the sort of information required.

For instance, call detail records, user information, and cell site information. A legal notification is sent to the service provider by an investigator. The first step is to keep the gadget safe. To avoid activities, it should disengage from all sorts of wireless connections, such as cellular networks and radio frequencies (deletion, wiping, and alteration). There are two ways to disconnect: the first is to put the smartphone in airplane mode, and the second is to put the device in a Faraday enclosure [14]. A Faraday box is a container that protects against external and non-external static electric fields by conducting current.

(ii) Social Media

Changes in the social media dynamic can be tricky. Distinct demographic or geographic groupings have different preferences for social media sites. Investigating agencies look to social media as a source of evidence and a method for gathering intelligence. Counterterrorism, criminal enforcement, demonstrations, and trends can all benefit from intelligence.

Investigators will need to manage the user's login and password on social media platforms such as Facebook, Twitter, Instagram, LinkedIn, WhatsApp, Snapchat, and Kik to gain additional information on browsing internet history, user information, and platforms. This data provides potentially useful information for analysis.

(iii) Internet Protocol Addresses

An Internet Protocol (IP) address is a one-of-a-kind identifier for a device connected to the internet or a local network.

IP addresses are viewed by investigators as a tool for internet research. IP addresses are divided into two types: IPv4 and IPv6. IPv4 addresses are the most widespread, whereas IPv6 addresses allow more devices to connect to the internet. The limitation of IPv4 is the scarcity of IPv4 addresses. IP addresses are used by investigators to trace suspects' internet usage. 172.50.120.254 is the IPv4 address.

IPv6 address: 2001:db8:3333:4444: 5555:6666:7777:8888

(iv) Internet of Things

Internet of Things (IoT) is an interconnection of physical devices, smart devices, buildings, and other electronic devices, sensors, software, network connectivity devices, actuators, and other things that allow these objects to communicate and gather data. IoT devices may show trends, activities, or other data that are the missing piece of the jigsaw.

TABLE 7.2
Generation of Electronic Devices and Their Evolution

First Generation	Printers
	Universal remote devices. E.g. Smartphones, Tablets.
	Internet access devices. E.g. Routers
	Printers, Copiers
Second Generation	Digital sensors. E.g. Thermostats, Smoke detectors, Water detectors/sensors, Fire alarms.
	Digital media devices. E.g. Digital cameras, CCTV cameras, Audio recorders, Mics.
Third generation	Wireless communication technology. E.g. Lifi (light fidelity), Smart watch fitness bands.
	Self-driving cars.
	Health devices. E.g. Heartrate devices, Glucometer, Blood Oxygen meter, etc.
	Digital security devices. E.g. Digital locks, Safes, Security sensors.

(v) Infotainment and Telematics Systems

Telematic devices are devices or technologies that send, receive, and store information and data, such as acceleration, speed, fuel consumption, position, and so on, utilizing telecommunication technology to operate remote control objects, such as self-driving autos.

To avoid data destruction, the investigator should treat the data with care. The digital systems in automobiles are comparable to those in other digital/electronic devices/systems. They save important information such as car information, phone logs, messages, e-mail history, contact list, media data (videos, music, photographs, social media feeds), preferred destinations, and navigation history. There are methods available to extract important data from vehicles; Berla iVe is a tool that facilitates the extraction of infotainment data from autos. Berla was first confined to Ford, Chevrolet, and GMC vehicles, but it is currently quickly expanding its decoding skills to an increasing number of vehicles. For over 5200 automobile models, both software and hardware offer data extraction on a logical and physical level.

7.3 TECHNIQUES USED IN CYBERCRIME INVESTIGATION

Creating and establishing the crime's backdrop using known facts can assist investigators to set a starting point for identifying what they're up against and how much information they have when dealing with the initial cybercrime complaint. The first part of a digital forensics investigation is identification, in which an investigator determines the episodes that are significant for pursuing a case and the evidence relative to those occurrences.

7.3.1 GETTING THE CHAIN OF CUSTODY STARTED AND SECURING THE DIGITAL EVIDENCE

After recognizing the evidence, an investigator must gather it from various digital media such as a mobile phone, hard disc, network, and so on. Early data or evidence security raises the chances of a successful investigation and litigation. The first custodian must be able to provide a more detailed description of the first document's appearance [4]. Many national and federal authorities employ interviews and surveillance reports to gather evidence of cybercrime. Surveillance covers not just security cameras, films, and photographs, but also electronic device surveillance, which includes information on what and when it is used, how it is used, and any other digital behavior.

7.3.2 IDENTIFYING AND TRACKING THE AUTHORS

This step may be performed during the information collecting phase, depending on how much information is already accessible. To identify the criminals behind the cyberattack, both private and public security agencies frequently collaborate with ISPs and networking companies to obtain valuable log information about their connections, as well as historical service, services, and protocols used during the time they were connected [19]. This is generally the most time-consuming stage since obtaining the essential material requires legal approval from prosecutors and a court order.

7.3.3 DATA FORENSICS

After researchers have obtained sufficient information about the cybercrime, it is time to investigate the digital systems that were impacted or those suspected of being involved in the attack's genesis. Examining raw data from network connections, hard discs, file systems, caching devices, RRAM and other sources is part of this technique. When the forensic inquiry begins, the researcher will look for fingerprints in system files, network and service logs, e-mails, online browsing history, and other locations.

7.3.4 IMAGE STORAGE DEVICES

It is the process of extracting data from a digital document and saving it to a storage device.

The following information is reviewed from the digital device: We studied the data by making a duplicate of the original evidence and loading it into a forensic instrument for further examination.

7.3.5 REPORT CREATION

In the last step, an investigator creates a structured report to convey his or her conclusions about the case, which should be acceptable in court. The cybercrime investigation tools give a profusion of capabilities depending on the tactics we choose. However, we must keep in mind that the majority of those technologies are intended for forensic knowledge analysis once we have the proof. Because there are thousands of tools for every type of cybercrime, this isn't meant to be a comprehensive list, but rather a quick look at some of the most basic resources for conducting forensic activities.

7.4 TOOLS USED FOR CYBERCRIME INVESTIGATION

7.4.1 THE SLEUTH KIT

The Sleuth Kit, abbreviated TSK, is a collection of forensic analytical techniques for UNIX-based command line files and disc systems (The Sleuth Kit (TSK) & Autopsy: Open-Source Digital Forensics Tools, n.d.). The file devices enable us to investigate a suspicious machine's filesystems discreetly. Deleted and hidden files are displayed because the tools do not rely on the operating system to process filesystems. Sleuth Kit accepts only the command-line programs. Whereas Autopsy simplifies and the same technique. Autopsy includes a range of tools for activities such as Keyword Search, Hashes Filtering, Acquiring Web Artifacts, Carving Data, Timeline Analysis, Exif Data, and so on that help in the gathering and analysis of critical data. Autopsy employs a large number of cores, performs background tasks in parallel, and warns you when something of interest surfaces, making it a very fast and dependable tool for digital forensics. Using the volume system tools, we may look at how discs and other media are laid out. We can also recover files that have been deleted, retrieve data from slack regions, examine a filesystem's journal, and analyze the partition layout on discs or images, among other things. It is important to note, however, that the Sleuth Kit only affects the present filesystem. The Sleuth Kit supports Mac partitions, DOS partitions, Sun slices (Volume Table of Contents), BSD partitions (disc labels), and GPT disks. These commands can be used to locate partitions and extract them so that system analysis applications can inspect them. TSK now supports the following filesystems: ExFAT, HFS+, FAT, Ext3, Ext4, UFS, NTFS and YAFFS2 [15].

7.4.2 SIFT WORKSTATION

The Sans Investigative Forensics Toolkit (SIFT) Workstation is a suite of free and open-source incident management and investigative techniques that may be used to undertake comprehensive digital forensic investigations in a variety of circumstances. SIFT was created by the SANS Forensics team as a computer forensics distribution for digital forensics. This release includes the vast majority of tools necessary for digital forensics investigation and incident response assessments. It is compatible with any present incident management and investigative techniques set. SIFT underscores the importance of utilizing advanced open-source tools, which are consistently maintained and accessible to the public, in order to improve incident management capabilities and digital forensic approaches. [13]. SIFT is scriptable, which means that users may combine instructions to make it act the way they want it to. SIFT may be run on any Ubuntu or Windows PC. SIFT takes evidence in several forms, including AFF (Advanced Forensic Format), E01, and raw format (DD). SIFT is also compatible with photos from memory forensics. HFS+, NTFS, FAT 12/16/32, EXT2/3/4, UFS1/2v, swap, vmdk, RAM data, and RAW data are all supported.

7.4.3 CAINE

Computer-Aided Investigative Environment (CAINE) is a live Linux/GNU system developed in Italy as part of a Digital Forensics project. Currently, Nanni Bassetti is the project manager (Bari – Italy). CAINE is a full forensic environment with a graphical user experience that blends current computer software into software systems. CAINE is a complete Linux distribution for digital forensic analysis, rather than just a cybercrime investigation software or suite (CAINE Live USB/ DVD – Computer Forensics Digital Forensics, n.d.). It is straightforward to set up on a real or virtual machine. CAINE may perform LIVE operations on file storage items without running the operating system.

CAINE Linux contains a variety of forensic software tools, modules, and scripts that may be run from the command prompt or in a graphical interface. It can extract data for several of the operating systems, including Unix, Linux, and Windows, and operates on a live CD. Among the most unusual aspects of CAINE Linux version 9.0 is that it defaults to read-only mode for all block devices. CAINE can extract data from any file system, memory, or network by integrating the greatest forensic tools with command-line and graphical user interfaces. Wireshark, PhotoRec, Sleuth Kit, Autopsy, Tinfoleak, and other well-known digital crime investigation programs are included.

7.4.4 X-Ways Forensics

X-Ways Forensics is an innovative workplace for digital forensics professionals. It runs on 64-bit/32-bit systems, and standard/FE/PE platforms, and supported operating systems. It simply takes a few seconds to download and install. Based on the WinHex hex and disc editors, X-Ways Forensics is a component of a pipeline concept that allows computer forensics experts to share data and engage with researchers via X-Ways Investigator [20].

7.4.5 PALADIN

SUMURI created PALADIN, a bootable Linux distribution based on Ubuntu. The boot procedure has been tweaked to ensure that no changes or mounts are made to the internal or external media of machines and devices. The ISO file for PALADIN can be used to create a bootable DVD or USB drive. When the user boots up, he or she will find a number of precompiled open-source forensic tools that can be used to do a variety of tasks. The PALADIN Toolbox simplifies a variety of forensic procedures by providing "Numerous forensic tools" — 30 or more categories, 100 or more instruments, including Autopsy and The Sleuth Kit. This virtual research facility on a disc is one of the most widely used forensic suites available since it is available in both 32-bit and 64-bit versions. Given that it is utilized by law enforcement, the military, the federal, state, and business sectors, PALADIN is the perfect ally for any computer fraud investigator. The heart of these instruments is the PALADIN Toolbox. The PALADIN Toolbox combines and simplifies a variety of forensic operations into a user-friendly Graphical User Interface (GUI) that takes little training and does not require the use of the command line. The PALADIN Toolbox's "engine" is a collection of apps that have been utilized by forensic examiners and investigators for years and have held up to the examination of numerous courts of law. Most PCs and Intel Macs are automatically booted into a forensically sound environment. It supports the most common forensic image formats, including. E 01, Ex01, RAW (.dd), SMART, AFF, VHD, VMDK, and VHDX. Devices can be cloned here. Conversion from one forensic image to another, including the VMDK format, is possible in PALADIN. Mounting and imaging across a network are both possible in PALADIN. Disk Manager makes it simple to see and identify attached drives and partitions. ExFAT, HFS+, EXT4, FAT32, and NTFS are all formats that can be used.

A forensic software platform called Oxygen Forensic Detective harvests, decodes, and analyzes data from many internet resources, such as IoT and mobile devices, UICC and media cards, device backups, cloud services, and drones. Oxygen Forensic Detective can locate and retrieve a variety of evidence, credentials and system files from Windows, macOS, and Linux PCs. The innovative and creative methods employed in Oxygen Forensic Detective include bypassing screen locks, tracking down passwords to encrypted backups, extracting and parsing data from protected programs, and retrieving deleted data, to name just a few. Furthermore, several extractions may be examined in a single interface to gain a full perspective of the data. The integrated industry-leading analytical tools may be used by enforcement agencies, corporate investigators, and other authorized personnel to identify social connections, create timelines, and classify photographs, all of which will contribute to making the world a safer place. Oxygen Forensic Detective comes as a USB dongle with a single-user license. It is possible to utilize it for the following:

  I. Data from over 19,500 devices can be collected (Android, BB, iOS, WP, etc.).
 II. Backups and pictures can be imported (iTunes, Android, JTAG, Chip-Off).
III. Analyze data from 430 different apps and 7,320+ different app versions.
 IV. Recover a wide range of data that has been destroyed.
  V. Analyze the information (social graph, timeline, key evidence).
 VI. Data can be searched using a variety of parameters, including keywords.
VII. Passwords to encrypted backups and photos can be recovered.
VIII. On common Android OS smartphones, bypass the screen lock.
 IX. Drones can be used to collect location records and media assets.
  X. Data are extracted from cloud sources (iCloud, Google, Microsoft, etc.).
 XI. Call data records can be imported and analyzed.
XII. Visualize a user's path and common location.
XIII. Data can be exported to a variety of file formats, including PDF, RTF, XLS, SML, and others.

7.4.6 ProDiscover Forensic

ProDiscover Forensics is a comprehensive digital forensics solution that enables investigators to extract crucial data from computers. ProDiscover is capable of handling all aspects of a forensic investigation, including evidence gathering, preservation, filtering, and analysis. ProDiscover's tools and capabilities may be used by an investigator to locate and combine different bits of evidence into a coherent picture. ProDiscover provides the capacity to study cybercrime's nature and methods. Reports of evidential quality can be generated and submitted into court. Researchers may utilize this digital forensic tool to swiftly locate files, gather, process, preserve, and analyze data, as well as create evidence reports. Using a number of diagnostic and evidence procedures, investigators may utilize ProDiscover's product suite to explore evidence and extract crucial investigative artifacts. Among its characteristics are cloud forensics, memory forensics, extensive automation, file previews without changing data on disc, including metadata, and data investigation at the sector level.

7.4.7 Digital Forensics Framework

This approach is used by digital forensic investigators to gather a list of user actions from digital artifacts obtained at the crime scene. The list may be used to figure out specific details about the crime, such as the motive, method, date, and place. It can recover data from both deleted and present files and directories in EXT 2/3/4, FAT12/16/32, and NTFS file systems. It also helps with the inspection and recovery of lost items network connections, local files, and program which are all stored on memory sticks [5,7].

7.4.8 BULK EXTRACTOR

Bulk Extractor is a system that gathers information from digital evidentiary files such as credit card numbers, URLs, e-mail addresses, and other forms of data. It's a multi-purpose forensics investigation application that may be used for malware and intrusion detection, visual analysis, and password cracking, among other things. The application has various distinguishing characteristics.

It can handle incomplete or partially damaged data as well as zipped data (such as GZIP, ZIP, and PDF files), which enables it to locate hidden tools like e-mail addresses, URLs, and credit card numbers. It can automatically identify and extract encrypted RAR files, office documents, JPEG files, and other sorts of files from compressed data chunks. Make a word list depending on all the terms identified in the data, or in zip files with no allotted space. These word lists can be used to crack passwords; quick turnaround; multithreaded. It can also create a histogram using the URL, search terms, domain name, email address, and other data after the analysis.

7.4.9 EXIFTOOL

ExifTool (Exchangeable Image File Format) is a command-line interface to ExifTool, a program that reads and writes metadata in image, audio, and video files. We may analyze every hidden meta info on our provided file. In today's post, we'll extract all possible data, including GPS, meta-data information, information about captured camera, and time. It is a platform-agnostic Perl library with a full-featured command line implementation for accessing, editing, and changing data in a variety of format files, including JPEG pictures. This metadata may include information on the exposure, shutter speed, and whether or not the flash was used, as well as information on the camera model, file type, permissions, and file size. ExifTool is perhaps the simplest way to extract information from files because it is a free and open-source program.

7.4.10 SURFACE BROWSER

Surface Browser is a fantastic tool for identifying a company's whole online infrastructure and obtaining important intel from domain names, DNS records and previously exposed subdomains, WHOIS records, SSL certificate data, and other sources. In order to get significant information about crimes, it is just as necessary to look at the outside of any firm or domain name on the Web as it is to look at local discs or RAM sticks. Whenever it pertains to cybersecurity, DNS records are a never-ending supply of information. You may use Surface Browser to get up-to-date DNS information. All publicly available online sources, including as the internet, e-mails, and other services, are completely under their control. Surface Browser displays present AAAA records quickly. Online criminals frequently change DNS records when committing crimes, leaving a trail. When it comes to investigating AAAA, A, SOA, MX, NS, and TXT records, regardless of the kind of DNS record they used, Surface Browser is our savior [8].

7.5   ADVANTAGES OF BIG DATA IN CYBERSECURITY

Gone are those days when the investigators would be at the crime scene spending a huge chunk of their time finding physical clues. With a digital transformation happening for good, so are the criminal activities. Activities related to banking frauds, identity theft, phishing, online data breach, etc. are commonly caused by crime that takes place over the internet.

A common binge-watch is a crime show wherein they are often found sketching an image of a suspect and run in across a database to check for either the identity or past criminal records. This is a very basic application of Big Data in crime. Another example is identifying the last location by tracing the cell phone. In the era of cybercrime, being able to defend your data is vital and Big Data can be a potential armor to shield your data. While it's true that cybercriminals utilize large data to plan their assaults, businesses can use the same data to their advantage through data analytics and machine learning. Although Big Data in cybercrime/security can act as a double-edged sword, it brings a variety of advantages. Below are a few examples that demonstrate the same. A conglomerate had reported multiple cases of equipment being stolen across various sites. They suspected the thievery was occurring after hours based on their access record. But they had several people working late regularly at the site, thus making them uncertain of suspects. However, by applying analytical intelligence to attendance the situation was resolved. Their first step was to define a "usual" behavior (areas the personnel have access to the most and at what time). Further anomalies were to be spotted (if an individual/group accessed an area at times that was not a part of their usual behavior.)

By doing this analysis, an employee was captured with strange patterns (unusual behavior). When any employee entered a new area at an interval besides their normal hours, a notification alert buzzed. A sentry would then follow the employee(s) and inspect the building. This led to the capture of the culprit red-handed. Additionally, a plan was devised to prevent such activities in the future.

In the case of a bank employing thousands of people over various sites, the bank was looking for cases when people were "remotely" accessing their IT systems even if they were (physically) within their buildings. Such exceptional behavior led to identification of record duplication, which is a major risk. Basic data integration and visualization principles might be used in their logical and physical access control systems, which is a reasonable approach. As a result, any such exceptions were immediately reported to the security team. The bank's risk was greatly reduced as a result of the prompt examination [6].

7.5.1 PREVENTING CYBERCRIME

One of the best defenses to an attack is to prevent its occurrence. Big Data can help to develop a predictive model that predicts future attacks based on past attacks. Thus reducing the risk of potential cybercrime. In case an organization has a history of victims, they can quickly understand the weak points and patterns which were utilized by the hackers to gain illicit access. Moreover, processes like ethical hacking, security auditing, penetration test, security scanning can help prevent future attacks and strengthen security [17]. Alternatively, if a business has never been attacked, it can utilize present and past data to identify tactics used by hackers. As a result, attackers would follow identical measures to get access to its system and, as a result, would find a solution before they did.

7.5.2 REAL-TIME CRIME COMBAT

In addition to prevention, Big Data can also help with real-time responses to data breaches and other fraudulent activities. Machine learning algorithms that take Big Data as input can interpret the information to identify vulnerability patterns. One famous system is the Intrusion Detection System (IDS). As the name suggests it detects an intrusion and fights against it. Such a process eliminates the potential threat of the network illicitly. For instance, an enterprise's real-time monitoring of databases, proxy logs, and domains can improve the technical health of the organization's network [17].

Government agencies and big conglomerates companies are highly vulnerable to lawsuits and investigations. Big Data poses the ability to produce evidence from multiple data sources and showcase the one real story. For instance, the ability to spot red flags can be done only from a broad view including audio, video, messages, e-mails, and financial records. Finding the leak from one place is far from tough as criminals avoid leaving traces. However, connecting to multiple data sources and trying to spot the red flag is much faster, easier, and a better approach.

Some of the other advantages are:

- Website utilization – to what extent a site is being used, an abrupt surge in traffic may be a potential threat.
- Key Performance Indicators (KPI) – e.g., performance of the security team based on their service level agreements.
- Identifying risk indicators such as tailgating (a physical security breach in which an unauthorized person follows an authorized individual to enter a secured area) unused access cards, etc.

Going digital also supports the go-green agenda which reduces energy usage in possible areas based on the patterns from the data. Big Data facilitates the analysis of colossal data and aids in better decision-making. Past criminal records can help predict susceptible crime areas. This ultimately improves the allocation of manpower and resources, e.g., series finder algorithm (cybercrime); delve deep in past performances and understand wrong decisions made in the past.

Needless to mention, Big Data plays a crucial role in time efficiency, be it real time or historic data, it can yield crucial results within a short span of time as compared to traditional methods.

A real-time case of Big Data being used as a new security concept by Abu Dhabi's defense companies. Having known all of the above points, one can say that it is inevitable in the future for Big Data to intervene in cybercrime activities.

7.6 CHALLENGES/ LIMITATIONS OF CYBERCRIME INVESTIGATION

According to Gantz et al. Big Data necessitates a generation of young architects and new technologies that allow for slightly elevated data capture, discovery, and analysis in order to effectively mine valuable information from vast amounts of diverse data. Unfortunately, typical cybersecurity and technologies are not built to manage large amounts of data. It is not always good to give low priority to significant data security and postpone the stages of extensive data adoption programs. "Security comes first" is not a cliche for nothing. At the same time, we acknowledge that guaranteeing significant data security comes with its own set of problems and challenges, which is why familiarizing yourself with them is highly beneficial [10].

7.6.1 FRAUD DETECTION

A large organization generates quintillions of bytes of data and 10 to 100 billion events every year. The company needs to add additional equipment and hire more employees, and operate more software for post hoc forensic analysis when events are generated from various and heterogeneous sources. As a consequence, via useful data analysis and data categorization prediction, the effectiveness of Big Data is achieved. Big Data analytics has piqued the security community's interest because existing analytical methodologies are insufficient for significant research and processing of significant data events [3]. The most evident concern in society right now is fraud detection, which necessitates Big Data analytics. Commercial banks, credit card companies, and phone companies are among the most affected businesses that require fraud detection. However, mining Big Data with a custom-built infrastructure is not cost-effective. As a result, Big Data technologies are beneficial since they provide a cost-effective infrastructure for security monitoring to an extensive range of institutions. In particular, Big Data technologies such as Hadoop map-reduce, which comprises Mahout, Pig, Hadoop, and Hive are available on the market. Analysis methods also function faster and on a larger scale when applied to Big Scale heterogeneous datasets, such as stream mining, complex event processing, and NoSQL databases. Only these solutions make it simpler to save, preserve, and analyze security data. On the other hand, the examples of efficient data processes for security depend on MapReduce, which is being employed by WINE and BotCloud2.

7.6.2 Data Privacy Issues

An organization's usage of data will determine how confidential it is. Utilization of data must only be for the reason for which it was obtained and nothing else. The information should be kept confidential to increase corporate earnings or gain market recognition. However, various tools and approaches extract private data and make infractions easy in the Big Data environment. Security policies and privacy policies must be followed by all parties participating in the process. To avoid privacy violations, it is now necessary to create an application while understanding the privacy policies and procedures [11]. A critical role is played by architects and designers in ensuring the security of data repositories and data privacy. Due to data availability to multiple parties for marketing and advertising purposes, privacy cannot be protected. Law enforcement agencies sometimes exploit private data for objectives of global safety. Additionally, the risk of intrusion and data theft exists while posing as authorized staff. The privacy issues surrounding data mining are examined from a broader perspective and in several ways that can support the protection of sensitive data.

7.6.3 Data Provenance Problem

The phrase "data provenance" relates to the origin of data, or when and where it was first generated, as well as its location. One of the problems with large data is data provenance because it comes from many sources, some of which are trustworthy and others that are not. Confidentiality, integrity, and availability are the three most important aspects of security. The term "confidentiality" refers to the shielding of data against disclosure. The confidentiality of sensitive information, such as commercial or personal information, is required. Access control mechanisms are covered by provenance information [16]. As advanced software applications advance, more complicated security procedures will be required. Traditional access control techniques are designed for specific objectives and are challenging to configure to meet the demands of today's complex world. If we can track the dependencies of access, it will reveal critical security information. Data provenance can lead to issues with data trustworthiness. For example, outdated journals or broadcast regarding a firm perhaps published by Big Data analytics techniques, resulting in a drop in the company's stock price (*Just a Moment. . .*, n.d.). As a result, when using Big Data tools to analyze data, we must consider authorized and reliable data. When it comes to data analysis, the two factors that we must consider are integrity and authenticity. To investigate malicious data, we must use statistical and machine learning algorithms. To solve the challenge of data provenance, researchers will need to develop some novel methodologies. Though data provenance has its drawbacks, it also has its benefits, such as following data from its source through analysis. More research on data provenance is required, and visualization approaches will assist in quickly identifying data provenance issues.

7.6.4 Fake Data Generation

The production of bogus data is one of the most severe security challenges confronting Big Data today. You can choose the best sort of data processing and apply a range of security measures. However, if you cannot recognize bogus data stored in your central repository, you will be exposed to substantial risks that compromise your capacity to secure client data. Fake data are a significant data security threat since it makes it more difficult to spot other problems. For example, false flags from phony data could make it difficult to detect fraud. False reports may also lead to unneeded activities that reduce output or other critical areas of a company's operations. Cybercriminals can fake data and "dump" it into your data lake to purposefully impair the quality of your extensive data analysis [22]. For example, suppose your manufacturing organization relies on sensor data to detect failing production processes. In that case, cybercriminals can hack your system and cause your sensors to display false findings, such as incorrect temperatures. If you do it this way, you may overlook dangerous trends and the opportunity to remedy problems before they cause significant damage. Such issues can be overcome by employing a fraud detection strategy. For fake data, there are false flags. Data can also drive inefficient activities that may result in decreased output or other essential business processes. One approach to avoid this is for businesses to be critical of their data to improve their business processes. Validating data sources through frequent evaluations and evaluating machine learning models with various test datasets to discover anomalies is an appropriate technique.

7.6.5 ENDPOINT VULNERABILITIES

Numerous devices, including PCs, laptops, cell phones, tablets, as well as barcode readers and scanners, can be located at the endpoints of a network or nodes within a corporate network. Each of these poses a security risk to the company's network. Endpoint security currently refers to firewalls and anti-virus software that are installed on the server and updated regularly. Endpoint security includes intrusion detection and behavior-blocking devices that continuously monitor devices and check for an activity generally launched by rootkits – this action is also linked to cloud anti-virus. After the device has been verified for vulnerabilities and compliance with network security standards, this security check works by checking the individual's credentials to the network and then giving them access to the network [12]. Cybercriminals can tamper with data on endpoint devices and send erroneous information to data lakes. Security solutions that analyze logs from endpoints must verify the endpoints' authenticity. Hackers, for example, can get access to industrial systems that use sensors to detect process flaws. Hackers gain access to the sensors and manipulate them to provide false findings. Fraud detection systems are typically used to address such issues.

7.6.6 ADMINISTRATION AND STORAGE CHALLENGES

The scope of Big Data has been changing rapidly since its inception. Big Data, according to IBM's 5Vs model, has a vast scale and rapid expansion characteristics. In particular, the size of data has grown from PB to EB. It continues to grow in response to the needs of practical applications and the growth of businesses, rapidly approaching the ZB level. Take, for example, Taobao, China's largest e-commerce website, which has in excess of 400 million registered users and creates over 400 million product details daily, or precisely, more than 50 TB of daily activity data. If such a massive amount of personal data is a leak, the ramifications would be unthinkable.

But the majority of currently used Big Data storage solutions, including Ceph, Tachyon, GlusterFS, HDFS, and QFS., and others, store data in a distributed, horizontally scalable fashion. Although these schemes meet cloud environments' storability and scalability requirements, they do not always match cloud applications' concurrency and security requirements. Furthermore, it might be challenging to secure dispersed data that are kept on a cloud server. Directly manipulating the cloud-based data server is inconvenient for users, and they have no control over who else may access the data. For management digital security and cloud platform security, a password is used. Administrators of cloud servers with considerable power, on the other hand, may conspire to share valuable Big Data. It is challenging to keep track of some high-ranking managers who have access to sensitive data and passwords. Meanwhile, the need for safer distributed systems with trustworthy storage and resilience is skyrocketing.

7.6.7 EMPLOYEE THEFT

Every employee now has access to a certain amount of vital company data thanks to the advancement of data culture. While it promotes data democratization, it also raises the chance of a sensitive piece of information being leaked, whether purposefully or unintentionally. Data loss by employees is not always unintentional. In reality, up to 70% of departing employees admit to stealing some data from the company. Even more upsetting is that most intellectual property theft by former workers occurs within three months of their notice of resignation. This could put your trade secrets, such as client and employee lists, in jeopardy. Employee theft is a problem not only in large corporations but also in small businesses. Companies must create legal procedures and secure the network with a virtual private network to prevent employee theft.

Furthermore, companies can use Desktop as a Service (DaaS) to eliminate the functionality of data saved on local storage. There are several techniques for lowering your chances of encountering this Big Data security issue. They are as follows:

- Examine your most important information and who has access to it.
- Ensure that policies and procedures are communicated to staff promptly.
- Monitor sensitive data-holding applications, as well as who is accessing them and why.
- When an employee leaves, immediately disable physical access to your network.
- Multi-layer authentication should be used.
- Implement a disciplinary policy and make sure staff are aware that they are being watched.
- Create a culture of security and responsibility.

Employees can either help to ease or exacerbate considerable data security challenges. Fortunately, their potential to cause harm is highly dependent on how much attention you pay to this problem, and this was demonstrated when an Apple employee exited the building carrying reams of data relating to the company's autonomous vehicle development. If the FBI had not apprehended him, the firm might have fallen behind in the race to self-driving cars.

7.6.8 Lack of Security Audits

One of the most severe problems with extensive data security is the failure to conduct proper audits. These audits should be conducted regularly to discover security flaws that could put a business in danger. Unfortunately, due to a lack of time, money, clarity on security requirements, and qualified employees, this critical work is sometimes postponed or overlooked entirely. Significant data security audits assist businesses in identifying security flaws. Although it is recommended that they be done frequently, this is rarely followed in practice. Working with large data already has issues and worries, and an audit would add to the list. Security audits should be carried out on a monthly or quarterly basis, depending on the size of your firm. However, they can also be carried out on a department-by-department basis if a company-wide audit would cause significant disruption. According to Forbes, data gathered during an audit may also be at risk; thus, this procedure must be carried out correctly.

7.6.9 User Access Control

Access to sensitive data, such as medical records containing personal information, is sometimes restricted by companies. However, others who do not have access permission must use this information, such as medical researchers. Granular access is a common approach in many organizations. This implies that people can only view and access the information they need. Granular access is not possible with Big Data technology. Copying essential data to a separate Big Data warehouse is one solution. For medical research, for example, only the medical information is copied, leaving outpatient names and addresses. Despite the fact that user access management is the most fundamental network security mechanism, few businesses utilize it extensively because of its high operating costs. This poses considerable risk at the network level. For the Big Data platform, it can be devastating. Effective user access management necessitates a policy-based approach to user access control that automates access based on user and role-based factors. Complex layers of user control, such as a large number of supervisor configurations, are managed by policy-driven automation, which protects the big data platform from inside threats. Companies can assure data integrity while simultaneously protecting data privacy by limiting which data individuals can view or alter. However, controlling access control is difficult, especially in larger organizations with thousands of employees. However, the transition from on-premise systems to cloud-based services has made dealing with Identity Access Management (IAM) easier. IAM is in charge of data flow control through identification, authentication, and authorization. Following relevant ISO standards is an excellent place to start to ensure that enterprises follow the best IAM practices.

7.6.10 ENCRYPTION

Encryption is a cybersecurity strategy that secures private and confidential data by scrambling it with unique codes that make it impossible for outsiders to read. Encryption ensures that an institution's data is safe even if attackers get past the firewall, even if there is a data breach. Businesses are progressively gathering a large amount of private user data. Thus, they must ensure that all data in their control are encrypted to prevent it from falling into the hands of unauthorized agents. Your encryption methods must safeguard data across huge data volumes, both in transit and while in storage [18]. Additionally, encryption must function with a variety of data types produced by both machines and individuals. The output data from various optimization algorithms, as well as common Big Data storage formats like Relational Database Management Systems (RDBMS), non-relational databases like NoSQL, and specialized filesystems like Hadoop Distributed File System (HDFS), must all be compatible with encryption technologies. A tabular schema with rows and columns is used in traditional relational databases. As a result, they cannot handle massive data due to its scalability and diversity of structure. Non-relational databases (NoSQL databases) were created to address the shortcomings of relational databases. The tabular schema of rows and columns is not used in non-relational databases. NoSQL databases, on the other hand, optimize storage models based on the data type. As a result, NoSQL databases offer greater flexibility and scalability than relational databases. Performance and flexibility are prioritized in NoSQL databases over security (*The Importance of Data Encryption in Cybersecurity*, n.d.). NoSQL databases must be set up in a trusted environment with additional security precautions for organizations that use them [9].

7.7 CASE STUDY

7.7.1 CASE STUDY: 1

A lady named Lucy had received a Facebook request from one of her school's friends. Having mutual friends and knowing the name (Aniket), she accepted the request. Soon after, she noticed that Aniket had initiated indirect interactions by liking her photos. Slowly they began texting. One sudden day Aniket posted a picture of himself with a BMW behind him. Out of curiosity, Lucy questioned Aniket how he managed to get so rich.

Aniket replied that a share-trading application using Artificial Intelligence (AI) helped him double his money within a day. Lucy was baffled. She began her Google search and was quite convinced that AI can indeed predict the future. Thus, having faith in Aniket's words, she asked if she could use the application as well. Aniket denied stating the reason that it is confidential.

Thus Lucy's desire to be a part of it increased. On further talks, Aniket agreed and shared the application link with Lucy within a few more texts. Lucy downloaded the application and invested Rs.500, and by the end of the day, her gross turned out to be Rs.1,100. She sensed ease and kept investing small amounts daily. For four months, her investment summed up to Rs.4,00,000 and gross earnings of Rs.9,00,000. One fine day she decided to withdraw the money, and on trying so, the application stopped functioning. She panicked and immediately tried to reach Aniket but could not connect by any means. Having no other option, she reached out to a cybercrime investigator. The investigator firstly decided to check out the application which Lucy had installed. Quickly he figured that the application was bogus and merely a means to transfer money from one account to another. The remaining magic was of the app's User Interface, making it look genuine. For example: The chart patterns of how the money multiplied, returns of the stocks, and more (all of it were just being an illustration and nothing in reality). The investigator was clear that retrieving the money would be uncertain but catching the culprit would be probable.

Approach: He initiated a plan of sending a link to Aniket, and upon opening it, it would help get the system's IP address. He got Lucy to send a link to Aniket and hoped he would click on it. Fortunately, he did, and within a short period, the investigator ran the IP address through a massive set of IP addresses and the respective information he possessed (Big Data). The investigator figured out the person's location and the IP and captured the culprit. It turned out the culprit, too, was an old school friend.

7.7.2 Case Study: 2

Adam worked as an engineer for a prestigious tech company for 2 years and abruptly resigned. He reasoned personal matters due to which he had to go back to his hometown. Upon brief discussion with his manager, he affirmed that he would be working for a tech company in his hometown. Soon after this, the company's database administrator notified the manager that confidential files had been downloaded from the database by an anonymous user.

Approach: The manager grew suspicious about Adam's decision and immediately set up a security check. The team went through Adam's work laptop and other devices. During the search, nothing seemed suspicious. Therefore, the manager decided to take a different approach and asked his data team to go through the activity log from the servers, firewalls, and other networks. Secondly, he asked them to run through the camera tapes to find a clue. The data team quickly spotted an oddity in video footage of the past week wherein an employee from the maintenance department had entered the server room for a minute and left. On interrogating, the employee confronted the activity. However, the activity log from servers and other networks showed a different story. A surprising pattern in the activity log showed up against Adam's network. The observation exhibited an all-time high activity by Adam since his entire time spent in the company. On interrogating Adam, he denied and defended stating he was working overtime and had several deadlines. He showcased the proof of them as well. Thus, the manager decided to investigate only the maintenance department further. On repeated questioning, the employee revealed that Adam was threatened and forced to go into the server room and connect a drive to the server. He also stated that Adam had threatened to leak all his intimate photos online unless he did as ordered. Now, connecting the dots, the manager opened a serious cybercrime investigation on Adam. In due course, it was found that the proof of overtime and several deadlines were all faked by Adam and had secretly used the maintenance employee as a route to get to the database and download confidential data. On further investigation, Adam's cyberattacks to access classified information were penalized as he sold it to a competitor. When investigated, Adam confessed he had stolen the company's data.

7.7.3 Summary of the Case Studies

The victim utilized Facebook to fake identity and build trust. Further, the victim went on with reverse phishing, enticing the victim to fall for the trap voluntarily and run away with the money. However, he was caught by tracking his IP address. The maintenance department employee fell prey to Adam's phishing attack (sending an e-mail or attachment impersonating someone known to gain access to personal files or the entire system illegally). Adam had faked being a friend and dubiously got him to click on a link sent via e-mail. Giving Adam complete control over the data further led to threatening and extortion (illegal activities) [9].

7.8.   FUTURE OF BIG DATA IN CYBERSECURITY

Strategic and sophisticated tactics have been developed to exploit the weak links of organizational and individual systems. Enterprises collect data regularly, especially security-relevant data, for future forensic analysis. This proves helpful in detecting and fighting off the more recent and complicated attacks on systems, as traditional tools are slowly failing because of the humongous amount of data generated every day [21].

If we talk about computing with reference to cybersecurity, great shifts are happening in this domain – all thanks to Big Data and Data Science.

In this section, we will delve into the application of Big Data in the domain of cybersecurity and the way it aids the process of conceptual model creation, which in turn, are used for decision-making and automation. It is common knowledge that large amounts of data are required to detect patterns or anomalies. The key to making robust, secure applications with the help of Big Data is achieved through the extraction of security-incident patterns from the available cybersecurity data and consequentially leads to a data-driven model, which makes security automated and intelligent.

We are well aware of our increasing dependency on digitization. But this also leads to various security-related issues such as:

*   Unauthorized access.
*   Malware attacks.
*   Zero-day attacks.
*   Breach of data.
*   Denial of services.

Now, we need to look into how we can tackle these challenges and lay the foundation of the future of Big Data in cybersecurity. Data-driven security is the next big thing waiting to take over the world, and we are here to witness it!

Big Data, however, cannot do it alone. Coupled with AI, Big Data can deliver top-notch solutions to existing and forthcoming problems in the world of cybersecurity.

7.8.1   FUTURE PREDICTION

By incorporating tools like Statistics, Machine Learning, AI, Computing Systems, and Prediction Models, we can use Big Data to proactively enhance our response to threat detection. Predictive analysis gathers historical data from cyberattacks of the past. The job of Cyber Defense Engineers revolves largely around analyzing this historical data and then building relevant AI-based algorithms [2]. This also allows them to establish a baseline for the normal scenarios and equip the system with the skills to highlight the anomalies.

Once the threat and attack patterns are identified, the engineers can work on making tailor-made cybersecurity solutions.

7.8.2   REAL-TIME DETECTION

The Intrusion Detection System (IDS) is the best prospect of combining Big Data and cybersecurity. Big Data analytics coupled with network flows, sensors, cloud systems respond to the intrusions in real time.

The IDS can be classified into two main types:

*   Network IDS.
*   Host-based IDS.

- Signature-based systems form the basis of IDS. These can detect the malicious automated monitoring.

Modern cyber defense operations rely heavily on automated monitoring and threat detection. Automated monitoring greatly facilitates a continuous monitoring environment, real-time actionable insights, real-time risk management tools, and even alerts for incoming threats.

Endpoint Protection Platforms (EPP) and Security Information and Event Management (SIEM) platforms are efficient Big Data analytics tools that provide continuous monitoring capabilities [1].

The endpoint devices have EPPs deployed in them, which aid them to detect, respond, investigate, and prevent threats. Logs are collected by SIEMs, and it even contains the data recorded within an organization's internal infrastructure. The efficient way to lessen the risk of a breach is to limit access to sensitive information. This is rightly done so by authorizing users and their credentials. In this domain, automated monitoring plays an essential role as it monitors and analyzes user behavior automatically whenever unusual activity is detected. These days, most enterprises are opting for Big Data to shield themselves from malicious attacks. And this involvement will grow further in the future. Let's look into some areas of cybersecurity that are bound to grow exponentially.

7.8.3 RISK MANAGEMENT

Highly intelligent tools supported by Big Data can prove to be a great asset to the domain of cybersecurity. We should have tools that can interpret the huge amount of data efficiently and then categorize the threats. This ensures that the threats are handled in the right way and in a timely fashion.

7.8.4 VISUALIZING THE THREATS

Big Data analytics allow us to visualize threats quite effortlessly. The complexity of the attack can be easily judged by doing an in-depth data source evaluation. Some more advanced tools would definitely give us the leverage to compare the historical and present data. This helps us to understand the stats of the trend.

7.8.5 PENETRATION TESTING

Planning, Scanning, Gaining, Maintaining, and Analysis are the five stages of Penetration Testing. It gives us insights into the infrastructure of a business. It is nothing but a simulated cyberattack against our vulnerable systems. We can implement our knowledge of Data Science, Machine Learning, and AI to enhance Penetration Testing further and even automate it! No IT enterprise can skip this step if they are working with data.

7.8.6 DEEP INFORMATION ANALYSIS

Big Data analytics enables businesses to do in-depth analyses collected on a daily basis, suggesting a potential threat to the integrity of company data. When there is a deviation from the usual, AI and machine learning could be used to create new paradigms and possibilities.

7.8.7 BEHAVIORAL ANALYTICS

Another example of potential research is behavior analytics, which involves the use of context tools to support the probability of detecting trends and anomalous behaviors that indicate fraud, theft, or other cybersecurity breaches. Outsider intrusions were successfully detected by traditional cybersecurity systems, while insider ones were not. Using anomaly detection in interaction behavior, such as how many times a file is downloaded, Big Data analytics systems can predict unexpected behavior and uncover intrusion attempts by observing the behavior of normal and legitimate users. How frequently is the database accessed? To conclude, some kinds of insider threats will be difficult to detect unless users' normal and unusual behavior is simulated.

7.8.8 VISUALIZATION

Advanced visualization tools are needed to give security analysts insights that help them identify cyber threats quicker. Some security-related visualization dashboards, such as Keylines, are already in use; however, more improvements are needed, chiefly as the number of data sources increases, making graphical analysis more complicated and as the demand for real-time processing of streaming data grows.

7.8.9 INTERNET OF THINGS

Smart cities, ITs, habitat monitoring, and other IoT applications are examples of Big Data programs that demand the generation of streaming data and real-time processing. As a result, Big Data analytics must be used to address security problems with IoT applications. Each application has its own set of necessities and demands in terms of security and privacy, requiring suitable design enhancements to satisfy this requirement.

7.9 CONCLUSION

Data are being used by almost 84% of enterprises to block hackers and safeguard their software, and that is why data breaches have seen a gradual decline. Nevertheless, even then, we should be using data as an advanced analytics tool, which can give us valuable insights on cybersecurity threats such as ransomware/malware attacks, compromised or weak devices, and even malicious insider programs.

Many experts have confessed that they have not utilized Big Data to its full potential. Moreover, that is where the future of Big Data begins – the possibilities are endless!

REFERENCES

1. Al-Yaseen, W. L., Othman, Z. A., & Nazri, M. Z. A. (2017). Real-Time Multi-Agent System for an Adaptive Intrusion Detection System. *Pattern Recognition Letters*, *85*, 56–64. https://doi.org/10.1016/j .patrec.2016.11.018
2. Ashabi, A., Sahibuddin, S. B., & Haghighi, M. S. (2020). Big Data: Current Challenges and Future Scope. *2020 IEEE 10th Symposium on Computer Applications & Industrial Electronics (ISCAIE)*. https://doi.org/10.1109/iscaie47305.2020.9108826
3. Bekker, A. (2021, May 31). *Buried under Big Data: Security Issues, Challenges, Concerns*. ScienceSoft. https://www.scnsoft.com/blog/big-data-security-challenges
4. Brayne, S. (2017). Big Data Surveillance: The Case of Policing. *American Sociological Review*, *82*(5), 977–1008. https://doi.org/10.1177/0003122417725865
5. *CAINE Live USB/DVD - Computer Forensics Digital Forensics*. (n.d.). CAINE. https://www.caine-live .net
6. City Security Magazine. (2019, February 19). *The Benefits of Big Data Analytics in Security*. City Security Magazine. https://citysecuritymagazine.com/security-technology/big-data-analytics-in-security/
7. Dimitriadis, A., Ivezic, N., Kulvatunyou, B., & Mavridis, I. (2020). D4I - Digital Forensics Framework for Reviewing and Investigating Cyber Attacks. *Array*, *5*, 100015. https://doi.org/10.1016/j.array.2019 .100015
8. Dutta, P. (2021, March 9). *Surface Web and Dark Web: Exploring Layers of Web*. Kratikal Blogs. https:// www.kratikal.com/blog/surface-web-and-dark-web-exploring-layers-of-web/
9. *The Importance of Data Encryption in Cybersecurity*. (n.d.). Techwell. https://www.techwell.com/tech-well-insights/2019/10/importance-data-encryption-cybersecurity

10. Kumar, D. (2021, November 17). *Top 7 Big Data Security Issues and Their Solutions.* Learn | Hevo. https://hevodata.com/learn/big-data-security/#dpg
11. Maayan, G. D. (2020, February 9). *Big Data Security: Challenges and Solutions.* Dataversity. https://www.dataversity.net/big-data-security-challenges-and-solutions/
12. Paladin Security. (2019, May 23). *Online Safety and Cyber Security.* https://paladinsecurity.com/knowledge-centre/cyber-security-awareness-month-practicing-safety-online/
13. Ripa, K. (2022, February 25). *The Truth About USB Device Serial Numbers – (and the Lies Your Tools Tell).* Sans. https://www.sans.org/tools/sift-workstation/
14. Shalaginov, A., Johnsen, J. W., & Franke, K. (2017). Cyber Crime Investigations in the Era of Big Data. *2017 IEEE International Conference on Big Data (Big Data).* https://doi.org/10.1109/bigdata.2017.8258362
15. The Sleuth Kit (TSK) & Autopsy: Open Source Digital Forensics Tools (n.d.). Sleuth Kit. https://www.sleuthkit.org
16. Smallcombe, M. (2020, June 24). *11 Big Data Security Concerns.* Integrate.Io. https://www.integrate.io/blog/big-data-security-concerns/#multi
17. Tanveer, A. (2021, September 5). *5 Promising Ways Big Data Deters Cybersecurity Threats.* Dzone.Com. https://dzone.com/articles/promising-ways-big-data-deters-cybersecurity-threats
18. Taylor, C. (2021, December 22). *What Is Big Data Security? Challenges & Solutions.* Datamation. https://www.datamation.com/big-data/big-data-security/#challenges
19. Turner, P. (2005). Unification of Digital Evidence from Disparate Sources (Digital Evidence Bags). *Digital Investigation, 2*(3), 223–228. https://doi.org/10.1016/j.diin.2005.07.001
20. *X-Ways Forensics: Integrated Computer Forensics Software* (n.d.). X-Ways Software Technology AG. http://www.x-ways.net/forensics/
21. Yaqoob, I., Hashem, I. A. T., Gani, A., Mokhtar, S., Ahmed, E., Anuar, N. B., & Vasilakos, A. V. (2016). Big Data: From Beginning to Future. *International Journal of Information Management, 36*(6), 1231–1247. https://doi.org/10.1016/j.ijinfomgt.2016.07.009
22. Zawoad, S., & Hasan, R. (2015). Digital Forensics in the Age of Big Data: Challenges, Approaches, and Opportunities. *2015 IEEE 17th International Conference on High Performance Computing and Communications, 2015 IEEE 7th International Symposium on Cyberspace Safety and Security, and 2015 IEEE 12th International Conference on Embedded Software and Systems.* https://doi.org/10.1109/hpcc-css-icess.2015.305

8 Low-Cost High-Impact AI Tools vs Cybercrime

P. Durgadevi, A.S. Mohammed Shariff,
S. Nagaraj, M. Dinesh Babu, and Savita

8.1 INTRODUCTION AND MOTIVATION

With the plan to investigate the capability of cutting-edge innovation in administration and policing, the Hyderabad city police and the state government-led incubator We Hub facilitated a hackathon. The invitees were youthful pioneers, new companies, and corporates called to discuss issues in areas like network safety and violence against women and children, among others. Innovation utilizing AI and man-made consciousness is the need of the hour. The hackathon focused on handling issues in the fields of cybercrimes, violence against women and children, street security mindfulness, and web-based media observing for handling counterfeit news. The members were entrusted with creating applications and security arrangements utilizing emerging technologies like artificial intelligence and information investigation. The goal of the hackathon was to evoke coding arrangements from the members for the proclamation of issues like cybercrimes, violence against women and children, street security and mindfulness, and online media checking. "Successful programs will be the models based on which we will plan the items to further improve policing work and resolve policing difficulties", said Indian Police Service Officer Shikha Goel.

The aim of this chapter is to investigate and comprehend the effects of computerized reasoning in the fields of public safety and security; to distinguish the political, international, and vital issues of AI [1]; to examine AI's place in clashes and cyberconflicts, and all the more, by and large in different types of savagery; to clarify the use of man-made brainpower by military organizations, as well as law enforcement agencies and the police; to talk about the enquiries made using the advancement of man-made consciousness and the increase in utilization of man-made consciousness in armed forces, police, and knowledge organizations, at the strategic, functional, and key levels. the molecular time and length scales are not sufficiently small compared to the characteristic macroscopic flow scales. Bit defender conveys direct danger insight to organizations and security operations centers by means of top danger knowledge stages (TIPs), SIEMs and Security Orchestration, Automation, and Response (SOAR) applications. Bit defender labs connect a huge number of indicators of compromise (IoCs) gathered through the global protective network (GPN), safeguarding countless frameworks all around the world and providing timely and relevant information on current threats [2].

Lawbreakers are using the Internet to commit numerous digital offenses, thanks to improvements in data innovation information technology (IT). The emergence of complicated scattered and Internet figuring patterns raises serious concerns regarding data security and protection. Digital systems are highly vulnerable to outages and other threats. Actual devices, such as sensors and indicators, are insufficient for monitoring and securing these frameworks; hence, there is a need for more refined IT that can exhibit common behaviors and distinguish unusual ones. These digital security frameworks must be adaptive, agile, and robust, with the ability to detect a wide range of threats and make informed ongoing decisions [3].

DOI: 10.1201/9781003251781-8

8.2 CYBERCRIME

New technological improvements have opened doors for new thieves, but the types of crime have remained the same. What distinguishes cybercrime from traditional crime? Clearly, one contrast is the use of a sophisticated computer, but innovation alone is insufficient to distinguish among diverse criminal realms. To propose falsehoods, traffic in children's sexual amusement, and preserve innovation seize a person's identity, or breach someone's security, lawbreakers don't need a computer. Before the "digital" prefix became popular, there was a plethora of exercises. Cybercrime, which includes the Internet in particular, comprises both the increase in existing criminal activity and certain new illicit activities. The majority of cybercrime focuses on data about individuals, businesses, or governments. Although the assaults don't happen on an actual body, they truly do occur on the individual or corporate virtual body, individuals are defined by their own set of enlightened qualities and organizations on the Internet [4]. At the end of the day, in this computerized age, virtual characters are fundamental components of regular day-to-day existence: We are a heap of numbers and identifiers in numerous PC information bases possessed by legal bodies and organizations. Cybercrime highlights the need of organized PCs and the fragility of personal identities.

8.2.1 DEFINITION AND ISSUE

Cybercrime, often known as computer crime, is the use of a computer to carry out further illegal activities, such as extortion, dealing with child sexual entertainment and protected innovation, stealing identities, or disregarding security. As the PC [5] has become a vital aspect of trade, entertainment, and government, cybercrime, particularly through the Internet, has grown. Because of the early and unavoidable acceptance of PCs and the Internet in the United States, many of the first victims and adversaries of cybercrime were Americans. By the twenty-first century, however, there is barely a town left on the earth that has not been affected by cybercrime in some way.

8.2.2 TYPES OF CYBERCRIME

Cybercrime encompasses a range of criminal activities. On the one side are wrongdoings that include critical threats to individual or corporate security, for example, attacks on the trustworthiness of data stored in computers and the utilization of wrongfully acquired advanced data to coerce a firm or a person. Likewise, at this end of the spectrum is the emergence of fraudulent activities. Halfway along the spectrum lies exchange-based violations like extortion, dealing with youngster sexual entertainment, computerized robbery, illegal tax avoidance, and forging. These are explicit violations with explicit casualties, yet the lawbreaker escapes uncaught owing to the general namelessness rendered by the Internet. Another type of wrongdoing involves people in enterprises or government administration who purposely adjust information for one benefit or the other or for political targets. At the other end of the spectrum are those wrongdoings that include endeavors to upset the genuine activities of the Internet. These range from spam, hacking, and disavowal of administration assaults against explicit locales to demonstrations of cyberterrorism, that is, utilization of the Internet to cause public aggravations and even demise of the public. Cyberterrorism focuses on the utilization of the Internet by nonstate entertainers to affect a country's financial and mechanical foundation. Since the September 11 attacks of 2001, public attention toward the danger of cyberterrorism has developed significantly. Digital crooks and organizations present huge danger to worldwide business and society. The utilization of the Internet for criminal activities is perhaps the most basic challenge faced by the FBI and law enforcement agencies overall [6]. Comprehension and utilizing the Internet to battle Internet extortion is fundamental for law enforcement. The impact of a solitary, fruitful digital assault can have expansive ramifications including monetary misfortunes, burglary of protected innovation, and loss of buyer certainty and trust. In general, the money-related effect of digital wrongdoings on society and government is assessed to be in the range of billions of dollars a year.

8.3 THE IMPACT OF AI ON CYBER SECURITY

As cyber-attacks grow in volume and intricacy, Artificial intelligence (AI) is helping underresced security activity examiners stay ahead of dangers. Arranging danger knowledge from a large number of research papers, sites, and reports, AI advancements like AI and normal language handling give fast experiences to slice through the commotion of everyday alarms, definitely diminishing reaction times. Watch the instructional videos to perceive how AI assists experts in drawing an obvious conclusion regarding dangers. Artificial intelligence is changing the game for online protection, dissecting enormous amounts of hazard information to speed up reaction times and increase under-resced security tasks. Artificial intelligence works on its insight to "comprehend" online security risk and digital risk by consuming billions of information artifacts. AI dissects connections between dangers, like noxious documents and dubious IP locations or insiders right away or in minutes [7]. AI gives organized danger investigation, decreasing the time security investigators take to convey basic choices and remediate intimations. Simulated intelligence (also called machine knowledge) arose as an examination regulation at the Summer research mission of Dartmouth institution in July 1956. Simulated intelligence can be portrayed in two ways: (i) As a science that expects to find the substance of knowledge and foster clever machines, or (ii) as a study of observing strategies for taking care of mind-boggling issues that can't be settled without applying some knowledge (for example, settling on best choices in light of a lot of information). In the use of AI for digital safeguarding, we are more intrigued by the latter definition. Research interest in AI incorporates ways of making machines (PCs) reproduce canny human conduct like reasoning, getting the hang of things, thinking, arranging, and so forth [3–5].

8.3.1 MAIN CHALLENGES CYBER SECURITY FACES TODAY

Difficulties in the network safety industry are just as powerful as the actual field. The online security chrome is always showing signs of change as new advances arise and change the actions of companies to achieve their goals. Regardless of whether it's the Internet of Things (IoT) filling in size and scale or the presentation of 5G innovation, organizations across all enterprises should urge their IT [8] divisions to upgrade their network safety framework and give significant online protection ready to become tremendously influential leaders in the organization. Organizations should get their resces and guarantee that their staff is prepared all of the time to react to a digital assault, to push ahead safely and forestall misfortunes because of digital crooks or pernicious danger entertainers. By and large, over the long haul, network protection dangers become more intricate as noxious hackers become more brilliant. So this is the ideal opportunity to execute preventive measures and assure security against cybercrime. The new challenges of cybersecurity in 2021 are as follows:

1. **Getting Used to Working with a Remote Team**
   It's no secret that the number of people working remotely has increased significantly, irrespective of whether offices are reopened or remote workforces are hired. The quantity and scope of cybersecurity concerns for remote employees grow as a result of a distributed work environment. Remote workers who use their home networks are far more likely to be victims of security breaches. In-person employees are safeguarded in traditional office environments, but it's more difficult to assure protection for remote employees. When it

comes to protecting remote workers and the business itself in a remote environment, a remote-working checklist is a smart place to start with.

2. **Emerging 5G Applications**
   When 5G was first introduced this year, several businesses were eager to make use of its capabilities, whether it was mobile phone carriers selling it to their clients or manufacturing industries trying to boost operational efficiency. 5G will improve the speed and responsiveness of wireless communications, and this new technology has a promising future. New technologies, on the other hand, bring new dangers to bear with, and cybersecurity professionals must be on the lookout for threats to these evolving networks.

8.3.2 How AI Improves Cyber Security

AI can be used to detect cyber dangers and potentially malicious behavior. AI systems are being trained to detect malware, execute pattern recognition, and detect even the tiniest characteristics of malware or ransomware attacks before they enter the system, using sophisticated algorithms. In the field of security, AI can identify and prioritize risk, detect malware on a network quickly, lead incident response, and detect intrusions before they occur. Complex cyber-attacks will be easier to carry out, thanks to machine-learning and deep-learning techniques, allowing for more focused, faster, and devastating strikes. AI's impact on cybersecurity is predicted to extend the threat landscape, introduce new dangers, and alter the nature of current threats. Artificial intelligence (AI) has become an indispensable component of cybersecurity measures in recent years. AI can forecast cyber-attacks with uncanny accuracy, and it can aid in the development of improved security features that can reduce the amount of cyber-attacks and their impact on IT infrastructure. Artificial intelligence is more difficult to learn than cyber security in terms of learning difficulty and job growth rates, but both are equally significant. Artificial intelligence is being used by a lot of companies in cyber security applications. AI is used by businesses to model and track the behavior of system users. The goal of watching how a system interacts with its users is to spot takeover attempts. These are attacks in which malicious employees steal other users' login information and exploit their accounts to perpetrate crimes.

8.4 ARTIFICIAL INTELLIGENCE

The traditional safety measures in the cyber security arena are antivirus software and firewalls. To identify and prevent web security threats, a variety of methods are utilized. In this case, the level of security on the digital platform would be defined by timely antivirus software upgrades in accordance with the most recent threats and the attitude of the person in charge of security. AI relies on innovative breakthroughs such as machine learning, deep learning, natural language processing, and others to make it difficult for programmers to access servers and other critical data kept on PCs [9]. AI has already accomplished a lot, and now it's time for it to tackle cyber security. Let's take a look at how artificial intelligence can help with cyber security. Finally, artificial intelligence techniques have progressed rapidly from their humble beginnings to become highly specialized. These assist cyber security professionals in dealing with actions related to the identification and prevention of cyber-attacks. Artificial intelligence (AI) can detect cyber security issues and advise specialists on how to respond. As a result, AI's function is expanding across numerous facets of data innovation in the advanced, including artificial intelligence in cyber security, software testing, and data security.

8.4.1 Application of AI for Cyber Security: Examples from Real Life

Machine learning is capable of scanning enormous volumes of data quickly and performing statistical analysis on them. It's no surprise that modern businesses generate massive volumes of data; therefore, machine learning is such a great device for data scanning.

8.4.1.1 DEFENSE SCREENING

Immigration officials and customs officers can spot those who are lying through security screening. Regardless, the screening mechanism has a proclivity for errors. Furthermore, human-based screening might lead to errors because people grow tired and can easily be diverted. The US Department of Homeland Security has developed AVATAR, a framework that monitors people's body movements and appearances. This simply employs artificial intelligence (AI) and big data to collect small variations in facial expressions and body language that could trigger suspicion.

8.4.1.2 SECURITY AND WRONGDOING EVASION

The New York Police Department has been using the Computer Statistics (CompStat) AI framework since circa 1995. CompStat is a type of early AI that combines authoritative administration and reasoning with a variety of programming tools. This framework was the primary tool for "predictive policing", and many police departments around the United States have been using CompStat to investigate security violations since then. AI-based misconduct investigation tools, such as Armorway, based in California, use AI and game theory to predict psychological militant threats. Armorway is also used by the Coast Guard for port security in Los Angeles, Boston, and New York.

8.4.1.3 DISSECT VERSATILE ENDPOINTS

A search engine uses machine learning to analyze the risks associated with mobile endpoints. This evaluation can be used by businesses to protect the growing number of individual cell phones. Zimperium and MobileIron have announced a partnership to assist organizations in embracing adaptable anti-malware systems that incorporate artificial intelligence. Zimperium's AI-based threat detection combined with MobileIron's consistency and security engine can solve issues including organization, device, and application threats. Skycure, Lookout, and Wandera are some of the other companies that offer flexible security plans. To distinguish expected hazards, each merchant uses its own AI computation.

8.4.2 ARTIFICIAL INTELLIGENCE IN THE FIGHT AGAINST ONLINE FRAUD

Companies must have the ability to detect a digital attack in advance. This is so that you can hinder anything the enemies are trying to accomplish. Artificial intelligence (AI) is a type of artificial intelligence that has been established to be extremely helpful in detecting digital threats. It all boils down to examining data and detecting a threat before it leverages information system vulnerabilities. AI allows computers in the direction of use in addition to altering computations based on the data they receive, learning from it, and determining the necessary improvements. In the context of cyber security, this means that the intention of AI is enabling the computer to forecast hazards in addition to monitoring some deviations by means of far greater accuracy than some person.

8.4.3 Drawbacks and Limitations of Using AI for Cyber Security

Cybercriminals are also well versed in artificial intelligence: Hackers can employ AI security technologies as well. Cyberthreats also evolve; therefore, just because you use AI in your company doesn't mean you're immune to all risks. While initial concerns regarding AI's progress in cyber security systems may be regarding the loss of much-needed human skill, intuition, and judgment, AI's true disadvantage is its unpredictability. AI implementation costs are extremely high. Humans cannot be replaced by AI-based machines, computers, and so on. Machines, without a doubt, perform far more efficiently than humans do. AI can be used to detect cyberthreats and potentially malicious behavior. AI systems are being trained to detect malware, execute pattern recognition, and detect even the tiniest characteristics of malware or ransomware attacks before the malware or ransomware enter the system using sophisticated algorithms. Any exploitable weak spot that jeopardizes your organization's cyber security is referred to as cyber security vulnerability. For example, if your business doesn't have a lock on its front entrance, it's a security risk because anyone may easily break in and steal anything valuable. There are significant limits to AI technology that prohibit it from becoming a popular security solution. Organizations require a large number of resources, including data, memory, and processing power.

To train the AI system, security businesses must use a variety of data sets containing abnormalities and malware codes. Creation of data sets need a significant amount of time and effort, which some organizations cannot afford.

Hackers also employ artificial intelligence to build and enhance their virus. Because AI-based malware may learn from existing AI tools to execute more complex attacks, it is extremely dangerous.

Neural fuzzing is a technique for detecting software flaws by putting vast volumes of random data through its paces. A threat actor can use a combination of neural fuzzing and neural networks to gather knowledge about a target software or system and uncover the weaknesses of the target software or system.

8.5   CYBER SECURITY AI SOLUTIONS

Europoll and E3 statistics suggest that we might be in the midst of an arms race. Organizations expect that in the near future, hackers will begin actively using AI, and let's face it as traditional solutions can't handle such dangers. Most businesses are now unprepared to deal with extremely intelligent viruses, malware, ransomware, and other cyberthreats. One thing is certain: Using AI solutions may already save businesses time and effort while also ensuring that businesses are better prepared for future threats. IT is both a weapon against current dangers and a long-term investment. Because technology is becoming more widely available, no firm will be able to avoid using AI in the near future. As more technology is interwoven into daily life, the contact of AI taking place lives will prolong in the direction of expand. Some experts feel AI has a negative impact on machinery, while others believe artificial intelligence has the potential to significantly improve human lives. The key advantages of cybersecurity include faster threat analysis and mitigation. Hackers can conduct both virtual and technology-based attacks, which is a matter for concern.

Artificial intelligence and machine learning aren't limited to known virus types; they can also have an impact on viruses that have not been discovered yet. The AI system can look up a threat in an existing database, use clever algorithms to discover similar patterns, and devise a counterattack strategy. With practice, such a system improves its ability to recognize and respond to unforeseen threats, thereby increasing its speed and efficiency. For example, thieves frequently hide malicious code among a jumble of meaningless combinations, making it nearly impossible for a traditional antivirus software or system to detect dangerous bits. OceanLotus, a Vietnamese hacker firm, employed this method, which was spotted by machine learning-based security software. Modern, potent viruses, as well as future AI-based viruses, necessitate a fresh approach toward cybersecurity. It's self-evident that businesses must stay one step ahead of risks. Even if cybercriminals haven't actively targeted us with AI-based attacks, that doesn't rule out the possibility of such attacks. For a variety of reasons, firms must include artificial intelligence in their security strategies.

Artificial intelligence has already infiltrated numerous industries, including cybersecurity. The majority of firms already believe that without AI support, they would be unable to detect and withstand attacks. According to a Capgemini poll, more than 80% of communications companies utilize AI for security, and 75% of banking executives have adopted the AI technology – a trend that can be seen across all major industries. Artificial intelligence is certainly taking over day-to-day security concerns, but it has also demonstrated its ability to solve difficult challenges – not only in terms of security but also in terms of hacking. Let's look at how AI is used for both security and hacking and what businesses can learn from looking at AI use cases. AI is well suited to solving some of the world's most complex challenges, and cybersecurity is undoubtedly one of them. Machine learning and AI can be used to "keep up with the bad guys" in today's ever-evolving cyber-attacks and proliferation of gadgets by automating threat detection and responding more efficiently than traditional software-driven ways. Cybersecurity, on the other hand, has certain particular challenges: With a large attack surface, with tens or hundreds or thousands of devices per company, there are hundreds of assault avenues to choose from. There are significant shortages of competent security personnel. Massive amounts of data are no longer in the range of a human-scale issue. New AI applications in cybercrime care for human groups in various network safety classifications, such as the following.

IT Asset Inventory – It deals with acquiring a total, precise stock of all gadgets, clients, and applications with any admittance to data frameworks. Arrangement and estimation of business criticality likewise assume enormous parts in stock.

Danger Exposure – Programmers pursue their goals in the same way that everyone else does, therefore what's fashionable among programmers changes on a regular basis. Man-made intelligence-based online protection frameworks can give prior information on worldwide and industry-related explicit dangers to assist with deciding on basic prioritization choices not just with respect to what could be utilized to assault your endeavor, but in view of what is probably going to be utilized to assault your venture.

Controls Effectiveness – It is vital to comprehend the effect of the different security devices and security processes that you have utilized to keep a solid security foundation. Man-made intelligence can assist with getting where your information security program has strengths and where it has weaknesses.

Security Breach Risk Prediction – Accounting for IT rescue stock, vulnerability to danger, and controls adequacy, AI-based frameworks can foresee how and where you are probably going to be penetrated, with the goal of allowing you to anticipate asset and device distribution toward areas of shortcoming. Prescriptive bits of knowledge got from AI examination can help you design and upgrade controls and cycles to further develop your organization's digital flexibility.

Occurrence Reaction – AI-fueled frameworks can provide a further developed setting for prioritization of and reaction to security alarms, for quick reaction to danger episodes, and to surface underlying drivers to alleviate weaknesses and stay away from issues in the future.

Reasonableness – The key to outfitting AI to enhance human infosec groups is the logic of suggestions and examination. This is significant in getting input from partners across the organization for understanding the effect of different infosec programs and for detailing pertinent data to every single partner involved, including end clients, security activities, CISO, inspectors, CIO, CEO, and directorate.

8.5.1 Wearable Plan as Key Achievement Factor

The present wearable-device security plan engineers face various challenges. Despite its conservative construction, shrewd groups and watches should provide convenience and natural representation. Other achievement factors incorporate high-transmission capacity availability, estimation precision, functional life span, low-power utilization, and solidness. Since wearable gadgets and tech gadgets for ensuring well-being record the user's data in evolving conditions, parts of the gadgets should be intended for functional soundness under various conditions, while continuously guaranteeing exact, strong estimation of tension and movement. Likewise, wearable devices should have foolproof security systems so that device users don't need to worry about their personal or confidential information falling into some unacceptable hands.

8.5.2 One-Stop Offering

Our comprehensive portfolio includes RF, sensing, remote networking, power, memory, and security building blocks to address current challenges and wow clients. Little in size, XENSIV™ sensors empower sport, well-being, and action checking to the best expectations of value and accuracy. XENSIV™ 60 GHz radar sensor, for example, is great for well-being monitoring, for example, pulse detection. Compared with past sensors, the RF portfolio improves user experience with consistent network and area following. Planners can choose between various charging modes, eliminating the issue of links and electrical plugs with remote/NFC arrangements or scaling down plans with USB-Type C regulators. Wearable architects can likewise depend on us for a rich and safety arrangement focusing on various use cases. The OPTIGA™ Trust family provides a variety of equipment-based trust services, including confirmation and device insurance. Specific relatives, for example, OPTIGA™ Connect Consumer and OPTIGA™ Authenticate S were intended to stretch out secure cell availability to wearable devices and to safeguard against fake new parts by providing every gadget a unique ID. The SECORA™ Connect family provides secure NFC abilities to wearable devices.

8.6 ARTIFICIAL INTELLIGENCE TO THE RESCUE

Artificial intelligence and machine learning have advanced to the point where they can accurately forecast outcomes as well as recognize and classify objects. These artificial intelligence applications can also be used to prevent disasters or respond quickly at the time of an emergency.

1. **AI for Designated Calamity Alleviation the Board**

   If a disaster occurs, the first step is to devise a basic support group to assist individuals who are in need. Before the team dives straight in, it's critical to deconstruct and assess the extent of the damage and to make sure to assign the correct guide to the people who need it the most.

   Computer-based intelligence strategies, for example, image recognition and order, can be very useful in surveying the damage as these can examine and observe images from satellites. They can quickly and productively collect these pictures, which would have needed a very long time to be done physically. From these images, computer-based intelligence can distinguish items and elements like damaged structures, flooding, and obstructed streets. They can likewise distinguish damaged settlements, which might show that individuals are in need of help, thus the main rescue operation could be coordinated toward helping them.

   Man-made brainpower and AI devices can likewise sum up and crunch information from numerous assets, for example, publicly available planning resources or Google Maps. AI moves toward consolidating this information together, eliminating questionable information, and distinguishing useful resource for creating heat maps. These heat maps can distinguish regions needing pressing help and can direct aid projects to persons in the affected area. Heat maps are likewise useful for administration in addition to additional philanthropic organizations in selecting any option for immediate aeronautical assessments.

   The digital world gives breathing space symbolism in addition to geospatial contented. Their unlock information agenda be an exceptional agenda intended for catastrophe reaction. By learning from the group, the product learns how to perceive structures from satellite images. Every year, Digital Globe releases pre- and post-event images for a few major disasters, and its publicly supported stage, Tomnod, will prioritize micro-entrustment to speed up damage assessments.

   Following the 2015 Nepal earthquake, rescuers and academics launched the Orchid program to use AI for safety measures. They employed pre- and post-catastrophe symbolism, publically backed information evaluation, and AI to identify regions affected by the shudders that had not yet received help. This information was then disseminated to assist labor forces with their activities.

2. **Cutting-Edge 911**

   If a disaster or debacle occurs, the number is quadrupled, if not significantly more. This necessitates supplementing traditional 911 contact centers with more cutting-edge technology for better management. Traditional 911 systems rely solely on voice calls. To obtain new types of information, cutting-edge dispatch administrations are revamping their crisis dispatch technology with AI. As a result, they can now consume data from calls, as well as messages, videos, music, and photos, in order to explore and make quick assessments. The bits of knowledge gleaned from this data can be distributed to crisis response teams in the field, allowing them to carry out fundamental tasks more efficiently.

   The Association of Public-Safety Communications (APCO) has been using IBM Watson to handle emergency calls. Using Watson's discourse to message and investigation programs, this drive aims to aid crisis call centers in further developing activities and public security. The setting of each call is taken into the AI's investigation program using Watson's discourse to message work, allowing improvements in how call centers react to crises. It also aids in reducing call times, providing accurate data, and speeding up time-sensitive crisis management.

3. **Feeling Examination via Online Media Information for Catastrophe the Board and Recuperation**

   Simulated intelligence-controlled chat bots can help occupants affected by a cataclysm. The Chabot can interface by means of the person in question otherwise different residents in the area through well-known online media channels and request that they transfer data like the area, a photograph, and some depiction. The AI can then approve and actually take a look at this data from different sources and give the applicable subtleties to the fiasco help panel. This kind of data can help them with surveying disaster continuously and assist with focusing on reaction endeavors.

   Artificial Intelligence for Disaster Response (AIDR) is a free tool that uses device intelligence to analyze and categorize web-based communication during crises, disasters, other compassionate situations. For this, it utilizes an aerial and a Tagger. The aerial aids in the collection and sifting of tweets by applying keywords and hashtags such as "twister" and "#Irma". The aerial serves as a word channel. The Tagger is a theme channel that orders tweets through subjects of attention, for example, "Framework smash up" and "Gifts", for instance. The Tagger consequently applies the classifier to incoming tweets gathered progressively utilizing the Collector.

4. **Computer-Based Intelligence Answers Trouble and Help-Calls**

   Crisis relief organizations are inundated with calls for assistance in the event of a crisis. When completed physically, managing such a large number of calls is time-consuming and expensive. It is possible that basic data gets removed without being noticed. In such situations, AI is able to function the same as an all day, every day dispatcher. Artificial intelligence frameworks and voice collaborators can dissect gigantic measures of calls, figure out what sort of occurrence happened, and confirm the area. They cannot just cooperate with guests normally and process those calls; however, they can immediately interpret and decipher dialects. Simulated intelligence frameworks can break down the manner of speaking for earnestness, separate repetitive or less dire calls, and focus on them in light of a crisis.

5. **Prescient Investigation for Proactive Catastrophe the Board**

   AI and different information science approaches are not restricted to helping in-ground alleviation groups or helping solely after a genuine crisis. AI approaches, for example, prescient investigation, can likewise break down previous occasions to recognize and separate examples and the populace powerless against normal cataclysms. An enormous number of regulated and solo learning approaches are utilized to recognize danger regions and further develop forecasts of future occasions. For example, grouping calculations can arrange deba-cle information based on seriousness. They can distinguish and isolate climatic examples that might cause nearby tempests with the cloud conditions that might prompt a broad tor-nado. Prescient AI models can likewise assist authorities with circulating supplies to where individuals are going, rather than where they were by breaking down constant conduct and development of individuals. Furthermore, prescient investigation procedures can likewise give knowledge to understanding the financial and human effect of normal catastrophes. Counterfeit neural organizations learn like district, nation, and cataclysmic event type to anticipate the expected money-related effect of catastrophic events. Ongoing advances in cloud innovations and various open-source devices have empowered prescient investigation with basically no underlying foundation speculation. So, organizations with restricted assets can likewise construct frameworks in view of information science and foster more modern models to dissect debacles. Optima Predict, a set-up of programming by Intermedix, gathers and peruses data about calamities like viral episodes or crime progressively. The product spots geological groups of revealed occurrences before people notice the pattern and cautions key authorities about it. The information can likewise be synchronized with First Watch, which is a web-based dashboard for emergency medical services (EMS) staff.

8.7   OTHER AI APPLICATIONS

Artificial intelligence (AI) is a type of computer intelligence that mimics human behavior or think-ing and may be educated to solve issues. AI is a combination of machine learning and deep-learning approaches. AI algorithms that have been trained with large amounts of data may make intelligent judgments. Some AI applications in day-to-day life are in the fields of e-commerce, education, lifestyle, navigation, robotics, human resource, healthcare, agriculture, gaming, automobiles, social media, marketing, chatbots, and finance.

8.8   CONCLUSION AND FUTURE WORK

Artificial intelligence and machine learning have the potential to boost security while also making it easier for thieves to break into systems without the need for human participation. Any business could suffer serious consequences as a result of this. If you want to reduce losses and stay in busi-ness, you should invest in some type of cyber security. AI, like any other evolving technology, will expand on its current ability. It has the potential to prevent outages from occurring and provide disaster response commanders with a more complete picture of the disaster region, thereby sav-ing lives. Academic materials reveal that AI approaches are already being used to prevent cyber-crime in a variety of ways. Planning and future research will be required for the application of AI approaches in cyber protection. One of the obstacles in network-centric warfare is knowledge man-agement; thus, the introduction of modular and hierarchical information architecture in decision-making software is a promising field for research. Only automated knowledge management can ensure rapid situation assessment and decision supremacy. It's also possible that the main aim of AI research – the production of artificial general intelligence – will be achieved in the not-too-distant future, leading to the Singularity, which is defined as "the technical fabrication of intellect smarter than human intelligence". Nonetheless, it is critical that we have the capability to deploy stronger AI technologies in cyber protection than criminals do. This chapter has summarized the progress made so far in the subject of using AI approaches to combat cybercrime and their current limitations and desirable qualities, as well as the scope for future research.

REFERENCES

1. Sutar Mega, G. M. U., "Intelligent safety system for women security", Associate Professor, EC and TC Department, DACOE, Karad, Maharashtra, India.
2. Dr. Mandapati, S., S. Pamidi, S. Ambati (2015). "A mobile based women safety application", *IOSR Journal of Computer Engineering (IOSR-JCE)*, 17, 29–34.
3. Tyugu, E. (2011). "Artificial intelligence in cyber defense", in *3rd International Conference on Cyber Conflict (ICCC 2011)* (pp. 1–11).
4. Wang, B., G. Y. Yang, Y. C. Li, D. Liu (2008). "Review on the application of artificial intelligence in antivirus detection system", in *IEEE Conference on Cybernetics and Intelligent Systems* (pp. 506–509).
5. Brunette, E. S., R. C. Flemmer, C. L. Flemmer (2009). "A review of artificial intelligence", in *Proceedings of the 4th International Conference on Autonomous Robots and Agents* (pp. 385–392).
6. Soni, V. D. (2020). "Challenges and solution for artificial intelligence in cybersecurity of the USA", Available at SSRN 3624487.
7. Wirkuttis, N., H. Klein (2017). "Artificial intelligence in cybersecurity", *Cyber, Intelligence, and Security*, 1(1), 103–119.
8. Taddeo, M. (2019). "Three ethical challenges of applications of artificial intelligence in cybersecurity", *Minds and Machines*, 29(2), 187–191.
9. Truong, T. C., I. Zelinka, J. Plucar, M. Čandík, V. Šulc (2020). "Artificial intelligence and cybersecurity: Past, presence, and future", in *Artificial Intelligence and Evolutionary Computations in Engineering Systems* (pp. 351–363). Springer, Singapore.

9 Computer-based (AI) Intelligence in the Field of Defense

T Akilan, U Hariharan, and P. Durgadevi

9.1 INTRODUCTION

The Defense Innovation Board (DIB) has developed AI Ethics Principles for the Department of Defense (DoD), and governments throughout the world have made significant investments in AI-based automation for defense. To establish an online marketplace for the purchase of AI, the DoD has taken action. AI is improving defense systems and has applications in the commercial, societal, and defense domains. Its application in speech recognition, object identification, picture analysis, and machine learning has expanded quickly. AI is now a crucial component of defense on a global scale, revolutionizing the use of AI defensive systems in cyberspace planning [1]. AI is a rapidly emerging field as a result of defense agencies' global interest on using it for a variety of military purposes. The capacity of AI to learn quickly and carry out tasks under a variety of settings without human intervention has piqued the curiosity of military intellectuals, foreign competitors, and political leaders. The AI application in the field of defense is illustrated in Figure 9.1. Defense Metrics in various aspects of AI are shown in Figure 9.2.

9.1.1 ARTIFICIAL INTELLIGENCE'S IMPACT ON DEFENSE SYSTEMS

Automated Weapons Targeting System were taken based on their accuracy and also on the ability to attach to a target immediately. Electronic focusing architectures should be improved to make them less resistant to counterattack when using this type of focusing approach. Defense measures for such methods are already commonly employed and Computer Vision is being used by automated weapon to recognize and follow goals. Whilst such frameworks are recognized as having the ability to monitor targets in regions where they can be dispatched, an automated weapon becomes basically self-sufficient [1]. The AI driving the targeting system should be equipped to determine which target is worth focusing its capabilities on and to advise the system administrator on how to use the available information for targeting. An adversary plane travelling into contested airspace at a fast pace, a missile fired at a city, or a militarily protected personnel carrier going along a mined street could all be examples of this. Currently, there no self-governing ballistic missiles are been fired or launched without the explicit approval of a monitoring controller. One of the most important advantages of autonomous weapons is that they can choose and identify targets without the need for additional human participation. Self-sufficient armaments allow Computer Vision's every 'eyes' to be fixated on the skies above, knocking back enemy missiles before they can detonate in a crowded place for preventing shock rocket attacks. If a human operator is engaged or nods off while on duty, valuable minutes may be wasted. In the cybersphere, AI can be used as a weapon.

DOI: 10.1201/9781003251781-9

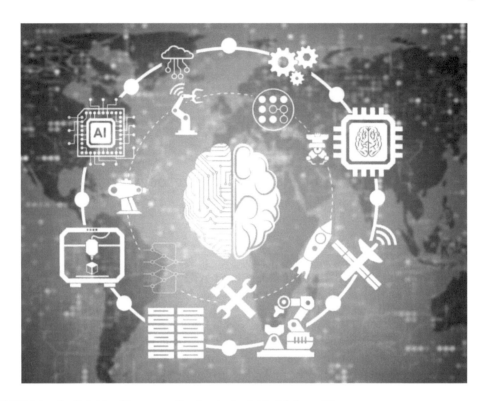

FIGURE 9.1   Artificial intelligence application in the field of defense [1].

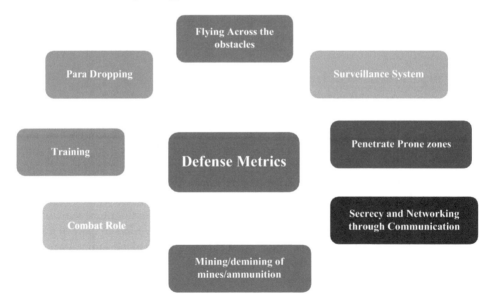

FIGURE 9.2   Defense metrics in various aspects in AI [1].

9.2   SECURITY ISSUES AND CHALLENGES IN COMPUTER-BASED AI

9.2.1   Resilience Testing and Monitoring

Breach testing is a crucial component of evaluating the security and resiliency of Information Communication Technology products and services. Because there are a plethora of dangers [2] in the field of AI that might severely impact the right functioning of AI technologies, AI penetration testing (pentesting) appears to be on the rise. Initial approaches and techniques have been presented or are in the process of being developed. Nevertheless, there is a significant void in the domain of AI pentesting products and particular methodologies for testing AI systems from an adversarial viewpoint [3]. Furthermore, assessing and analyzing resistance to even non-adversarial environmental changes brings up a new field of study. Figure 9.3 depicts the measuring and monitoring of various dimensions in research issues.

9.2.3   Resilient Malware Detection

Antivirus software has traditionally used a signature-based methodology: Pattern-matching techniques are being used to categorize coding as harmless or dangerous using source code signatures acquired from genuine harmful samples. Sadly, malicious code can elude identification by using code modification [4] or camouflage methods. To be resilient against such tactics, malware detection must include encrypted samples in its analysis. Owing to the increasing difficulties in malware direct code testing, a methodology is a viable alternative: The primary method for detecting malicious activity involves monitoring typical connections with (suspicious) instructions along with Operating System devices to detect finger impression for unusual activities. By contrast, innovative operations are likely to exhibit unique, unusual characteristics.

9.2.4   Technical Challenges of Defense System

9.2.4.1   Recognizing Various Targets

It can be very difficult to build a mechanism which can distinguish military personnel from the public. In certain scenarios, this is used to involve the rules needed by the Rules of Engagement (ROE) and Law of War (LOW) particularly when troublemakers' actions resembles those of normal citizens. Furthermore, robots will have to distinguish among enemy troops people who still are alive

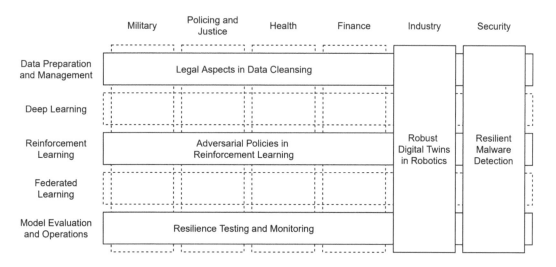

FIGURE 9.3   Measuring and monitoring of various dimension in research issues [2].

and those who have been killed or surrendered, which would be a difficult assignment [7]. Even though human troops find aim distinction to beat ought and blunder activity, we ought to be certain about just how accurate this discrimination should be. Therefore, we hold the system to a higher level when we can't seem to be doing it ourselves, at least not in the coming years.

9.2.4.2 Challenges of the First Generation

It would be naive to believe that yet another catastrophe involving military robots will not occur. Defects or bugs will inevitably occur, just as they do with certain developments. This issue can be addressed by technological advancements in the coming years. Original errors are really not hard to diagnose with internet advancements and can be remedied with code patches or upgrades. However, the stakes are much higher with army mechanical technology, because people's lives could end due to incorrect instructions or other faults [5]. However, it is important to note that testing scenarios may be significantly unique in comparison to increasingly unstable, unorganized, and changing front-line situations in which each possible opportunity can't be predicted.

9.2.4.3 Robots on the Amok

Some imagine it is possible that robots could break from their human programming, due to coding errors or intentional hacker attacks, resulting in robots that follow their own instructions, as depicted in science fiction films and book. Because robots could be taught to be robust and even strike in certain scenarios, it would be incredibly difficult to defeat them – which is indeed the point of using robots as super multipliers in the first place. A few of these scenarios are more likely than others; We are unlikely to see robots with the ability to transform themselves by radically expanding their knowledge and deviating from expected moral conduct any time soon[6]. However, various scenarios, like espionage, look to be relatively close possibilities, especially when robots are not provided sufficient self-protecting skills. The fear that robots will begin to run rampant is an upgraded version of the fear that enemies will use our own designs against us. This also relates to the fact that previous weapon architectures, in addition to their inherent limitations, required human support, which left robots defenceless and could be considered a "delicate underside" of system architectures. What safeguards are being put in place to prevent robots being seized, deciphered, or recreated in order to weaken our own commands? If we construct an 'off switch' capable of halting a robot, we create a potential weakness which could be exploited by an adversary.

9.2.4.4 Illegal Overrides

The concern with bypasses, particularly with respect to nuclear weapons, is that a corrupt authority may launch such terrible weapons without permission or, in any event, abrogate its coding to perform illegal actions. This is a multifaceted test that must be passed with any new disruptive technology: It's a human problem, an authoritative issue (procedural safeguards), and a specialized issue (creating moral, capable officials) (to give basic defense). So far, nothing has emerged which suggests that there was anything unique regarding this issue that could stymie the sequence of events. In any event, this issue should be taken into account at the designing and organization stages.

9.2.4.5 Challenging Ethical Frameworks

It is unclear whether moral theory can be used as our prototype if designers attempt to construct a moral framework of robotic operations. A half-and-half practise is the hypothesis which would seem to produce very less intuitive results. Moreover, any contemporary hypothesis says all the accounts ineffectual against discrepancies and competing requirements is a concern that is expressed in the principal specialized test depicted above, which states that integrating certain norms of conduct or coding it into the computer is much too difficult to contemplate. However, it should reconsider all the most critical. Our overarching goal is not to create a morally superior society. However, it should reconsider what can be deemed critical. The primary goal is not to create a very moral robot – especially one which exhibits greater moral conduct than individuals. Sadly, this may be a minimal thing to accomplish.

9.2.4.6 Synchronized Attacks

When deciding on a military strike, it is better to have some knowledge than none at all. Usually robots are designed to communicate well with other robots and frameworks. However, this might cause problems for robots designed solely as administrators. While robots work as a team, we have to establish tiers of leadership to ensure that its operations are coordinated. The danger here is that as the complexity of any framework increases opportunities for faults arise, and any mistake committed by defense robots could be fatal.

9.3. OBJECTIVE ANALYSIS OF AI TECHNOLOGY

9.3.1 ROBUSTNESS OF AI TECHNOLOGY

A competent AI program would theoretically be capable of passing both the Turing and Chinese room tests. Defense systems using AI-enabled surveillance systems can quickly identify attack patterns and build countermeasures. AI interface with military transportation can save the cost of transportation and at the same time reduce human operating efforts. AI improves defense systems' ability to identify target positions through gesture recognition. AI-enabled systems can harvest medical information from soldiers and assist in complicated diagnoses [8–10]. AI-assisted systems assist defense people in monitoring threats and improving real-time information. Various Forte of AI is shown in Figure 9.4.

9.3.2 AI TECHNOLOGY HAS ROBUST FUZZY DATA PROCESSING ABILITY

Artificial General Intelligence (AGI) is a term used to demonstrate coding. It resembles the cognitive capacities of the human brain. A robust AI system can employ fuzzy logic to adapt information from one field to another. It discovers a strategy independently while facing an unexpected problem

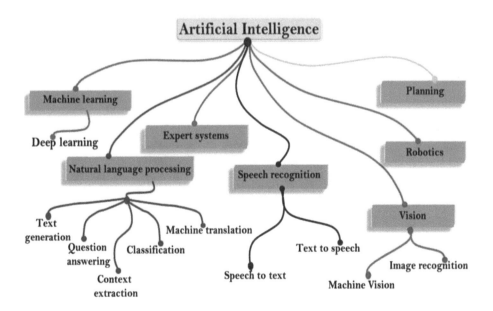

FIGURE 9.4 Various forte of artificial intelligence [5].

[11–12]. It's a reliable system that doesn't expect exact instructions. Those systems can handle a variety of inputs, including data that are ambiguous, skewed, or inaccurate. If the feedback sensor stops working, it can be reprogrammed to match our requirements. Because fuzzy logic methods may be programmed with minimal data, they don't take up a lot of memory [13, 14]. Such systems can handle complicated challenges with unclear inputs and rely solely on them because they resemble human reasoning. Those systems are adaptable, with rules that may be changed. The systems are easy to build and have a simple interface. Low-cost sensors can be incorporated into these systems, lowering the cost of the system [15].

9.4 IMPLEMENTATION OF COMPUTER-BASED AI DEFENSE SYSTEM

The early stages of AI development and deployment had a significant impact on people and governments. A much more productive discussion on the various applications of AI in defining resilience and mitigating foreign threats is required. AI can be used in both limited and generalized intelligence applications. They are expected to open up a slew of new possibilities, all of which have the potential to improve individual and group experiences in practically every aspect of human life. The superior weaponry system, with its major strengths in research and development and advanced AI know-how, may improve the world as a place to live in. AI encompasses a wide range of topics, including human tasks that can be completed with the assistance of robots and computers. There are many tasks that machine intelligence can execute with the same or near-human precision as humans. Several existing instances where the performance can be used for example IBM's Deep Blue, Google Maps, Google Translation, and Chatbots. This chapter also presents a few measures that can be used to illustrate the defense system's resilience. To begin with, the defense system should access the internet, and the data it accesses will be transferred from the defense system to the cloud storage, as well as to the corresponding users and can be able to process the data and return back with correct command for the next step. Figure 9.5 depicts the information shared by the defense system to authorized user.

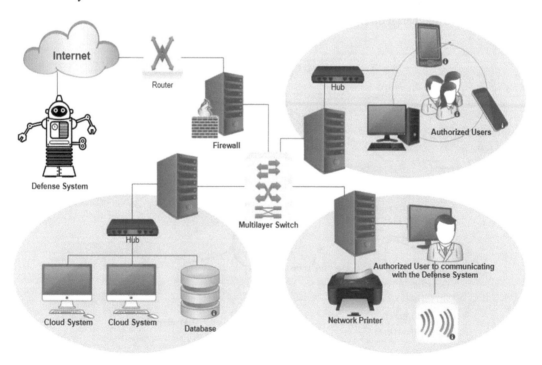

FIGURE 9.5 Information shared from defense system to authorized user.

9.4.1 Earth Object Extraction from Remote-Sensing Satellite Images

For military purposes, identifying warplanes in high-resolution satellite pictures is critical. Despite years of research and numerous publications [16], finding a generalist location algorithm and classifier to recognize airplanes in complicated airport settings remains tough. The spatial relationship between the ground components are an important interpretive aspect for correctly detecting the object. Such an interpretation component becomes even more important when compared to natural pictures because remote-sensing pictures actually reflect the ground covering, and whether naturally or artificially, the development of this exposure has principles that can be followed in most circumstances [17–18]. Because high-quality or high-pixels remote-sensing photographs make object borders more visible than ever, it's now possible to analyze the spatial relationship between earth items in these pictures. Buildings are a common type of artificial earth object, but there has been a lot of research into extracting buildings from remote-sensing photos. Pixel-based approaches are widespread, and the roof outline can be derived using classification, line feature extraction, and various contour evolution methods like the Level Set method, among others.

A panchromatic picture and a multispectral photograph are the two primary forms commonly provided by satellites. The panchromatic image is a single-tone picture that catches a broad frequency band with excellent spatial resolution, such as a major portion of the visible spectrum. Multispectral photos, on the other hand, are made up of many images acquired using equipment that are sensitive to certain frequencies and have a limited spatial resolution [19, 20]. Among these precise spectral bands, objects have distinct spectral reflection and absorption characteristics. Multispectral photographs are used to extract spectral data that are not visible to the naked eye. Furthermore, image-processing techniques like inter-channel operations are used to emphasize spectrum properties in satellite pictures that are analyzed using multispectral imaging. Because of its excellent spatial resolution, the panchromatic picture is commonly employed for satellite picture object classification. Newsam and Kamath, on the other hand, have performed image-processing techniques on multispectral satellite pictures using common texture features like the GLCM feature and the Gabor feature [21, 22]. Their findings show that employing all multispectral photos obtained in the visible and near-infrared bands gave better results than using merely a panchromatic photo. However, since such characteristics were essentially interconnected features derived from individual channels, it is also important to consider channel relationships when utilizing spectral data.

This chapter examines the efficiency of an image feature which incorporates the interactions amongst some of the channels in object-identification task trials using satellite images. It concentrates primarily on Higher-Order Local Autocorrelation Features (HLAC) from the standpoints of computation efficiency and accuracy in identification [23]. Since the feature extraction technique solely requires product-sum process, HLAC is quick to compute. As a result, the feature works well with large-scale photos, like satellite photographs. The functionality can record picture geometric patterns on a local level. Figure 9.6 shows the Earth Object Extraction from Remote Sensing Satellite Images.

9.4.2 Lidar-based Intruder Detection

The requirement to monitor a country's borders need assets for the creation of a wide range of skills – through simple wiring to high-tech sensors which have the capacity to identify infiltration of the hostile entity. Various physical as well as electromagnetic methods are presently used to monitor international boundaries and the line of control. Buried sensors, tracking radars, and unmanned aircraft are among the electromagnetic measures currently in use [24]. These measures each have their own set of advantages and disadvantages, as well as varying degrees of efficacy. Shackleton, Van Voorst, and J. Hesch [25] discuss the different LiDAR picture segmentation, clustering, attaching pixels to symbolic data structures, computing characteristics, and categorizing entities. Following that, basic algorithms for recognizing human forms in a wide range of postures

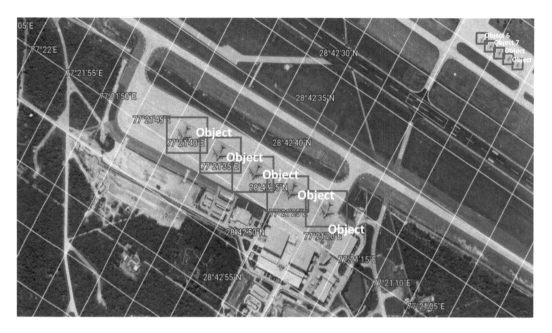

FIGURE 9.6 Earth object extraction from remote sensing satellite images.

in varied environments were designed. The human figures were segmented from the range image using this method. Colour segmentation process can be challenging, especially in natural settings with clutter and shadows. In addition to the qualities of luminosity or colour, a LiDAR range picture pixel has a range attribute [26]. A method was disclosed in which a unique stationary 3600 LiDAR sensor was used to recognize and identify persons wandering through an area in real-time basis. Surface monitoring is often used to segment a set of points depending on spatial separation over the scene using 3D occupancy grids [7]. On the basis of basic dimensions and orientation limitations, these point groups were regarded as candidate-specific targets.

The 3D Flash LiDAR (3DFL) illuminates scenes with a sole 5ns pulse with an energy of 1.5 to 2.8 mJ. The laser pulses return to an intelligent pixel array, particularly an Avalanche PhotoDiode (APD) array through the Complementary metal-oxide semiconductor ReadOut Integrated Circuit (CMOS ROIC), which captures and then saves analogue and digital information reflecting the flight duration. The APD identifier transforms photons into electrons with high improvement. The ROIC's timing circuit delivers a time-of-arrival and intensity output for every pixel. Relying on laser power and optics utilized for laser and reception, the system can accommodate varied ranges and horizontal fields of vision [27, 28]. This could easily detect motion targets using a series of 3D frames and then convey the data. ASC incorporation has designed and tested a surveillance system based on Flash LiDAR technology. The firm claims to be able to scan target areas ranging from 5 cms to 5 kilometres utilizing different lens pairings. The intensity of signal responses for each pixel is displayed using colour-coded pictures, as is the range distance to the surface at every pixel point. Figure 9.7 shows LiDAR vs. Flash LiDAR technologies and Figure 9.8 shows the object identification using LiDAR.

9.4.3 VIOOA 360-DEGREE LIVE STREAMING

360-Degree video, often known as omnidirectional or panoramic videos, provides enhanced interactive experience by spanning the viewers' whole angle of vision and enabling them to easily glance all around the environment with a complete 360-degree visual field. Furthermore, when

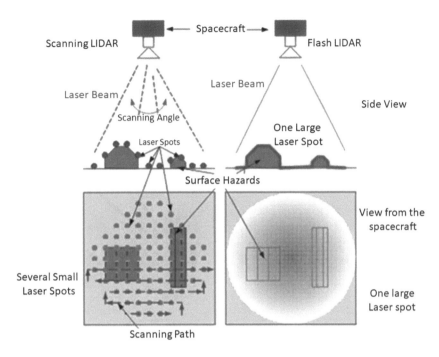

FIGURE 9.7 LiDAR vs. Flash LiDAR technologies [24].

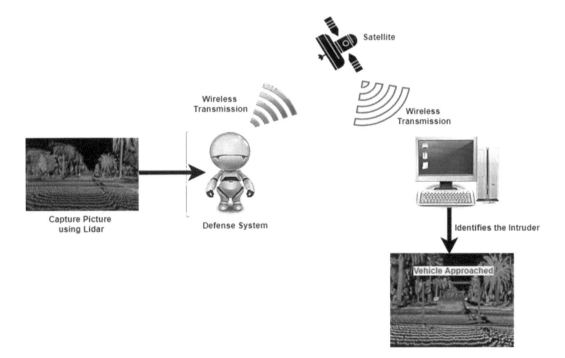

FIGURE 9.8 Object identification using LiDAR.

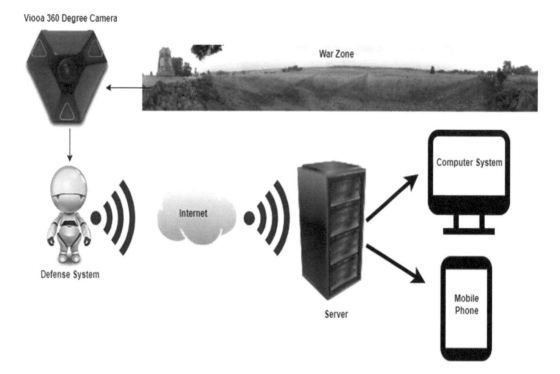

FIGURE 9.9   360ζ Live Video Streaming.

compared to broadcasting conventional videos, 360-degree video streaming systems transfer the whole 360-degree video frame result in much worse overall quality [29, 30]. Because the majority of pixels in 360° videos are out of sight or in the periphery, broadcasting 360-degree video around the same quality needs a greater resolution and frequency (Figure 9.9).

It can substitute the existing, unwieldy, wasteful gimbaled equipment with a next-generation 360-degree solid-state surveillance system that has a built-in 6-axis picture-stabilizing sensor with an easy plug-and-play ability [31]. Using this unique camera setup and innovative sewing technique, it can now shoot 4K beautiful videos or photos from literally any viewpoint whilst simultaneously broadcasting user viewpoint through HDMI. Instead of straining the drone to its limitations, think about how you can extend it. Viooa's small size, super light, lack of internal battery and aerodynamic shape would not only boost your drone's efficiency but also cut down on its energy usage, which is directly proportional to its overall durability: acquire more by flying longer. The proprietary camera configuration developed by Viooa takes airborne imaging technology to new heights. The autonomous system can perceive depth, identify motions, and is able to detect objects and more owing to the combination of Visual Detection and Ranging (ViDAR) technology and powerful 360-degree image-processing capabilities. It can simply add a self-awareness component to the quadcopter by a simple interaction with the autopilot, allowing it to securely fly about.

9.4.4   EMOTION DETECTION USING GOOGLE CLOUD VISION API MODULE

Numerous Emotion Detection Systems exist that can interpret emotions which are just deployed for the purpose of controlling. Emotional robots that are presently available have limited predictive accuracy in emotion. As a result, there is a demand for an Emotion Detection Robot that can forecast a person's mood. The person will be able to communicate with the robot based on their emotions. This should be a user's constant companion.

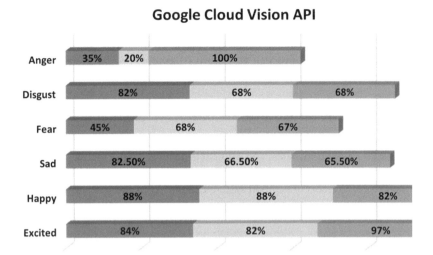

FIGURE 9.10   Forecast the accurateness, sensitivities, and precision of five persons with six various moods.

The Google Cloud Vision API was used to detect the emotion. This method employs a convolutional neural network that has been taught on a labelled dataset. Since it encapsulates strong machine learning models in a convenient REST API, the Google Cloud Vision API was utilized to interpret the information of a picture. The API accepts a JSON answer with the image as an input. Then it rapidly identifies the faces in images, predicts the expression, and outputs a JSON response with the sentiment. One of the most significant disadvantages of utilizing Google Cloud Vision API to forecast emotion is that it necessitates transmitting the image to Google's servers. This approach cannot be utilized if the application powered sensitive information, such as monitoring dementia sufferers.

With an accuracy of 80%, the Google Cloud-Based Vision API identifies feelings like joy, sadness, anger, and surprise. It accurately predicts anger feelings of the human and accurately recognizes the emotion of dread with 40% accuracy. As a result, each emotion involving rage will reduce the performance of the method. The entire test accuracy is 64.28% (Figure 9.10). This algorithm's total specificity and sensitivity in percentages are 60% and 78.67%, respectively. Table 9.1 shows, using the Google Cloud Vision API, the accurateness, sensitivities, and precision of five persons with six various moods.

9.5   ARTIFICIAL INTELLIGENCE IN NETWORK INFORMATION SECURITY DEFENSE

9.5.1   Data Aggregation, Data Processing, and Intelligence Analysis Made AI

AI could be used to improve situational awareness by effectively analyzing sensor information and raw intelligence, which includes intelligent sensing and automation of multi-sensor data fusion. In addition, incorporating deep learning algorithms into the satellite picture analysis process can considerably improve processing speed. Information processing and intelligence analysis are aided by AI.

9.5.2   Military Reasoning Using Computers (Tactical AI)

Computational military reasoning focuses on strategic AI or combat judgements and involves computer-resolving human-level defense problems. Tactical AI examines the battlefield and responds by generating a series of logical orders (often referred to as a Course of Action (COA) that utilize the holes in the enemy's position. Numerous worldwide laboratories have successfully demonstrated how an unsupervised machine learning algorithm could acquire this expertise and provide battlefield assessment which was statistically indistinguishable from SMEs' findings [32]. Landscape study, war games, and combat training can all benefit from this AI programme. DARPA's TIGER and MATE AI systems for combat analysis have proven to be successful.

9.5.3 UNMANNED WEAPON SYSTEMS THAT ARE INTELLIGENT AND AUTONOMOUS

Intelligent and autonomous defense systems, such as unmanned aviation, ground and undersea vehicles, army robots, and ballistic missiles, can all benefit from AI. Information collecting and management systems, knowledge base systems, support to decision systems, mission execution systems, and other components of this sort of weapon system can use AI to automatically track, identify, and defeat enemy targets.

9.5.4 CYBER DEFENSE AND CYBER WARFARE

AI can be used to improve the defense of important military networks and information systems, measure the impacts of cyberattack activities, and notify cyber warfare command decision-making. Pattern matching, data analysis, deep learning, and Big Data analysis can all be used to prevent and identify Distributed Denial of Service (DDoS) assaults. Deep neural networks could be used to address intrusion detection/prevention approaches, and software vulnerability research can be dependent on AI 'fuzzing' techniques that can be utilized in pentesting for defensive or offensive objectives. Given the rapidity with which cyber operations are conducted, AI could be a crucial enabler of quick command. Non-state actors can use AI applications in the cyber realm.

9.5.5 AIR COMBAT AI

AI demonstrates prospects in air warfare, wherein milliseconds count. The AI agent 'ALPHA' was constructed by the US Air Force Research Laboratory (AFRL). It has consistently beaten professional military pilots in a range of air-to-air combat situations in flight simulator trials. ALPHA will be improved in the future to improve autonomous capabilities for mixed battle groups of remotely piloted fighters operating in a crowded environment [32].

9.6 CONCLUSION

Even though the examples provided represent a tiny portion of the current attempts to deploy AI for defense reasons, they demonstrate that AI technologies have the potential to provide a variety of operational benefits. Relatively high situational awareness, greater efficiency, speed, higher cybersecurity, lower operating costs, higher unit integrity, higher complexity of combined arms manoeuvres, higher security of network communication, properly informed decision-making, increased operating consistency in network degraded situations, higher acceptance for physically dangerous operations, higher consistency and resilience are just a few of the benefits. In the field of defense, computer-based AI intelligence remains focused on signal recognition, intended detection, discrimination, and locating simplistic tactical weapon console planning, or specific data mining in information management system. However there is a significant trend that AI is having a big impact on tactical decision-making, assisting commanding officers in putting available resources on full display.

REFERENCES

1. CRS Report on "Artificial Intelligence and National Security" - Prepared for Congressional Research Service. https://crsreports.congress.gov/, R45178, November 2020.
2. European Union Agency for Cybersecurity (ENISA), *Artificial Intelligence Cybersecurity Challenges: Threat Landscape for Artificial Intelligence*. Publications Office of the European Union, 2020.
3. N. Das et al., MLsploit: A framework for interactive experimentation with adversarial machine learning research. In *Proceedings of the of the 25th ACM SIGKDD International Conference on Knowledge Discovery and Data Mining, ACM*, 2019.
4. O. Eigner et al., Towards resilient artificial intelligence: Survey and research issues. In *2021 IEEE International Conference on Cyber Security and Resilience (CSR)* (pp. 536–542). IEEE, 2021, July.
5. V. Rastogi, Y. Chen, and X. Jiang, Catch me if you can: Evaluating android anti-malware against transformation attacks. *IEEE Transactions on Information Forensics and Security*, pp.1-6, 9(1), 2013.
6. S. Selvaganapathy, S. Sadasivam, and V. Ravi, A review on android malware: Attacks, countermeasures and challenges ahead. *Journal of Cybersecurity and Privacy*, 10(1), 2021.
7. P. D. ManjuPayal et al., *Robotics, AI, and the IoT in Defense Systems, on AI and IoT-Based Intelligent Automation in Robotics* (pp. 109–127). © 2021 Scrivener Publishing LLC, 2021.
8. A. Kayid *The Role of Artificial Intelligence in Future Technology*, March 2020. http://doi.org/10.13140/RG.2.2.12799.23201.
9. D. Chen et al., *Autonomous Driving Using Safe Reinforcement Learning by Incorporating a Regret-Based Human Lane-Changing Decision Model*, 2019. arXiv:1910.04803 [cs.RO].
10. A. Ferdowsi, U. Challita, W. Saad, N. B. Mandayam, Robust deep reinforcement learning for security and safety in autonomous vehicle systems. In *2018 21st International Conference on Intelligent Transportation Systems (ITSC)*, 2018. http://dx.doi.org/10.1109/ITSC.2018.8569635.
11. P. Palanisamy. *Multi-agent Connected Autonomous Driving Using Deep Reinforcement Learning*, 2019. arXiv: 1911.04175 [cs.LG].
12. S. Wang et al., Deep reinforcement learning for autonomous driving, 2018. arXiv Preprint ArXiv:1811.11329.
13. E. Sallab, M. Abdou, E. Perot, S. Yogamani, Deep reinforcement learning framework for autonomous driving. *Electronic Imaging*, 2017(19), pp. 70–76, 2017.
14. Z. Xu, C. Tang, M. Tomizuka, Zero-shot deep reinforcement learning driving policy transfer for autonomous vehicles based on robust control. In *2018 21st International Conference on Intelligent Transportation Systems (ITSC)* (pp. 2865–2871). IEEE, 2018.
15. https://www.upgrad.com/blog/fuzzy-login-in-artificial-intelligence/.
16. D. Koc San and M. Turker, Building extraction from high resolution satellite images using hough transform, 2010. http://www.isprs.org/proceedings/xxxviii/part8/pdf/ic02_20100306204833.pdf.
17. Z. Li, Z. Liu, and W. Shi, A Fast level set algorithm for building roof recognition from high spatial resolution panchromatic images. *IEEE Geoscience and Remote Sensing Letters*, 11(4), pp. 743–747, 2013.
18. X. Jin and C. H. Davis, Automated building extraction from high resolution satellite imagery in urban areas using structural, contextual, and spectral information. *EURASIP Journal on Applied Signal Processing*,14, pp. 2196–2206, 2005.
19. K. Uehara, H. Sakanashi et al., Object detection of satellite images using multi-channel higher-order local autocorrelation. *2017 IEEE International Conference on Systems, Man, and Cybernetics (SMC)*, pp. 1339–1344, October 5–8, 2017.
20. X. Wang, B. Wang, and L. Zhang, Airport detection in remote sensing images based on visual attention. *International Conference on Neural Information Processing*, vol 7064, pp. 475–484, 2011.
21. X. Bai, H. Zhang, and J. Zhou, VHR object detection based on structural feature extraction and query expansion. *IEEE Transactions on Geoscience and Remote Sensing*, 52(10), pp. 6508–6520, 2014.
22. W. Zhang, X. Sun, H. Wang, and K. Fu, A generic discriminative partbased model for geospatial object detection in optical remote sensing images. *ISPRS Journal of Photogrammetry and Remote Sensing*, 99, pp. 30–44, 2015.
23. S. D. Newsam and C. Kamath, Retrieval using texture features in high resolution multi-spectral satellite imagery. *Proceedings of the SPIE*, 5433, pp. 21–32, 2004.
24. B. Lohani et al., "Surveillance system based on flash LiDAR" on Indian. *Cartographer*, XXXII, pp. 77–85, 2012.

25. J. Shackleton, B. Van Voorst, and J. Hesch, Tracking people with a 360-degree lidar. In *Proceedings of the 2010 7th IEEE International Conference on Advanced Video and Signal Based Surveillance, Ser. AVSS '10.1em plus 0.5em minus 0.4em* (pp. 420–426). IEEE Computer Society, 2010. http://doi.org/10.1109/AVSS.2010.52.

26. J. S. Albus, T. Hong, and T. Chang, Segmentation and classification of human forms using ladar data. In *AIPR.1em plus 0.5em minus 0.4em IEEE Computer Society*, 2006. http://dblp.unitrier.de/db/conf/aipr/aipr2006,html#AlbusHC06.

27. Y. Guan, C. Zheng, X. Zhang, Z. Guo, and J. Jiang, Pano: Optimizing 360° video streaming with a better understanding of quality perception. In *Proceedings of the ACM Special Interest Group on Data Communication, SIGCOMM '19* (pp. 394–407). Association for Computing Machinery, 2019. http://doi.org/10.1145/3341302.3342063.

28. F. Qian, L. Ji, B. Han, and V. Gopalakrishnan, Optimizing 360 video delivery over cellular networks. In *Proceedings of the 5th Workshop on All Things Cellular: Operations, Applications and Challenges, ATC '16* (pp. 1–6). Academic Medicine, 2016. http://doi.org/10.1145/2980055.2980056.

29. Y. Guan, C. Zheng, X. Zhang, Z. Guo, and J. Jiang, Pano: Optimizing 360° video streaming with a better understanding of quality perception. In *Proceedings of the ACM Special Interest Group on Data Communication, SIGCOMM '19* (pp. 394–407). Association for Computing Machinery, 2019. http://doi.org/10.1145/3341302.3342063.

30. F. Qian, L. Ji, B. Han, and V. Gopalakrishnan, Optimizing 360 video delivery over cellular networks. In *Proceedings of the 5th Workshop on All Things Cellular: Operations, Applications and Challenges, ATC '16* (pp. 1–6). Academic Medicine, 2016. http://doi.org/10.1145/2980055.2980056.

31. R. Sridhar et al., "E-Bot: A facial recognition based human robot emotion detection system" by BCS learning and development Ltd. In: Proceedings of the British HCI 2018. Belfast, UK, 2018.

32. http://www.indiandefencereview.com/news/artificial-intelligence-in-military-aviation/.

10 Assembly of Cyber and Illegal Intimidation

Jaya Sinha, M. Chandraprabha, and T. Akilan

10.1 INTRODUCTION

Crime is an unlawful activity that endangers society's well-being while also posing a serious threat to a country's economy. Lack of education, unemployment, poverty, corruption, resentment, and mental frustration are only a few of the primary factors contributing to the global surge in crime rates [1]. In today's Covid-19 situation, rise in unemployment, poverty, and frustration have exacerbated criminal activity in society. Theft, burglary, murder, assault, financial fraud, and cybercrime are some examples of criminal activity, and crime investigation is a legal process for identifying suspects, determining the likely destination of a crime, and anticipating the occurrence of a crime in order to protect society and people from such illegal activities [2–6]. Intimidating people in society either by cybercrime as cyberbullying or threatening people physically is a major concern that has to be focused upon in recent scenarios. As a result, a system based on Artificial Intelligence (AI) techniques is needed to be developed to assist in the area of cybercrime investigations and provide predictions and recommendations on various criminal actions to counter or reduce the effect of intimidation by cybercrimes.

Deep Learning (DL), a subspace of AI and Machine Learning (ML) is a promising approach that has been effectively utilized for efficiently recognizing objects, faces, and gestures, in the area of other Natural Language Processing (NLP) tasks, self-driving vehicles, precision agriculture, weather forecasting, and genomics. DL technology has piqued the curiosity of many in the area of cyber and computer security community recently. Many researchers have been inspired by the success of DL models in the above-mentioned areas to use DL-based techniques and architectures to develop recommendation systems that do not require human intervention in the area of crime analytics and investigation to aid various investigation agencies, including the police. Different neural network architectures are used in DL-based models, as well as ML techniques such as supervised methods, unsupervised methods, semi-supervised methods, and reinforcement learning, that includes many classification and clustering algorithms, data mining techniques such as association to identify common criminal behavior trends or underlying patterns in criminal pieces of evidence such as in text and speech. Many well-known supervised ML methods, such as k-Nearest Neighbors (k-NN) refers to classification method which is a non-parametric technique; Support Vector Machine (SVM) which may be applied for solving regression related and classification problems; Naïve Bayes is also a means of classification technique that uses Bayes' Theorem; Decision Trees are a rule-based approach suitable for classification and regression; and Ensemble learning, which combines several models to improve model accuracy, has been appropriate for classification and regression. Boosting, bagging, and stacking are important ensemble methods. K-means clustering, an unsupervised ML technique, and hierarchical clustering are two other common techniques [1].

There is also a range of models on the concept of deep learning that employs Convolutional Neural Network (CNN), popular neural architecture applied for classification of images and categorization.

DOI: 10.1201/9781003251781-10

Some of the popular computer vision algorithms for image classification and object detection that work well in real-time include Deep Neural Network (DNN), Region-based CNN (R-CNN), Fast Region-based CNN, Faster Region-based CNN, You Only Look Once (YOLO), Visual Geometry Group VGGNet, and Residual neural net (ResNet) [1, 7]. Pre-trained neural network architectures containing CNN layers include ResNet, YOLO, and VGGNet. All these ML and DL techniques and architectures have been elaborated in Section 3–5 with an overview of related literature in the field of crime investigation and analytics.

Pieces of crime evidence can take several forms, ranging from structured data saved as official records in relational databases tracking attributes, crime type, location, occurrence date, and time to unstructured data in the form of photographs, messages, e-mails, speech samples, and DNA samples, depending on the type of crime. To explore such vast amounts of heterogeneous data, a formal advanced system for data acquisition, integration, storage, and analysis must be developed. Integration of DL methods with Big Data and cloud services is one of the promising approaches to design and develop a generic crime analysis system for the investigation process. Such a system will enable investigating agencies to forecast and prevent cybercrimes including other crimes also, in real time, ensuring the safety of society and people as cybercrime is a cause of worry for businesses, as it can result in financial losses, damage to their reputation, productivity decrease, and legal concern.

10.2   TYPES OF CRIMES

Numerous forms of criminal activities are prevalent in present-day society which requires thorough police investigation. This section presents only some typical crimes that have been analyzed by various researchers using data mining, ML, along with DL approaches. All of these crimes have been categorized as cybercrimes and other crimes.

10.2.1   CYBERCRIMES

As cybercrime has a negative effect on both countries' governmental and private sectors, it is one of the primary areas that need constant surveillance and rigorous police investigation. Cyberspace has become more easily accessible to cybercriminals as a result of technological advancements, leading to an upsurge in cybercrimes. Cybercrime was the highest reported crime investigated from 2016 to 2018 [8]. According to 2021 crime statistics, cybercrime has increased by 600% owing to the current Covid-19 predicament. Globally, in 2025, cybercrime cost can escalate up to $10.5 trillion [5]. These figures suggest that dealing with and anticipating cybercrime is a pressing issue, and AI with DL, as an emerging trend, can be a backbone technology for efficiently predicting such crimes and assisting police investigations in the process, saving lives and money.

Cybercrimes have been categorized as Hacking, Phishing, Malware Dissemination, Software Piracy, Fraud, Spoofing, Cyberstalking, Cyberbullying, Spam, Denial of Service, Net Extortion, Cyber Defamation, Cyber Warfare, Cryptojacking, Cyber terrorism, and others which severely affect individuals, individual's property, organizations, and society as described below and shown diagrammatically in Figure 10.1 [5, 6, 8–12].

10.2.2   HACKING

It is referred to as getting unauthorized ingress into a computing machine and altering its hardware and software parameters. A **spoof** e-mail has a falsified e-mail header such that although the message appears to come from one source, it was actually transmitted by another. **Spam** is defined as unintended or unwelcome e-mails sent in large numbers to e-mail accounts. **Software piracy** is defined as making copies of software without permission and engaging in commercial activities [9].

FIGURE 10.1   Cyber Crime Categories

10.2.3   PHISHING

Phishing scams are one of the most popular types of cybercrime, accounting for 36% of all incidents in 2021. Phishing scams are those where e-mails are sent to a large group of people at random in the hope of tricking them into supplying sensitive information like account passwords, warning the user of attack, and pushing the user to install updated security software which is essentially malware. A link towards a bogus website could also be included in a phishing e-mail. It uses a mix of social engineering and spoofing tactics [9].

10.2.4   MALWARE

It refers to malicious software that obtains information without the user's permission. Malware, particularly ransomware, poses a serious concern for many small and big business organizations. It employs social engineering tactics to deny user accessibility of their data, demanding ransom with an assurance of restoring their contents [9].

10.2.5   CYBERBULLYING

It is also a rising and serious issue nowadays. Cyberbullying is a sort of cybercrime that encompasses behavior that is damaging to an individual. Identity theft, stalking, credit card fraud, bullying, and psychological manipulation are examples of cyberbullying. Cyberbullying can take the form of text, photos, photographs, video, and audio carried out through social media, e-mail, and text or SMS messages. Cyberbullying has the potential to linger for a long time. Youngsters and females are mostly victims of these crimes. Cyberbullying has been proven in several studies to indulge in raising stress factors and work unhappiness in employees. Such consequences at the workplace because of cyberbullying may result in a decline in worker productivity, if not addressed [9].

10.2.6 CYBER WARFARE

It is a sort of warfare that employs cyberattacks rather than weapons. It can be carried out without the consent of the government by organizations or gangs of hackers, and it can result in political issues between countries. Cyberwarfare is now the most common form of conflict. In the previous 20 years, there have been numerous cyberwars. In 2008, countries such as Russia and Georgia were involved in a cyberwar that included Distributed Denial-of-Service (DDoS), cross-site scripting attacks, and SQL injection on Georgian government websites [9].

10.2.7 CRYPTOJACKING

Cryptojacking is the unlawful mining of cryptocurrencies on another person's computer. Hackers accomplish this by convincing the victim to proceed using a malicious link which is sent in their e-mail that tries to install cryptomining malware on the machine. It can also be done when a website is infected with JavaScript code that executes as and when it is loaded in the victim's browser. Cryptojacking is now a recent concern for cybercrime since 2017 [9].

10.2.8 DENIAL OF SERVICE (DoS)

DoS occurs due to the website taking an excessive amount of time to load and work properly. A typical online danger is DoS assaults, in which an intruder disrupts the availability of a service. DoS attacks cause the computing system to crash and stop providing the intended service, compromising systems by flooding them with several requests, as Smurf and SYN floods. Distributed DoS, a sort of attack where the attacker has access to multiple channels in a network and each victim acts as an agent to attack another system DDoS attacks are a type of DoS assault where the attacker may access numerous network channels in a network. In this type of attack, each victim acts as an attacker agent for other systems [9].

According to Xingan Li's article, illicit cyber criminals may be satisfied by having conducted an illegal activity against a person or by having committed an illegal activity against a property. The study focuses on different motivations such as proving self-ego, testing the security of a system, as part of the adventure, due to hatred, for financial gain, and others, which influence actors to commit illegal cybercrimes. The study claims that maybe illegal online activities have a wide range of motivations, but they all have one thing in common – they are frequently geared towards gray regions of social life. The research on the motivations for unlawful cyber activities will aid in the development of practical penal policies that will eliminate the fertile ground for such crimes and make them more difficult to perpetrate in the cyber world [13].

DL techniques are emerging technology that can aid with such real-world economic threats and risks. There exists different DL architectures that can outperform in identifying cyber infiltration and phishing offenses. For areas of NLP, Image Detection, and Speech Identification, DNN, RNN, and CNN are promising architectures that will provide an effective platform for cybersecurity as well [14].

Berman et al. (2019) conducted a comprehensive literature survey that focuses on lity of DL techniques and its applications for cybersecurity, which included contributions from various authors. The paper provides a quick overview of several DL approaches. The paper also examines how Dynamic CNN, Deep Belief Network (DBN), CNN, Recurrent Neural Networks (RNN), Deep Neural Network (DNN), and Generative Adversarial Network (GAN) architectures are ideal architectures for analyzing and predicting various cybersecurity attacks mainly detecting malware and its classification, Domain Generation Algorithms (DGA) preventing spams, stealing personal data, and useful in implementing distributed DoS attacks, Botnet detection, network intrusion detection, spam identification and more [15].

Choi et al. aim to provide a complete view on recent research while using DL models on computer security issues. Applicability of DL techniques on defending network attacks, fighting Return-Oriented Programming (ROP) assaults, malware categorization, attaining Control-Flow Integrity (CFI), system-event-based anomaly detection, security-oriented program analysis, and memory forensics attaining secure software are covered in the review. According to the findings of the research, the literature on using DL techniques to address computer security vulnerabilities refers to a suitable approach and is still in its infancy [16].

Ravi et al. have described existing traditional ML techniques and DL architectures to counter zero-day threats in this comprehensive work. The article conducted a one-of-a-kind analysis on employing DL on the applications of cybersecurity with a variety of parameters, including applied datasets, the architecture of DL among others. Significance of NLP, image, signal processing with Big Data in cybersecurity applications was also highlighted. Authors have conducted a thorough literature study of several DL architectures used for cyberspace security to combat various threats and state-of-the-art AI learning techniques [17].

10.2.9 OTHER CRIMES

Other criminal acts, aside from cybercrime, continue to pose a threat to people and society. Individuals may suffer physical or mental injury as a result of it. It could also result in harm to public or private property. All of these common crimes have been classified in this area [2–4]:

10.2.9.1 Property Crime
Property crimes are related to stealing property without physically harming an individual. Burglary, theft, larceny, vehicle theft, and arson are few examples of property crimes.

10.2.9.2 Traffic Crime
Traffic crimes are those traffic offenses that are punishable by law. Driving under the influence of alcohol, reckless driving, overspeeding, hurting, or killing an individual while operating a vehicle are examples of traffic crimes.

10.2.9.3 Violent Crimes
Violent crimes are forcible felonies. Criminal homicide, rape, sexual assault, harming an individual using weapons while robbery, sex trafficking, terrorism are some examples of violent crimes.

10.2.9.4 Fraud and Financial Crimes
Embezzlement, banking fraud, forgery, deception of identity, corruption, money laundering, tax evasion, and bribery are some examples under fraud and financial crimes.

In addition to all these crimes there are other crimes also. These crimes include hate crimes, which cause societal discontent among races, religions, or genders as a result of derogatory words, crimes against mortality, such as illicit gambling and drug distribution, and white collar crimes, such as embezzlement and tax evasion, among others.

Steven Walczak (2021) has conducted a detailed analysis of the literature on the usage of several neural network-based architectures to forecast crime hotspots. Their research examines the performance of neural network architectures as Multi-Layer Perceptron (MLP), Recurrent Neural Network (RNN), Convolutional Neural Network (CNN), and Supervised Learning on property crimes as burglary, robbery, larceny, theft, and car theft, as well as other crimes such as assault and murder, to efficiently predict crime hotspots by identifying key attributes or recurring patterns of crime. As a result, the study demonstrates that ML and neural network designs are effective approaches to crime analytics [18]

Oatley et al. address data mining and decision-making tools for cops, taking into account a wide spectrum of computing techniques to aid cops with their work. This topic is quite practical, including study on authors' actual experimentation with three departments of police in the United Kingdom. Decision-making strategies based on geographical statistics, as well as a variety of data mining tools such as case-based reasoning, survival analysis, logic programming and ontologies, Bayesian networks, and model comparison are discussed and experimented with. Authors have investigated soft forensic evidences collected as crime scene data especially about burglary from

Knowledge Discovery and Dissemination 1999 dataset (KDD-Cup'99). They have elaborated with an example data containing some attributes such as crime reference number, date of crime at which it was committed, data about victim and culprit and crime type information. Authors claimed that logic programming technology is very useful when it comes to comparing a series of crimes to earlier series of crimes [19].

Stalidis et al. in their work present a detailed investigation for classifying and predicting crimes utilizing DL architectures. Using available data from police reports, authors have investigated the performance of DL algorithms in the sector of crime analysis, offering guidelines to construct, train and test systems for forecasting crime regions. A comparative analysis of ten state-of-the-art approaches with three alternative configurations of DL systems is undertaken using crime types per location as training data from five publicly available datasets. The experimentation shows that DL-based algorithms routinely beat previous best-performing methods in this area. Furthermore, work also assesses the efficacy of various parameters in DL architectures and provides guidance on how to configure them for enhanced crime classification and, ultimately, crime detection [20].

10.3 STATE-OF-THE-ART AI TECHNIQUES

AI is a growing field in the area of science and technology that is related to the computational model of perception that deals with intelligent movements and results in intelligent machines development. AI encapsulates a set of tools, methods, and algorithms, such as neural networks, genetic algorithms, symbolic AI, and DL [1], as shown in Figure 10.2. These key areas significantly show the growth and have dominant impacts on various areas such as healthcare, space, crime detection, robotics and military.

One of the main objectives of the AI field is to construct autonomous intelligent agents that interact with the environment, identify best behavior and look up over time in trial and error is almost human. There is a long-time challenge by starting with a robot that can notice and act in response to it. Modern AI technology is used in aviation, driving, medical and internet advertising, image recognition, personal support and crime detection. Two main sub areas of AI are ML and DL and it deals in machine training by taking the help of neural networks and prediction techniques. In Section 10.3.1 and 10.3.2, we are going to look into ML and DL concepts.

10.3.1 MACHINE LEARNING

ML is meant as a technique that allows computer systems to gain knowledge and improve the results or predictions without being explicitly programmed based on previous experience. After looking at the data, it is not always possible to identify the exact pattern or information. In these situations, ML is used to interpret specific patterns and data. The premise behind ML is that by accessing the right data, machines can learn and solve both complex mathematical and unique problems. Otherwise, the approach of learning by example used by a computer system is known as ML. Users get access to various categories of ML techniques that can be used on datasets. However, supervised and unsupervised learning algorithms are the two main types of learning algorithms. The function of supervised learning is nothing but inferring information or "the appropriate answer" from labeled training data. To anticipate, the algorithms are given a certain attribute or group of qualities. Unsupervised learning algorithms, on the other hand, are designed to uncover hidden patterns in unlabeled class data. Cybersecurity is not about shielding a company's private information. With the creation of the GDPR

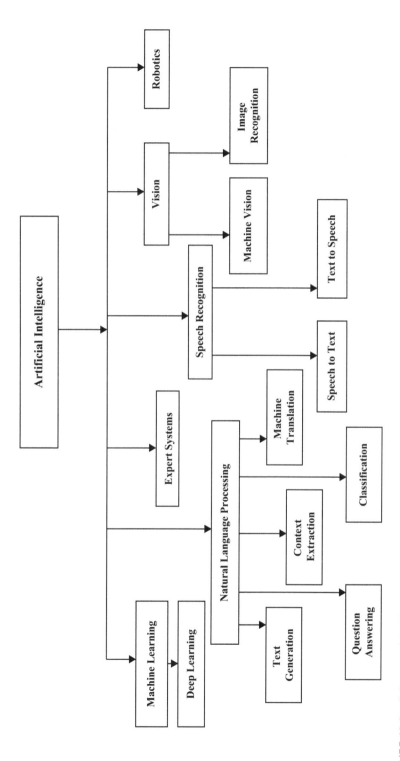

FIGURE 10.2 Sub areas of Artificial Intelligence

and the CCPA, it has additionally end up a prison matter. Therefore, protection and governance of facts are more critical than ever. As a result, AI and ML are certain to end up extra outstanding figures in cybersecurity. They are crucial at the international level, wherein protection professionals are already understaffed and crunched for time. User and Event Behavioral Analytics, or UEBA for short, is one of the ML approaches. To identify the behavioral patterns of individuals utilizing the corporate network and construct models of these users, UEBA uses ML and DL. The goal is to be able to recognize any unusual conduct and report it. Other statistical tools, on the other hand, flag threatening conduct based on previous patterns; UEBA, on the other hand, does not require predetermined patterns or rules to detect the same behavior. Varonis, a business specializing in data security and insider threat detection, provides machine learning-based solutions. The software can create a behavioral baseline for each user and keep track of what data they're accessing. Changing user permissions when a user no longer requires access to a certain piece of data because they haven't accessed it in a long time or their behavior profile differs from that of other users of the same data.

10.3.2 Deep Learning

Deep learning is an AI subset of ML. Artificial Neural Networks (ANNs) [1] are used in DL to emulate the functionality and describe the connections related to neurons in the human brain. The depth of an ANN is determined by the number of layers it contains. In DL architecture, the initial layer is fed with an input that it goes and processes through the different layers of the network architecture. Layers in the network include different types of scales and functions that make corrections in the input that can be crossed via layers based on specific sequence, and it finally gives an output, as prediction. The framework of DL includes TensorFlow and PyTorch that help us to build our personal DL models and conduct researches and evaluations. To learn the DL framework, both TensorFlow and PyTorch will act as a wealth of resources for beginners and aficionados. DL, Convolutional Neural Networks, and Recurrent Neural Networks (RNNs) [14] are used to build smarter ID/IP systems by determining traffic very accurately, minimizing false alerts, and assisting security teams in distinguishing between harmful and positive network activities. Some of the notable examples in applications of DL in the areas are Web Application Firewalls (WAF), Next-Generation Firewalls (NGFW), and User Entity and Behavior Analytics (UEBA). DL systems help to detect more advanced threats without relying on established signatures or attack patterns. Figure 10.2 shows the growth graph of DL in the IT industry. According to Figure 10.3, IBM demonstrates

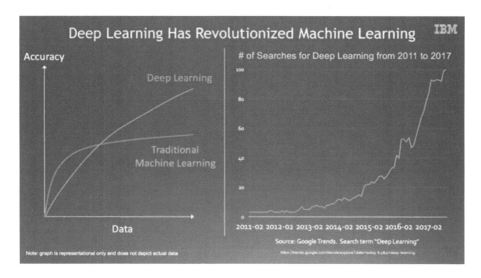

FIGURE 10.3 Growth of Deep Learning (Source : IBM)

that DL shows higher accuracy than ML from 2011 to 2017. This is because DL uses neural networks to achieve accuracy.

10.4 ML METHODS

ML algorithms are used to detect and respond to cyberattacks in apps before they have a chance to take hold. This is usually accomplished through the use of a model established by large data sets analysis of security events and the identification of malicious behavior patterns. As a result, when comparable behaviors are discovered, they are dealt with automatically. Due to the usefulness of ML in cybersecurity challenges, ML for cybersecurity has lately become a hot topic [4]. Intrusion detection, malware categorization, spam identification, and phishing detection are just a few of the key concerns in cybersecurity that have been tackled with ML techniques. Although ML cannot completely automate a cybersecurity system, it can assist to discover cybersecurity threats faster than other software-oriented approaches, easing the strain on security analysts. Effective adaptive approaches, such as ML techniques, can lead to higher detection rates, lower false alarm rates, and cheaper computing and communication costs are obtained as a result. Four categories of ML methods are namely, (i) Supervised Learning, (ii) Unsupervised Learning, (iii) Semi-Supervised Learning, and (iv) Reinforcement Learning.

10.4.1 SUPERVISED LEARNING

Supervised learning is an ML task that transforms an input into an output based on an example input / output pair [22] by using a learning function. It uses training data with labels and a set of training examples to derive the function.

Supervised learning is used when it is determined from a particular input set that a particular goal that needs to be achieved [23] is a task-driven method. Classification means separation of data based on some property and "regression" means fitting of data according to a special category. These are the most typical supervised tasks. Figure 10.4 depicts an example of supervised learning. In this, images that are classified as an apple are said to be a known data. The known data serves as input into the computing device that evaluates, identifies the correlation in images according to their shape, size, sharpness, and other characteristics. As soon as a novel image is supplied in a system that is unlabeled, the computing device can now properly anticipate that it is an apple based on previous data.

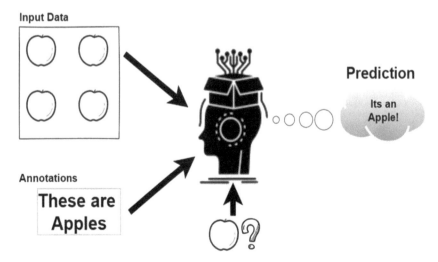

FIGURE 10.4 Example of Supervised Learning

There exist two categories of supervised learning namely, classification and regression. Whenever the output variable is categorical, involving two and above two classes, i.e., either no or yes, either female or male, either false or true, and so on is called classification. Example for classification is to separate spam messages from other messages. The first step involves tutoring the machine in order to forecast whether it is a spam mail or not. Various spam filters are used for this, which scan the e-mail body, header, and content for any deceptive information. All these factors are taken into consideration to rate the e-mail and a spam score is thoroughly assigned. The likelihood that an e-mail is a hoax decreases with the e-mail's overall spam score. The algorithm determines whether new incoming mail should go to the inbox or spam with regard to the content, label, and spam score. Supervisory ML task is classification. Spam detection is successfully applied in cybersecurity via ML-based classifiers, which entail classifying a particular e-mail message as spam or not. Spam filter models can distinguish between spam and non-spam messages.

When either the real or continuous output variable is used, then it is said to be regression. An example for this can be given as salary depending on job experience or weight on height. There is a relationship between two or more variables. In the preceding example, a change in one variable is related to a change in the other. Let's look at two different variables: humidity and temperature. Temperature is considered an independent variable, but humidity is considered a dependent variable. The humidity level decreases as the temperature rises. The machine learns the interdependence between the above two variables when fed into the model. Following training, the system can predict humidity with accuracy given the temperature.

Algorithms of ML are used to train and detect if a cyber assault has occurred. An e-mail message can be issued to security engineers or users as soon as the threat is discovered. Any classification algorithm [21] can be used to determine whether or not the attack is a DoS/DDoS attack. Support Vector Machine (SVM), called a supervised learning approach that implements the data analysis and recognizes patterns, is an example of a classification algorithm.

10.4.2 Unsupervised Learning

Unsupervised learning is called data-driven learning which helps to analyze unlabeled datasets without the help of humans [22] and it is generally used to extract generative features, discover relevant patterns and structures, result groupings, and experimental reasons. Otherwise, unsupervised learning is nothing but making machines to learn from unlabeled data without any supervision.

Previous examples can be referred to, except that this time we don't inform the machine whether the object is a different type of fruit which is shown in Figure 10.5. The algorithm recognizes data patterns and categorizes them according to their patterns, similarities, and other factors. In unlabeled datasets [24], an unsupervised approach is also used to discover an anomaly in smart grids.

There are two major categories in unsupervised learning. They are (1) Clustering and (2) Association.

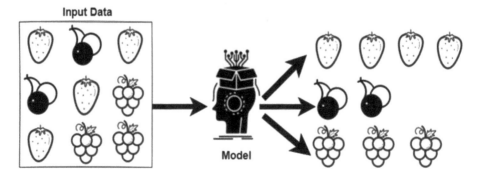

FIGURE 10.5   Example of Unsupervised Learning

The process of grouping things into clusters that are comparable to one another but not to the objects in another cluster is said to be clustering. Finding out which customers bought identical products is the example for clustering.

Another ML and data mining technique is association learning that is used to discover meaningful relationships between variables or features in a data set by implementing rules. Intrusion recognition [25] can be defined as the pattern identification process based on program implementation and behaviors of customers in the form of association rules. Unlike traditional association algorithms that use degrees of similarity to find hidden relationships in databases, association rule learning uses a measure of interest to produce an association rule for fresh searches. Also, association creates cybercrime dataset rules based on frequent occurrences of crime patterns. These generated regulations support the defense society's assessment producer in taking a deterrent action. The steps in the technique are as follows: Intrusion recognition is a way of detecting reccurring item sets in a cybercrime database by identifying patterns in program execution and customer behavior as association rules.

10.4.3 Semi-Supervised Learning

Semi-supervised learning (together with the methods created to solve it) is a learning problem in which a model must learn and predict on new examples from a limited number of labeled examples and a large number of unlabeled examples. As a result, it's a learning problem that falls between supervised and unsupervised learning. Semi-supervised learning is needed when labeling instances is difficult to handle or expensive.

10.4.4 Reinforcement Learning

The last important ML technique is reinforcement learning which focuses more on how software agents should behave in a given environment and it is a part of DL technique that allows you to optimize a fraction of your total reward. We can say that, RL is a division of ML that deals with how an agent should operate in a given environment in order to maximize some kind of cumulative reward. The agent is the entity that interacts with the environment and makes decisions at each time interval, and we will use the transmitter as an example. An agent must be able to detect some element of its surroundings and make actions that influence its state. Reinforcement learning, for example, can be used to teach a robot to walk without having to write the motion directly. We could, for example, teach an RL agent to do a penetration test or "hack" an API. This technology can be used by businesses to evaluate their applications for security both proactively and reactively (or at least as secure as the capabilities of the client). A secure RL system is a cornerstone for AI's security-critical applications, which has sparked greater worry than ever before. Recent studies have discovered that the intriguing attack mode adversarial assault is also successful when targeting neural network policies in the context of reinforcement learning, inspiring further study in this area.

10.5 DEEP LEARNING FOR CYBER AND OTHER CRIME DATA CLASSIFICATION AND ANALYSIS

Neural networks are a type of ML that show the applicability of neural networks for crime analytics. Models were constructed which indeed helps to predict specific types of crime by taking location and time information as an input, as well as to forecast a crime's location when given the crime and time of day. The neural network crime prediction models make use of geo-spatiality to deliver real-time crime information to help law enforcement make better decisions.

Two NN prediction fashions are created to reveal how NN fashions may be used to forecast and put together for police crime. In each fashions, the supervised mastering NN architectures are used. Opportunity schooling strategies include back propagation and radial foundation features.

All NN models are trained for at least 150,000 training epochs, with training preventing errors that are less than 0.05 or consistent over 1,000 training epochs. Because back propagation is the maximum widespread NN schooling method, it permits for extra correct cross-examine comparisons.

When simply the fundamental kind of crime (i.e., cluster) and time of day and week are known, the second one NN model's aim is to be expecting the area of a crime. This replicates the situation in which a crime reporter, whether victim or not, receives an emergency call and is unclear of their whereabouts.

10.5.1 Popular Deep Learning Architectures

DL is built on training neural networks with example data and rewarding them based on their performance, the more data available, the better. The structures and algorithms utilized in DL are numerous and diverse. There are six architectures based on DL that have been developed over the last 20 years. Long short-term memory called LSTM and Convolutional Neural Networks (CNNs) are two oldest systems, but they're also two of the most popular. Nowadays, VGGNet in CNN are also used for image recognition and prediction, along with that ResNet and YOLO is also used in Neural Networks. In this section, VGGNet, ResNet, and YOLO architectures of DL will be discussed.

10.5.2 Visual Geometry Group (VGGNet)

In the ImageNet Large Scale Visual Recognition Challenge (ILSVRC) in 2014, VGGNet was a neural network that did distinctly well. It works really excellent in photo localization and moderately well in photo classification. Finding the place of a certain object in a photo, as defined by way of a bounding box, is referred to as localization. The term "classification" refers to the approach of describing what the object within the photo is. The VGGNet architecture comprises 21 layers that are shown in Figure 10.6.

There are five distinct groups of layers in VGGNet. Three fully connected (or "fc") levels are found at the network's end. VGGNet is activated by placing an image in the first layer, conv1

1. This layer transforms the pixels of the image before sending it to the following layer, conv1
   2. The data transformation is carried out and the output is sent to pool1, and so on, until the image reaches the final layer, fc8. The softmax function is applied to the data in the last layer to generate a probability distribution.

For example, 1,000 different categories of images are used. A test image is given as an input to layer 1, the output will be a probability distribution for that image. A probability is calculated (a value

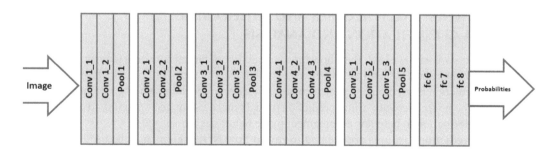

FIGURE 10.6 VGGNet Architecture

between 0 and 1) for these inputs, the highest probability category can be used as an output. This process is mentioned in Figure 10.7.

10.5.3 RESIDUAL NEURAL NETWORK (RESNET)

ResNet, short for Residual Network, is a form of neural network, while it allows us to add more layers to the CNNs to perform more difficult computer vision tasks, it comes with its own set of problems. It has been discovered that as the number of added layers increases, training neural networks gets more complex, and in some situations, accuracy decreases.

ResNets, which are made up of Residual Blocks, make it feasible to overcome the problems of training very deep neural networks. ResNet was created specifically to address this problem. In deep residual nets, model accuracy has been increased with the help of Residual blocks explained in Figure 10.8. The concept of "skip connections," is a very important concept in ResNet which is at the heart of the residual blocks. In two ways, these skip connections will work. For starters, they solve the problem of vanishing gradients by creating an alternate path for the gradient to follow and allow the model to learn an identity function. This ensures that the model's upper levels perform equally well as the lower layers. In short, residual blocks make learning identity functions much easier for the layers. As a result, ResNet [18] boosts the performance of deep neural networks by adding more neural layers while lowering the error rate. To put it another way, skip connections combine the outputs of prior layers with the outputs of stacked layers, allowing for far deeper network training than previously feasible.

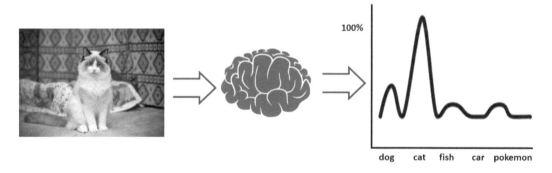

FIGURE 10.7 Process to find highest probability using VGGNet

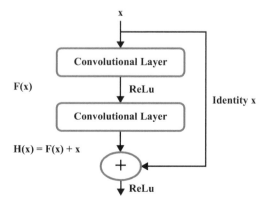

FIGURE 10.8 Architecture of Residual Net (ResNet)

In intrusion detection systems, a Residual Network (ResNet) is used to extract the temporal patterns in network traffic events. These patterns are then organized in order to find anomalies in IoE networks.

10.5.4 YOU ONLY LOOK ONCE (YOLO)

Real-time object identification technique called YOLO is explained in Figure 10.9 uses neural networks. This algorithm is very well-liked due to its speed and precision and it has been used to recognize traffic signals, pedestrians, parking meters, and animals in various applications.

Because every photograph and video collected for evidence from a particular crime scene gives a tangible documentation of the crime scene, the way of digital forensics can be quite tough and may comprise pretty specialized assessment of large contents within the route of a forensic investigation. Main software program of YOLO is an object-identification model based absolutely on the You Only Look Once (YOLO) Convolutional Neural Network (CNN) architecture [26] that has been created to apprehend topics at a crime scene without the need for human intervention. The goal is to find topics at a crime scene without the need for human intervention resulting in an advanced approach to criminal evidence computation.

10.5.5 DEEP LEARNING CAPABILITIES FOR COMBATING AND DETECTING CYBER AND OTHER CRIMES

Criminals are increasingly leveraging cyberspace to perform a variety of cybercrimes as technology improves. Intrusions and other cyber threats pose a serious threat to cyber infrastructures. Also, an alarmingly increasing rate of other physical crimes are threats to societal infrastructure. Physical equipment and human interaction are insufficient for monitoring and protecting these infrastructures, necessitating the development of more sophisticated crime analysis systems capable of detecting a varied range of attacks and making intelligent judgements in real time. Several AI techniques such as DL discussed in Sections 10.4 and 10.5 have become more essential in the identification and prevention of cyber and other crimes due to its various phenomenal capabilities in the area of object detection and classification, speech recognition, text analysis and cyber forensics among

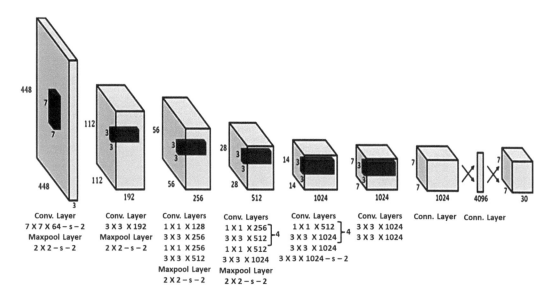

FIGURE 10.9 YOLO Architecture

others. This section discusses work of various researchers in this area motivating the usage of DL in preventing cyber and other crimes.

10.5.6 Object Classification and Detection

Face and object recognition are crucial for identifying criminal suspects and detecting crime weapons such as pistols, guns, and knives in order to complete a criminal investigation. Figure 10.10 gives an idea of object detection in case of criminal activity and it also shows how image and video processing methods along with ML techniques can help in tracking and analyzing criminal behavior from identifying and detecting faces and objects. Major Feature for Burglar Abnormality Detection is shown in Figure 10.11. Face identification and verification have been successfully implemented using CNN, a deep neural network architecture. Below is a summary of some of the related research in this field.

In their paper, Garg et al. claim that YOLO, a pre-trained DL architecture with CNN layers, can perform efficiently for face and object detection with high prediction accuracy. The experiment uses image data from the video stream as input, with each image measuring 448ζ448 pixels, and applies YOLO for face recognition. The experimental results show that YOLO, a CNN-based architecture, is capable of effectively detecting faces and objects in real-time with high precision [27].

A deep CNN-based automatic handgun detection system was presented by Olmos et al. (2017). By evaluating images recorded from surveillance recordings, the proposed system uses faster R-CNN on VGG16 architecture to classify an object as a pistol or not. The results reveal that even for low-quality films, faster R-CNN with a VGG16-based classification model produces a prediction accuracy of 84.21%. Systems with such accuracy can be further optimized to work better, and will undoubtedly aid crime investigators in making timely decisions regarding forecasting crime hotspots and crime kinds, increasing the likelihood of preventing criminal activity [28].

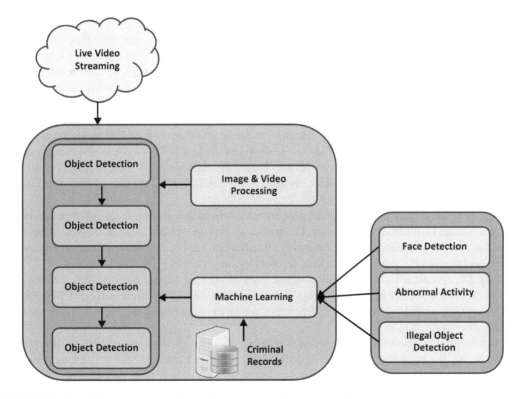

FIGURE 10.10 Video Processing Methods to detect the Burglar Activities

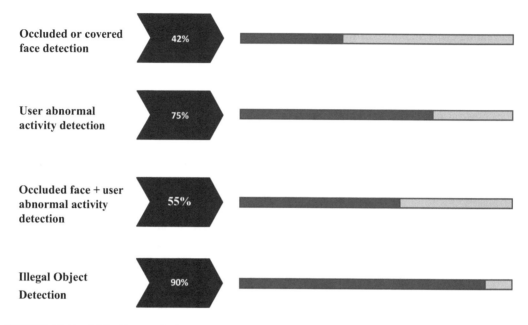

FIGURE 10.11   Major Feature for Burglar Abnormality Detection

Saika et al. (2017) have presented and tested a pre-trained VGG16 architecture with a faster R-CNN-based model for detecting different objects in an indoor context. Experimentation shows that 74.33% accuracy was achieved by the proposed model for detecting objects in real time [29].

10.5.7   SPEECH RECOGNITION AND TEXT ANALYTICS

Speech and text are the most elegant ways of expressing one's feelings and thoughts. One of the grounds for committing hate crimes is giving a speech or writing text with the wrong aim, which can lead to enmity among people of different religions, races, and genders [3, 4]. As a result, a computer-assisted intelligent system that can forecast and recognize malicious speeches and remarks in real time can assist an investigation team or the police in preventing societal disturbance. Malicious and non-malicious speech can be classified using varied methods of ML and DL.

For classifying malicious speeches, Rahman et al. in 2020, developed DL-based architecture using Long Short-Term Memory (LSTM), a learning measure in RNN. The paper also compares the suggested system's performance to that of other classic ML methods as SVM, KNN, Decision Tree, and logistic regression. The experimental results show that DL-based models outperform classic ML algorithms in terms of accuracy [30].

Zang et al. have also proposed a deep neural network-based system to detect speeches with malicious content collected from Twitter. The model was composed of Convolution Neural Net and Gated Recurrent Unit (GRU) for implementing classification of speech data. GRU was applied with an aim to eliminate the vanishing gradient problem in the network [31].

Many DL techniques can be applied in the area of speaker recognition as well. Jahangir et al. performed a comprehensive study on diverse work employing DL architectures DNN, CNN, AlexNet, VGGNet, RNN, ResNet, and Encoders that offer a promising way to construct speaker identification systems [32].

Cyberbullying is one of the serious concerns when it comes to workplace. It may cause severe mental health issues to the victims. Kompally et al. presented that ML and DL approaches are utilized in existing automated cyberbullying detection tools. They have proved that DL-based algorithms yield greater text-based classification accuracy than previous methods. For detecting offensive textual content, MaLang, a revolutionary decentralized DL technique has been created. The proposed model examines the user message data and categorizes it as abusive or non-abusive and using DL bidirectional LSTM and GRU, predicts the likelihood of message having various types of hazardous text material, for example, "Toxic," "Insult," "Threat," or "Hate." MaLang exceeds other contemporary cyberbullying detection algorithms with a classification accuracy of 98.2% [12].

10.5.8 CYBER FORENSICS

As is mentioned in Section 2.1, cybercrimes are increasing at alarming rates and will continue as technology advances and so there is a need to keep a strong check on these crimes and the process of investigation of cybercrimes have to be fastened and smoothened by applying DL algorithms which is a subset of AI.

Karie et al. have provided a generic prototype of a framework that demonstrates the value of bringing DL techniques and algorithms to the field of Cyber Forensics (CF) and have proposed a framework named Deep Learning Cyber-Forensic Framework (DLCF). It analyzes the evidential data collected called Potential Digital Evidence (PDE) using ML classification and clustering methods. The framework greatly aids cyber forensic crime investigators' decision-making and could be useful for implementing CF processes using various DL approaches [8].

Harikrishnan et al. in their work have introduced a prototype model to uncover and detect cybercrimes utilizing ML methods and DL architectures. On the Knowledge Discovery and Dissemination 1999 (KDD-Cup-99) dataset, the paper also examines performance of trained, unsupervised algorithms for intrusion detection and phishing. Suggested model tunes the architecture using supervised DNN and the ADAM optimizer, and the experimental results demonstrate that DNN-based classification outperforms various classic ML classifiers mainly Naïve Bayes, KNN, Decision Tree, Random Forest, AdaBoost, and SVM [14].

10.6 DATA SOURCES FOR CRIME DATASETS

In general, criminal statistics and crime data evidence for various crimes can be gathered from a variety of sources, including all digital gadgets like smartphones, mobile, tablets, laptops, desktops, etc., accessing social networking sites such as Twitter, Facebook, and others, data from electronic surveillance systems such as CCTV footage, Camera, Sensors Data, Crime Record and DNA evidence maintained by crime investigation agencies or police departments as official records, online transaction data, YouTube videos on internet, accessing many open-source data repositories available freely online, different cities of the world also maintain open public offense data set [2, 7]. In the section below, we've listed some of the most popular open datasets. Researchers must make sure to give due credit to all the sources from where they have collected the data in their work.

Kaggle is a massive online open-source collection of data and code that has been shared by the community. Users can also publish data, assist in the development of data science initiatives, and compete in numerous competitions. It also contains datasets containing samples of hate speech and offensive language [12, 33].

The most often used publicly available databases for detecting intrusions include the KDD-Cup'99 datasets, NSL-KDD, CICIDS2017, and UNSW-NB15. The KDD-Cup'99 dataset contains more than four million training network traffic data and was developed for the KDD-Cup'99 challenge. There are 41 features in the dataset, which are divided into three categories: basic, traffic, and content type features. The data are also divided into 22 different forms of cyberattacks, which are grouped into four categories: DoS, Remote to Local (R2L), User to Root (U2R), and Probing. This dataset has been used by several academics to train and test data on ML-based systems for predictive analysis. Another dataset NSL-KDD was also proposed due to limitations of KDD-99 that promotes no redundancy and duplicity in training and test datasets. The CICIDS2017 dataset is also quite useful because it contains statistics on recent frequent attacks [14, 15, 19, 34].

As previously stated in this section, researchers can also use crime datasets maintained by various cities around the world. For example, Walczak (2021) used a crime dataset publicly available from RMS Crime Incident for the city of Detroit, Michigan, to analyze crime statistics using neural networks [18]. In addition, Kim et al. used a publicly available crime dataset for the city of Vancouver, which primarily provides information on crime type, time, and place of occurrence. The crime dataset was studied using multiple ML algorithms to see how accurate each method was at predicting crime [1].

Many more open-source datasets can be used to recognize and detect faces and objects. The Face Detection Data Set and Benchmark (FDDB) is a freely available dataset that can be used for face and object recognition and detection. Within a set of 2,845 photos, this dataset contains 5,171 face areas with annotations. The images or photos are from the Faces in the Wild dataset [35].

Face recognition datasets such as Imagenet, MS-COCO, and the Karina dataset are also popular and freely available. Imagenet dataset provides researchers with an extremely large collection of images, with around 14,197,122 images and 21,841 synsets, for object detection. Microsoft Corporation's MS-COCO collection is also a large repository that contains around 330 K photos divided into 80 object types [36–38].

10.7 CRIME DATA ANALYSIS METHODOLOGY

This section presents a generic methodology based on a comprehensive review of several proposed efforts in this area. The steps proposed in the methodology can be suitably applied for modeling any crime analysis system. Ding has proposed an AI-based investigation model which employs data mining algorithms for criminal case investigation analysis assisting police for intelligent and efficient decision-making in criminal cases. To improve decision-making, the suggested approach contains three primary phases: Evidence Integration, Evidence Cleaning, and Evidence Extraction [39]. Proposed Crime Analysis Model is shown in Figure 10.12.

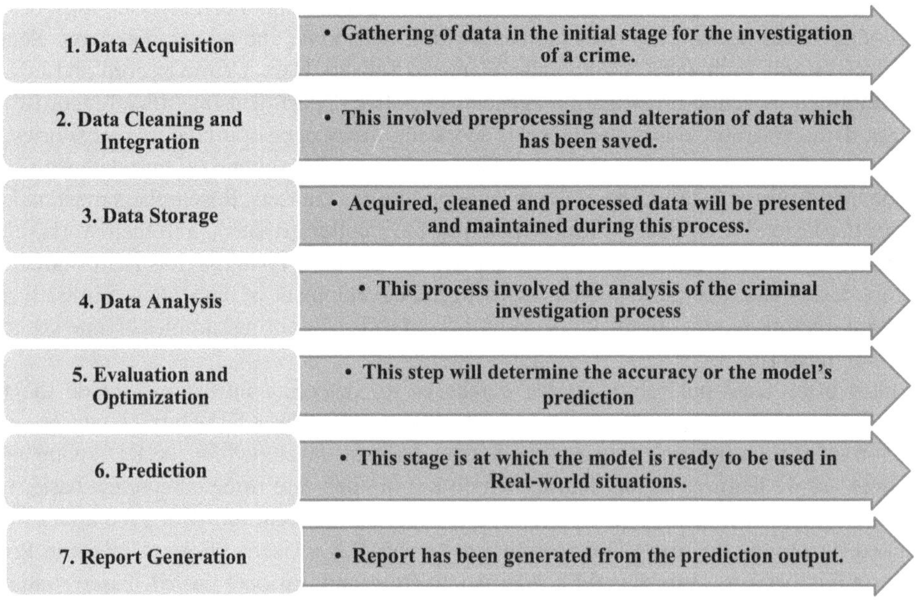

FIGURE 10.12 Proposed Crime Analysis Model

The following major phases can be formulated to develop a DL-based crime analysis model for crime investigation, which have been diagrammatically illustrated in Figure 10.11 based on work by Ding (2021) and Karie et al. (2019) [8, 39]. The proposed model presents Data Acquisition, Data Cleaning and Integration, Data Analysis, and Prediction as some of the major phases for crime data analytics to enhance decision-making, where employing ensemble learning methods is proposed in the prediction step.

STEP 1. DATA ACQUISITION

The gathering of data is the initial step in the investigation of a crime. Depending on the sort of crime committed, evidential elements of crime are acquired as input to the system from a variety of sources. Images, audio, video, and text (statements, conversations, and messages, for example) can be acquired from a range of sources, including social networking sites, digital devices, mobile phones, official records in databases, biological material, and others.

STEP 2. DATA CLEANING AND INTEGRATION

The second phase involves pre-processing and alteration of the data that have been saved. Pre-processing data that focuses on maintaining only relevant data properties while removing unneeded, redundant, and missing valued attributes is referred to as data cleaning. Dimensionality reduction techniques and data normalization can be applied at this stage. After the data have been cleaned, it now only contains useful and non-redundant data parts for the evidence collected. The data are combined and transformed in the integration step so that it may be processed by the system.

STEP 3. DATA STORAGE

The acquired, cleaned, and processed data will be preserved and maintained during this phase. The data can be stored in relational databases or, if the data are large and heterogeneous, as in Big Data, it can be stored in the Hadoop Distribution File System (HDFS).

STEP 4. DATA ANALYSIS

One of the most crucial aspects of designing a model is the analysis of evidence data. As a result, crime analysis is crucial in the criminal investigative process. The task of training, testing, validating, and optimizing the proposed model is mostly covered in this phase. All these tasks defined are an integral part of any analysis system, and they are iterated repeatedly to optimize output to a predetermined threshold or to function with expected accuracy.

The purpose of this step is to choose an acceptable DL architecture and learning algorithm for the proposed system's training such as CNN, DNN, R-CNN, and Faster-CNN, as well as from pre-trained neural architectures like as ResNet, YOLO, and VGGNet. For training and testing the system, various ML classification and clustering methods such as k-NN, SVM, Naïve Bayes, Decision Trees, Ensemble Learning, K-means clustering, and hierarchical clustering are used, each with its unique set of characteristics. The type of input to be processed by the system determines the neural architecture and training technique to be used. For example, CNN-based models are excellent for image and object recognition, RNN for voice recognition, and k-NN for creating recommendation systems. The entire collected dataset can be divided into three subsets for training, testing, and validation of the suggested system.

A training dataset is a collection of values that fits the suggested model. Validation dataset is a subset of the training dataset that is used to perform an unbiased assessment of a model's fit on the training dataset while tuning hyper-parameters, whereas the test dataset is a subset of the training dataset that performs an impartial assessment of the finalized model fit. A common example is modifying the suggested model's hyperparameters by applying k-fold cross-validation rather than a separate validation dataset.

In this work, we propose to employ the Ensemble Learning approach rather than classical ML classification algorithms to improve the model's performance as far as classification and prediction are concerned during crime analysis.

STEP 5. EVALUATION AND OPTIMIZATION

This step involves evaluation and optimization of the suggested model. The term "evaluation" refers to the process of determining the accuracy of a model's prediction and assisting in the selection of one model over another based on that accuracy. A utility function or loss function is another name for it. Model evaluation can be done using several evaluation functions such as Mean Square Error (MSE), Root Mean Square Error (RMSE), likelihood to assess expected probability of model on given observed data, and confusion matrix. A variety of optimization strategies can be used to fine-tune the model in order to generate or improve system performance or prediction accuracy. One of the most prominent strategies for optimizing the model proposed is stochastic gradient descent.

STEP 6. PREDICTION

The final step in the data analysis process is prediction. This is the stage at which the model is ready to be used in real-world circumstances. In order to estimate the possibility of occurrence of a specific event, "prediction" refers to an algorithm's or a model's output when we have trained it on "Prediction" and refers to the output of an algorithm after it has been trained on a past dataset and applied onto current and distinct data. As a result, an inference or output from the proposed system is generated at this stage.

STEP 7. REPORT GENERATION

Finally, a report can be generated from the inference or prediction output. In a single report, the report generating tool allows you to combine inferences generated by the system with manual recommendations from specialists. The report also includes specific information regarding criminal evidential data such as crime type, source, date, time, and location of occurrence, as well as any other relevant information that the investigating team can utilize in the future if a similar crime occurs.

10.8   EXPERIMENTATION AND PERFORMANCE ANALYSIS

In this section, in order to analyze the performance of ensemble learning techniques and compare their performance with some classical ML classification techniques as Naïve Bayes and Decision Tree, we have conducted an experiment for detecting DDoS Attacks, a category under cybercrime. Ensemble learning is regarded as a meta technique of ML that combines the predictions of numerous algorithms to improve predictive performance. Bagging, stacking, and boosting are common types of ensemble learning techniques. Bagged Decision Trees and Random Forest come under bagging techniques and AdaBoost for boosting.

The dataset for experimentation was derived from NSL-KDD (an open-source data repository) for predicting DDoS attacks, which has more than 20,000 instances with approximately 42 attributes. Some of the major attributes are protocol_type, service, src_bytes, dst_bytes, root_shell, serror_rate and dst_host_serror_rate among others.

Predictive performance of ensemble learning techniques Bagging on Decision Tree, Random Forest, AdaBoost along with classical Naïve Bayes and J48 Decision Tree model was determined and comparative analysis done. The whole experimentation was conducted using Weka 3.8.2, a

TABLE 10.1

Comparative Performance Analysis of different Machine Learning Methods

Machine Learning Methods	Attack Instances Correctly Classified	Attack Instances Incorrectly Classified	Prediction Accuracy of Correctly Classified Attack Instances	Prediction Accuracy of Incorrectly Classified Attack Instances
Bagged Decision Tree	22238	306	98.64 %	1.36 %
Random Forest	22252	292	98.70 %	1.30 %
Adaboost	22233	311	98.62 %	1.38 %
Naïve Bayes	18201	4343	80.74 %	19.26 %
J48	22228	316	98.60 %	1.40 %

popular ML tool and 10 cross-fold validation was used to train the system for each of the above-mentioned techniques. Result of the experimentation has been summarized in Table 10.1. The table stores values of DDoS attack instances which are correctly predicted, incorrectly predicted with their respective prediction accuracy, for ML techniques in order to perform a comparative analysis of their performance. In all, prediction accuracy of five ML algorithms has been analyzed: Bagging Decision Tree, Random Forest, AdaBoost, Naïve Bayes and J48, obtained after experimentation. Random Forest method has achieved the highest prediction accuracy of 98.7%, Bagging Decision Tree has achieved 98.64%, AdaBoost is the next method with 98.62%, J48 has achieved 98.6% in the order and the least prediction accuracy of 80.74% was achieved with Naïve Bayes method. Table 10.1 thus, clearly demonstrates that ensemble learning methods Random Forest, Bagging Decision Tree, and AdaBoost have achieved better prediction accuracy as compared to Naïve Bayes. In addition to this, it is also clearly visible that the J48 Decision Tree method has also performed well on this dataset.

10.9 PREVENTIVE MEASURES FOR CYBER AND ILLEGAL INTIMIDATION

The general public, businesses, financial institutions, and information technology firms are all common targets of cybercrime and so there is a need to create awareness measures for preventing and detecting these crimes. Cybercrime prevention emphasizes establishing multifaceted public– private alliances with government security organizations, non-governmental organizations, internet firms, and financial institutions to effectively combat cybercrime. This section elaborates on some preventive measures that internet users must take care of to keep their data safe from cyber criminals [9, 40]. Figure 10.13 shows the Preventive Measures for Cyber and Illegal Intimidation.

- **Building Strong Passwords**: For each account, use a separate password and username combination, and resist the urge to write them down. Use different passwords/usernames for different accounts.
- **Vigilant to social platforms**: Set your social media profiles as private on Instagram, Facebook, YouTube, Twitter, and others. When using/accessing social networking sites, you should enable your privacy settings and also, keep on updating the security settings.
- **Deploying Firewalls**: The use of a robust server firewall and an application-level firewall can help prevent DoS attacks.
- **Refraining Usage of Public Wi-Fi:** Wi-Fi in public places should be avoided at all costs. Verify safe data transmission standards with the provider's authorities. In case you are using public Wi-Fi of trusted internet in emergency, disconnect as soon as possible and reset the passwords of any accounts you've accessed via public Wi-Fi.

FIGURE 10.13   Preventive Measures for Cyber and Illegal Intimidation

- **User Awareness of Mobile and Website Usage**: Users should also be aware that computer viruses can infect their mobile devices as well. So, make sure applications should be downloaded from reputable websites. Maintaining the latest version of your operating system is also critical in this regard.
- **Preventing Phishing**: To avoid being a victim of a phishing scam, you must first recognize the phishing page or e-mail. Thoroughly verify the e-mail's sender, subject, and attachment, among other things. Opening email attachments from unknown senders is not recommended. Spam filtering features can be used to filter spam e-mails. Almost all major e-mail clients offer this service. Keep an eye out for trusted SSL certificate of any web page you visit. Other measures to defend yourself from phishing attacks include using anti-malware software, fire barrier walls, and anti-phishing tools menu, and only visiting guarded websites with the "https" prefix in the URL.
- **Antivirus Software**: Install the most up-to-date antivirus software on your smartphone, laptop, and other internet-connected devices. Also, make sure the Internet Security options are turned on. Using a secure lock screen on your smartphone is another good option to secure your personal sensitive information from unwanted individuals.
- **Safeguard Important Information**: Encrypt your most sensitive files, such as personal and financial documents to protect your data from unauthorized access.
- **Preventing Spoofing**: To avoid spoofing encourage the usage of Transport Layer Security (TLS), HTTPS, and Secure Shell (SSH). Also, make use of a more effective packet filtering process or instrument for prevention against spoofing.
- **Protecting an Individual's Online Identity**: Be cautious when providing any personal information over the Internet. During online shopping make certain that the website is secure.

- **Safeguard against Credit Card Fraud**: Users should not respond to fake callers and inform about their bank account and credit card details balance. Change your Internet banking passwords and personal identification of credit and debit cards on a regular basis. Download and use the authorized bank's mobile app. Also, don't swipe your card in places you don't know.

10.10 CONCLUSION

To combat the increasing rate of crime and identify offenders, new technology and tools are deployed. This chapter's comprehensive review addressed a variety of cybercrimes. The chapter surveys the DL methods and architectures which are promising modern AI techniques in the field of cyber and other crime analysis. Academic materials reveal that AI approaches as DL are already being used to prevent cybercrime in a variety of ways. The literature study conducted shows that the DL networks such as DNN, CNN, RNN, Adversarial Networks along with various pre-trained neural network architectures with layers of CNN as YOLO, ResNet, VGGNet can be applied to develop a crime analysis system that has the characteristic feature of being an efficient predictive tool for crime analysis and investigation. The work also explains fundamental steps to develop a deep learning-based decision support model for crime analysis. Police and other crime investigation agencies can benefit from such emerging technologies to combat cybercrimes. The study demonstrates that DL-based architectures may be efficiently utilized to aid in the detection of cybercrime. With cameras, video, and social media creating vast amounts of data, AI could discover crimes that would otherwise go unnoticed and assist in the greater public safety by probing probable criminal activity, boosting public trust in law enforcement and the criminal justice system. The accessible crime datasets were also extensively discussed in this study which have already been utilized in the research. This work has summarized recent progress in the realm of combating cybercrime with DL architectures. The experiment conducted shows that the meta learning approach in ensemble learning if used can significantly improve the model's prediction ability and the prediction accuracy is higher with respect to classical ML methods. The work also suggests various preventive measures users should be aware of to safeguard them against various cybercrime.

REFERENCES

1. Kim, S., Joshi, P., Kalsi, P. S., & Taheri, P. (2018, November). Crime analysis through machine learning. In *2018 IEEE 9th Annual Information Technology, Electronics and Mobile Communication Conference (IEMCON)* (pp. 415–420). IEEE.
2. Tyagi, D., & Sharma, S. (2018). An approach to crime data analysis: A systematic review. *International Journal of Engineering Technologies and Management Research*, 5(2), 67–74. https://doi.org/10.29121/ijetmr.v5.i2.2018.615.
3. https://www.statista.com/topics/780/crime/#dossierKeyfigures accessed 17/01/2021, Published by Statista Research Department, Jun 24, 2021.
4. Crossman, A. (2021). 7 Different types of crimes. *ThoughtCo*, Aug. 5. https://www.thoughtco.com/types-of-crimes-3026270 accessed 17/01/2021.
5. https://purplesec.us/resources/cyber-security-statistics/ accessed 17/01/2021.
6. https://www.packetlabs.net/cybersecurity-statistics-2021/ accessed17/01/2021
7. Olmos, R., Tabik, S., & Herrera, F. (2018). Automatic handgun detection alarm in videos using deep learning. *Neurocomputing*, 275, 66–72.
8. Karie, N. M., Kebande, V. R., & Venter, H. S. (2019). Diverging deep learning cognitive computing techniques into cyber forensics. *Forensic Science International: Synergy*, 1, 61–67.
9. Al-Khater, W. A., Al-Maadeed, S., Ahmed, A. A., Sadiq, A. S., & Khan, M. K. (2020). Comprehensive review of cybercrime detection techniques. *IEEE Access*, 8, 137293–137311.
10. https://www.embroker.com/blog/cyber-attack-statistics/ accessed 17/01/2021.
11. Ali, M. M. (2016). Determinants of preventing cyber crime: A survey research. *International Journal of Management Science and Business Administration*, 2(7), 16–24.

12. Kompally, P., Sethuraman, S. C., Walczak, S., Johnson, S., & Cruz, M. V. (2021). MaLang: A decentralized deep learning approach for detecting abusive textual content. *Applied Sciences, 11*(18), 8701.

13. Li, X. (2017). A review of motivations of illegal cyber activities. *Kriminologija & Socijalnaintegracija: Časopis za Kriminologiju, Penologijuiporemećaje u Ponašanju, 25*(1), 110–126.

14. Harikrishnan, N. B., Vinayakumar, R., Soman, K. P., Poornachandran, P., Annappa, B., & Alazab, M. (2019). Deep learning architecture for big data analytics in detecting intrusions and malicious URL. *Big Data Recommender Systems: Algorithms, Architectures, Big Data, Security and Trust, 303.*

15. Berman, D. S., Buczak, A. L., Chavis, J. S., & Corbett, C. L. (2019). A survey of deep learning methods for cyber security. *Information, 10*(4), 122.

16. Choi, Y. H., Liu, P., Shang, Z., Wang, H., Wang, Z., Zhang, L., & Zou, Q. (2020). Using deep learning to solve computer security challenges: A survey. *Cybersecurity, 3*(1), 1–32.

17. Ravi, V., Alazab, M., Soman, K. P., Srinivasan, S., Venkatraman, S., Pham, Q. V., & Simran, K. (2021). Deep learning for cyber security applications: a comprehensive survey, 10.36227/techrxiv.16748161.

18. Walczak, S. (2021). Predicting crime and other uses of neural networks in police decision making. *Frontiers in Psychology, 12.* https://doi.org/10.3389/fpsyg.2021.587943.

19. Oatley, G., Ewart, B., & Zeleznikow, J. (2006). Decision support systems for police: Lessons from the application of data mining techniques to "soft" forensic evidence. *Artificial Intelligence and Law, 14*(1–2), 35–100.

20. Stalidis, P., Semertzidis, T., & Daras, P. (2021). Examining deep learning architectures for crime classification and prediction. *Forecasting, 3*(4), 741–762.

21. Ramesh, B., Kumar, J. V., Vyshnavi, V., & Prem, M. Artificial intelligence framework for cyber attack detection and notifying using machine learning techniques, https://doi.org/10.3390/electronics11020198

22. Han, J., Pei, J., & Kamber, M. (2011) *Data Mining: Concepts and Techniques.* Elsevier.

23. Sarker, I. H., Kayes, A. S. M., Badsha, S., Alqahtani, H., Watters, P., & Ng, A. (2020). Cybersecurity data science: An overview from machine learning perspective. *Journal of Big Data, 7*(1), 1–29.

24. Karimipour, H., Dehghantanha, A., Parizi, R. M., Choo, K. R., & Leung, H. (2019). A deep and scalable unsupervised machine learning system for cyber-attack detection in large-scale smart grids. In *IEEE Access, 7*, 80778–80788. https://doi.org/10.1109/ACCESS.2019.2920326.

25. Lekha, K. C., &Prakasam, S. (2017, August). Data mining techniques in detecting and predicting cyber crimes in banking sector. In *2017 International Conference on Energy, Communication, Data Analytics and Soft Computing (ICECDS)* (pp. 1639–1643). IEEE.

26. Oladipo, F., Ogbuju, E., Alayesanmi, F. S., & Musa, A. E. (2020). The state of the art in machine learning-based digital forensics. Available at SSRN 3668687.

27. Garg, D., Goel, P., Pandya, S., Ganatra, A., & Kotecha, K. (2018, November). A deep learning approach for face detection using YOLO. In *2018 IEEE Punecon* (pp. 1–4). IEEE.

28. Olmos, R., Tabik, S., & Herrera, F. (2018). Automatic handgun detection alarm in videos using deep learning. *Neurocomputing, 275*, 66–72.

29. Saikia, S., Fidalgo, E., Alegre, E., & Fernández-Robles, L. (2017, September). Object detection for crime scene evidence analysis using deep learning. In *International Conference on Image Analysis and Processing* (pp. 14–24). Springer.

30. Rahman, M., Arefin, M. S., Hossain, M., Habib, M. A., & Kayes, A. S. M. (2020). Towards a framework for acquisition and analysis of speeches to identify suspicious contents through machine learning. *Complexity,* pp. 1-14, *2020.*

31. Zhang, Z., Robinson, D., & Tepper, J. (2018). Detecting hate speech on Twitter using a convolution-GRU based deep neural network. In *Proceedings Od the 8e Semantic Web. ESWC 2018* (pp. 745–760).

32. Jahangir, R., Teh, Y. W., Nweke, H. F., Mujtaba, G., Al-Garadi, M. A., & Ali, I. (2021). Speaker identification through artificial intelligence techniques: A comprehensive review and research challenges. *Expert Systems with Applications, 171*, 114591.

33. https://www.kaggle.com accessed 18/01/2021.

34. Al-Haija, Q. A. Top-down machine learning-based architecture for cyberattacks identification and classification in IoT communication networks, .2021

35. Jain, V., & Learned-Miller, E. (2010). *Fddb: A Benchmark for Face Detection in Unconstrained Settings* (Vol. 2, No. 4, p. 5). UMass Amherst technical report.

36. Saikia, S., Fidalgo, E., Alegre, E., & Fernández-Robles, L. (2017). Object detection for crime scene evidence analysis using deep learning. In Battiato, S., Gallo, G., Schettini, R., Stanco, F.(eds.), *Image Analysis and Processing - ICIAP 2017. ICIAP 2017. Lecture Notes in Computer Science 10485.* Springer. https://doi.org/10.1007/978-3-319-68548-9_2.

37. https://www.image-net.org/ accessed 18/01/2021 https://cocodataset.org/ accessed 18/01/2021.

38. Ding, J. (2021). Case investigation technology based on artificial intelligence data processing. *Journal of Sensors*, *2021*, pp. 1-9.

39. Biswal, C. S., & Pani, S. K. (2021). Cyber-crime prevention methodology. *Intelligent Data Analytics for Terror Threat Prediction: Architectures, Methodologies, Techniques and Applications*, pp. 291–312.

40. Lee, J., Lee, Y., Lee, D., Kwon, H., & Shin, D. (2021). Classification of attack types and analysis of attack methods for profiling phishing mail attack groups. *IEEE Access*, *9*, 80866–80872.

11 Computer-based Intelligence and Security

Sushma Tanwar, S. Vijayalakshmi, P. Durgadevi, and R. Girija

11.1 INTRODUCTION

Computers are an important part of our lives today. The use of computers is increasing day by day and so is the information saved in it. With this increase in information being stored there is a need to provide security to the information in terms of availability, integrity, and confidentiality. The information may be stored in a single machine or a system of machines. Most of the systems that implement security are implementing rule-based security. This means that the software has a set of rules that are to be implemented in case of any violation from security. These rules are prewritten either by the creators or the vendors of the computers. These rules are being updated from time to time with the help of security update procedures.

Different security systems have different possibilities of addition to the rules; some security systems may allow while some may not. When a security check is performed, if the computer does not have a rule defined for a particular attack then the system needs to be shut down or it has to restart in safe mode. Then the administrator finds a rule to handle the attack from either the attacked software creator or the system's vendor and adds the rule to the security update to repair the system. In case no update is found then the administrator has to manually remove the problem, which takes the time of the administrator in investing resources required for handling the problem. Such a situation may reduce productivity of the organization or the user.

The number of incidences of security attack is increasing at much higher rates today. A single attack has the capacity to get mutated and may get equipped in stealth mode. This situation may complicate the system as most of the systems that have prewritten security rules find it difficult to adapt to new attacks. In order to solve this problem some question needs to be answered like

1) Is there any possibility of creating a security system that can learn by its own and does not wait for any new security update?
2) Is there any possibility of creating a security system that is capable of repairing itself after a security attack?
3) Is there any possibility of creating a security system that has the capability to learn from attack experience and develop defense security updates?

This chapter provides some computer system security that is based on Artificial Intelligence (AI) which may help administrators in saving their time searching for repairing computer security problems. This may also help in implementing the security updates and repairs. These systems are capable of providing increased adaptability and availability.

11.1.1 Artificial Intelligence

A number of researchers have given various definitions of AI. Some of the definitions are as given below:

DOI: 10.1201/9781003251781-11

- AI is the study of ideas that help computers to become intelligent [1].
- AI is the study of how to make the computer do things which human beings can do in a better way [2].
- AI is the branch of computer science which provides the machine's reasoning and perceptual abilities [3].
- AI is the branch of computer science which helps in making computer systems intelligent. Intelligent computer means they can exhibit the characteristics like learning, understanding, problem solving, reasoning etc. [4].

The objective of research in AI is to get new ideas to endow the computer with behavior like human intelligence. This will lead to an increase in the usefulness of computers and will also help in better understanding of the human cognitive system, human intelligence and the mechanisms that are needed to produce intelligence [5]. The field of AI is historically related to psychology and philosophy. Initially it was made to understand and imitate human intelligence but now it is extended to understanding human beings at the biological level. This field is composed of the following subfields: logic, knowledge reasoning, reinforcement learning, neural network, pattern recognition, artificial immune system, genetic algorithm, classifiers, probabilistic reasoning, robotics, etc. [6].

11.1.2 COMPUTER SECURITY

Computer security can be defined as the protection endowed to a computer system in order to preserve integrity, confidentiality, and availability of the computer system [7] as shown in Figure 11.1. The given description of security can be further supported with the following definitions:

1) **Confidentiality:** It means to protect the information present in the computer system from unauthorized access [8]. Confidentiality is analogous to secrecy. There are many methods to implement confidentiality, one of them is encryption.
2) **Integrity:** It is the term used to allow only authorized users to access the desired information [8]. This can be implemented by granting identification to users and checking the identification of the user authorization at the time of granting access to information. The examples include asking for read and write permissions while trying to open operating system files.
3) **Availability**: It is the availability of service to the authorized users whenever the user wants [7]. This definition of availability is also known as CIA-Triad. Some malicious users

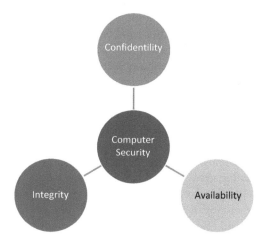

FIGURE 11.1   Components of computer security 1.3 Computer security types.

or hackers have created their DAD-Triad which means Disclosure, Alteration, and Denial [9]. Here, disclosure means when any unauthorized user is able to access confidential data. This compromises the confidentiality of information. Alteration compromises integrity of information, it means when any unauthorized person is able to make changes in the data or information. Denial compromises with the availability of information. In this the authorized person is denied access to the computer system.

Computer security can be divided into various categories or forms namely, network, application, and host security [10]. Network security is defined as protecting computer network from malicious users or attackers. There are different types of network attacks like DoS, spoofing, intrusion detection, etc. Security of network is dealing with all such attacks. Network security is also concerned with protecting the transmission of data, so it is also called communication security [11]. Some tools are available to protect the network like TippingPoint [12], Snort [13], and Wireshark [14]. Application security means preserving the functionalities of any application. It includes keeping a check on the application for vulnerabilities on performing abnormal operations. It includes providing confidentiality, integrity, and availability to applications and data in a computer. The host security means protecting the host from attackers or malicious entities. It involves protecting each firmware and hardware. The tools used to protect the hosts involve anti-virus installed in personal computers or server computers. It also involves physical security [11].

All the hosts present in any network should preferably have host security. Also the applications present in any network should own application security. In most of the security systems there is a network administrator who monitors the tools used for the security mentioned above. The network administrator takes action when there is a security breach in the network. This security breach is dealt with the help of analytical tools. Some rule-based security tools are Tipping Point, Snort and their variations. As they are rule-based security tools they have security rules implemented in them. But if any new rule is to be added the network administrator has the right for the same. Other than the network administrator the manufacturer of the tool can also add rules by providing updates. The anti-virus and anti-malwares can also be provided with new rules via updates. Most of the security software has built-in security rules. The administrator or user may or may not be able to add security rules as it completely depends on the type of software. The security rules that are added in anti-virus are called virus definitions.

11.1.3 NEED FOR ARTIFICIAL INTELLIGENCE IN COMPUTER SECURITY

The combination of AI and computer security may sound weird to researchers, but this can be stated by the fact that AI researchers are interested in giving computers the ability to perform tasks that human beings can perform while on the other hand the security researchers are concerned with protecting the computer from malicious or unauthorized users [15]. From this statement it can be seen that these two fields namely, AI and computer security may be combined. The upgradation in technology has combined both AI and computer security. Computer systems have started gaining intelligence. The increase in technology has given the computer systems the ability of self-configuration and automation, and with this it is likely that soon the computer systems will be able to protect themselves with less human interference. Keeping computers secure is a difficult and broad area. In a network the difficulty is caused by building a network skeleton which initially was from communication among two systems. This later became local area network and subsequently has now reached the point of creating network on cloud. The administration of a computer network is a complex task by a human being. So, there is a need of an intelligent network that can automatically detect, tell the administrator and repair the problems in network.

AI and computer security can also be combined to endow computer systems with adaptability. Intelligence is also becoming a key feature of malicious users. The types of attacks have increased from cracking a password to attacking a complete network in stealth mode and mutation attack. So, there is a need for computer security software to adapt to these changes and the increase in security attacks. This can be done using AI. AI gives computer systems the ability by which they can act based on the changes in the environment. Reinforcement learning, which is a part of AI, helps computers to learn to deal with new security issues and adapt themselves to that environment. It can be concluded that AI can help computer systems to cope up with the increasing security attacks. In future AI may be used either as a system administrator or an assistant as the world is dwelling more into adaptive and adaptive systems.

11.2 DETECTION

Figure 11.2 shows the list of the intrusion-detection techniques.

11.2.1 NEURAL NETWORK

A team of researchers at IBM used a single-layer neural network for detection of boot sector virus [16]. They extracted trigrams which was a special feature from the viral boot sector which was 512 bytes long. The length of each trigram was about 3 bytes. Out of the detected trigrams, the ones that were present in the non-infected boot sector were not considered. Also, some of the trigrams were rejected based on the fact that only those trigrams that had a minimum of 4 features in the list would be considered. At last, 50 features were left to provide as input to the neural network. A vector was created to record the presence represented by 1 or absence represented by 0 of any of 50 features in a boot sector. A vector that had 50 features was given as input to the neural network, to assign weight to each element. The neural network gave two outputs for the given inputs. It gave positive, if the boot sector had infection and negative if the boot sector was not infected. In training, a data set consists of 100 viral boot sectors and 50 non-viral boot sectors. When testing was performed on the same data set, 80% to 85% of accuracy was achieved for the viral boot sector and 100% accuracy was obtained for the non-viral boot sector. This approach was implemented in IBM anti-virus and was able to detect 75% of new boot viruses. Due to the limitation in training data, this approach had a large number of false results. The ratio of false positive and false negative was improved by keeping the activation threshold at 0.7.

11.2.2 PROBABILISTIC APPROACH

This approach is used to assign threat-level probabilities to the activities that took place in a network or computer. For example, network intrusion can be considered as a classification problem. A probability can be assigned to every activity. Based on the probability the activity can be classified into a specific class. According to some researchers, a probabilistic approach can be done using the Hidden Markov Model rule for developing host-based protection. Authors in [17] used the Hidden Markov Model on system calls of network connections. Authors in [18] recorded series of system calls and used them as observations for the Hidden Markov Model. These approaches proposed by [17, 18] started by creating λ, a normal set with the help of Hidden Markov Model for the training data. The number of the states

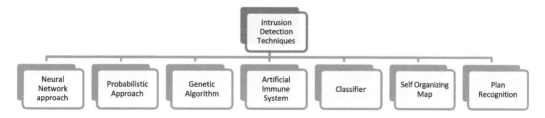

FIGURE 11.2 Intrusion detection techniques.

in training data was more specific for the model. After the completion of the training the system calls were used as observations. The Hidden Markov Model after training was able to calculate a probability that measured the possibility to which the observation was in λ. After calculating the probability, the system calls were classified based on a threshold. The system calls were classified as intrusion if the probability was below threshold. After these works the authors were able to conclude that the detection depended on the number of states of the Hidden Markov Model. More research can be done in order to find how computation depended on detection accuracy. Researchers in [18] were able to attain accuracy of 28% in abnormal activity detection on e-mail systems.

11.2.3 GENETIC ALGORITHM

Authors in [19] proposed the use of genetic algorithm or creating rules for detecting intrusions in networks. Based on the specification of the network, chromosomes were randomly obtained. The chromosomes were trained by capturing the real-time data by [13]. The data used for training were hand classified by experts in order to make separate categories of intrusion and non-intrusion data. The major goal behind proposing genetic algorithm was to produce rules that can deal with intrusion attacks.

The chromosomes were provided with a fitness value that helped them to match with the intrusion data by describing the accuracy. The steps involved in assigning fitness value to the chromosomes are as follows:

Step 1: Calculate outcome

$$\text{Outcome} = \sum{}^{57}_{i=1} \text{Matched} * \text{Weight} \tag{1}$$

The value assigned to Matched is 1 if a match is found, else 0. Two more variables were introduced while proposing this approach. The first variable was used to indicate the extent of match between two network connections. It was named as suspicious level and its value was computed based on the historical data. The other variable was named as ranking calculated the difficulty in detecting the intrusion from the historical data. The fitness was calculated by applying the following formula:

$$\Delta = |\text{outcome} - \text{suspicious level}| \tag{2}$$

$$\text{penalty} = (\Delta * \text{ranking}) / 100 \tag{3}$$

$$\text{fitness} = 1 - \text{penalty} \tag{4}$$

The researchers left the problem open for future work. Those interested can determine how different techniques namely, crossover, selection, crowding, and mutation can increase the efficiency of the approach. Authors in [20] used tree graph to express real network security rules. Chromosomes were created using tree graph data structure using the alphabets. New rules were created based on genetic programing by setting the value of mutation probability as 0.01 and crossover probability as 0.6. More work is required in this field to discover the correct mutation, crossover probabilities, and population size. Authors in [20] took help from DARPA and got 10,000 network connection records in order to train their genetic algorithm. The proposed algorithm had average false negative rate = 5.04%, average false positive rate = 5.23%, and average rate of detecting unknown attacks as 57.14 for each rule.

11.2.4 ARTIFICIAL IMMUNE SYSTEM

Researchers in [21] in LYSIS network security were the first to make use of the Artificial Immune System. They created a fixed length binary string and named it as detector. The detector was passed through negative selection, tolerization, and human co-stimulation. The goal behind this was to create an artificial neuron that can behave like biological immune system. The activity of the network was divided into two categories namely, self and non-self, self was for normal activities and non-self was for abnormal activities of the network. While performing the negative selection and tolerization, the detector that was able to match with the self of the network was removed and a new detector was placed in its place. To perform matching r-contiguous bits were used, two strings were considered to be matched if they had common r-contiguous bits. The detectors that were able to retain in the tolerization period were used to reduce the false positive rate by alarming the human operator in case an intrusion was found. The human operator can either validate or discard the intrusion alarm. In case of a validation operation, the detector that gave the alarm received a co-stimulation signal and had to remain active in the system and in case of discard the detector that gave alarm had to die and a new detector was placed in place of that detector. The authors in [22] used memory detectors for performing co-stimulation. They also used genetic algorithm to keep and multiply the detector that were fit. The fitness of the detectors was computed based on the negative selection process. Authors in [23] proposed an approach similar to that of [22], the only difference was that it used real values instead of binary values. They used Euclidean distance in place of the r-contiguous bits used in the previous approaches. They made use of two approaches namely positive and negative characterizations. The Positive Characterization (PC) took the help of self-detectors and removed non-self-detectors while the other characterization used negative selection. Among these approaches the first one, that is, PC, gave more accurate results, although it needed more time and space. The approach proposed by [23] that is negative characterization used data set given by DARPA. It was able to give an 87.5% detection rate and a 1% false alarm rate.

11.2.5 Classifier

The major goal behind intrusion detection was to classify an abnormal and normal packet. The data used here can be in different forms. Researches showed how classification can be used for detection of network intrusions.

Researchers in [24] used data mining to differentiate between normal and abnormal packets. Tcpdump was used as training data for this approach. For identifying the classification features the source and destination addresses, the ports numbers, services, message sizes, and connection flags were used. Although data mining needs a large amount of data set, it could enhance the efficiency of rule-based intrusion-detection system. While using this approach on DARPA intrusion dataset, it gave 95% detection rate and 6% false positive rate. Also, this approach can be easily added with any other currently available intrusion-detection systems. Some researchers also used support vector machine for classification of malicious and non-malicious packets [25].

For classification, the classes of the training data should be known before time. This created a lot of extra work for using classifiers as an intrusion-detection mechanism. To avoid these overheads the unlabeled data were clustered to detect intrusion [26]. Similar to previous approaches, this approach also took source address, destination address and port number from the TCP connections. The values extracted were converted into numerical values and normalization was performed on those values. Finally, clustering was performed on the normalized values, without using the class labels. The authors in [26] considered a cluster as normal if it had more than 98% of training data and else were considered as abnormal. Detection was performed by measuring the Euclidean distance of the incoming packets to the centroids of clusters. The calculated distance was compared with a threshold, if the distance was less than the threshold then the packet was categorized into the cluster from which distance was taken. So, it was concluded that the accuracy of the approach and false-positive rate depended completely on the training data. This approach was further tested with a different dataset named as KDD CUP 99 and gave 40% to 55% correct detection and was able to give 1.3% to 2.3% false-positive alarms.

11.2.6 SELF-ORGANIZING MAP

Self-Organizing Maps (SOM) are single feed forward neural networks. They are also called Kohonen Map [27] and are used mainly for data compression and pattern recognition. They transform data from higher dimension space to a lower one or two-dimensional array of neurons [27]. The dimension of the input vector is always higher than the dimension of the output vector in case of SOM. It works like clustering. The weights of the neurons in the network are adjusted based on the training data. If the input vector's weight is similar to that of a neuron then the weight of the neuron is updated by the weight of the neuron and the neuron is termed as the winning neuron [27]. The distance of other neurons is calculated from the winning neuron and their weights are adjusted according to the calculated distance. Authors in [27] performed intrusion detection using SOM. They created their training data by collecting packets from a real network. The packets were then labeled based on the network event corresponding to each packet. In their data set they also used some labeled data from the training data of DARPA website [27]. Feature extraction was performed on the packets and the extracted packets were used for training purposes. After completion of training the SOM classifier was tested with real network packets. So, the authors in [27] concluded that the SOM was able to successfully detect intrusion, but they did not give more details about the feature extraction technique used. The use of SOM for intrusion detection can provide intrusion detection with higher efficiency. But this approach was bit time-consuming as the training and labelling of data is a time-consuming task.

11.2.7 PLAN RECOGNITION

This area of AI is concerned with predicting the intention of the agent [28]. To use the plan prediction technique the actions performed by the agent are to be observed. If the actions are not observable then the changes made by the actions should be observable. Authors in [28] gave an approach to use plan recognition in intrusion detection. The observation behind this approach was that the intrusion-detection systems were able to report the intrusion after the intrusion had occurred not before the occurrence of the intrusion. But with plan recognition the intrusion can be reported before the occurrence of intrusion. The approach given was a theoretical approach and to test this the attack library was required. The attack library was to contain the actions or events that were related to each attack available in library for accurate prediction. For predicting the intentions, the intrusion-detection system made use of a partial sequence of actions of the intruder, which can infer multiple goals. In order to predict the occurrence of the goal from the available goals each goal was given a probability value which was computed based on the distance between the partial sequence and the possible complete sequence of actions. Hence, it was concluded that this approach can be beneficial for the network administrator as it can decrease the candidate intrusion attack responses that can be implemented. But, this approach was not able to deal with misleading attackers.

11.3 AUTOMATIC SOFTWARE REPAIR

11.3.1 SYSTEM'S MODEL

If an intrusion is detected, then there is a need to repair or patch the software or application that caused the intrusion. With the help of AI researchers have developed some intelligent patching systems that can automatically repair or patch any abnormal or broken software or application. Figure 11.3 shows all the automatic software repair models. ClearView [29] patch program is one such intelligent patching system. It used a technique that was similar to the artificial immune system used to create an intelligent patching system.

In case of detection of failure or abnormal activity, ClearView created candidate patches. The obtained candidate patches were filtered in order to get the most effective candidate patches. The candidate patches changed the value of registers and memory on execution. ClearView when applied on Firefox blocked 10 vulnerabilities and generated 8 out of 10 patches. Authors in [30], and similar

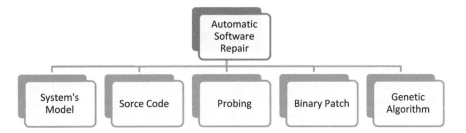

FIGURE 11.3   Automatic software repair.

to these works used neural networks for performing anomaly detection and they also used case-based reasoning in order to automate deploying patches tasks. These are stand-alone software not installed in the software they maintained. It worked similar to the network monitor.

11.3.2   SOURCE CODE

Authors in [31], Lin et al. (2007), used software patches of Microsoft and analyzed them for frequency. After analyzing the data they realized that the patches were generated after around 75 days after the security breach occurred. So, there is a need for automatic patch software. Authors in [31] designed AutoPag, which was an automatic patch software, that could patch the damages occurred due to buffer overflow attacks. It comprised three components namely, out of bound detector, source patch generator and root cause locator.

11.3.3   PROBING

Authors in [32], Cui et al. (2007), introduced an approach that was able to generate patches for anti-virus and firewalls automatically. They named their approach as ShieldGen and it worked as follows:

Step 1: Analyze the incoming file, network or data using an attack detector. Analyzing will check whether the incoming file or data contained arbitrary code execution, arbitrary code execution or arbitrary functions argument.

Step 2: If the data had any of the three exploits listed above then the data are forwarded to data analyzer, which checks the data format for any formatting violations.

Step 3: If a format violation is found the data analyzer will automatically create a probe, a duplicate data in order to amplify the violation.

Step 4: The probe generated is sent to the attack detector.

Step 5: The attack detector will analyze the probe, and if the detector triggers an alarm, then the new predicate rules are created for the violation and to the system rule of anti-virus or firewall.

11.3.4   BINARY PATCH

Authors in [33], proposed an approach named as PatchGen which was able to create patches from input and binary program. This approach targeted buffer overflows. On detection of overflow it modified the program. Modified binary program would go to the automatically created guard code. This approach made use of Windows operating system. It had the capability of patching all the buffer overflows that were produced by six random attacks. But it had a drawback; patches created would work fine only if program did not come to the program that caused the overflow. This is called control flow problem.

11.3.5　Genetic Algorithm

Researchers in [34] introduced an approach that was able to automatically repair a program using genetic algorithm. The approach was capable of automatically repairing the software during testing.

The genetic algorithm had to maintain the program variant population. The fitness of a variant depends upon the number of total test cases passed, both negative and positive. The variant also had the permission to mutate or crossover. In each iteration, half a population was replaced by genetic algorithm. The algorithm then created a program variant which could pass all test cases, then it stopped. This variant selected was used to repair the software.

Original program was modified by the statements in the abstract syntax. This approach was made for the C programming language but according to x tree. Although to the authors it was also able to detects like format string vulnerability, heap buffer overrun, infinite loop, integer overflow, segmentation fault, denial of service, incorrect output, non-overflow and invalid exception. An assumption was made in this approach that the path of negative and positive test case was different. Also the defects were considered to be detectable and repeatable.

11.4　AUTONOMOUS DEFENDER APPROACH

11.4.1　Risk Metric

A company named Symbiot Inc. introduced an AI-based network security defender [35], which was able to behave similar to biological systems. In figure 11.4 shows different types of autonomous defender approach. It was also expected to be autonomous and utilize humans as observers, so that network defenders can take lessons from them. The final defender made was given the name as iSIMS, which started with network environment modeling. The events taking place in the network were monitored and a risk metric was created based on these events and was used by iSIMS for performing actions. One of these actions was attacking the network attacker.

There is no discussion about the AI methods and processes involved in iSIMS. In future, more research can be done in this area to know more about the processes and AI behind iSIMS.

11.4.2　First Shooter Game

The authors in [36] Harrop and Armitage (2006) proposed a first shooter game to help the network administrator. A network administrator's job needs advanced skills and training. In order to engage the regular computer users in network management tasks authors in [36] converted a first shooter game into a visualization tool for maintaining network security.

The approach introduced by [36] converted the network environment into a three-dimensional game, where objects modelled to real network objects. The administrator had to login as a player and the actions performed by the administrator were converted into commands.

Their approach used a "Cube 1" game engine, a FreeBSD host and a router. The correctness and accuracy of the visualizations are not discussed in brief. Also there is a limitation on the network

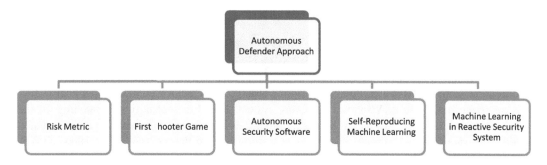

FIGURE 11.4　Autonomous defender approach.

operations that can be performed as it is based on the translation possible among the real network and game environment. In future more actions can be added for improving the use of this approach for becoming a network administrator.

11.4.3 Autonomous Security Infrastructure

The authors in [37] proposed to make the computer security infrastructure intelligent. In this approach a single software was used for responding to attacks, detecting failures, intrusion detection, and repairing security breaches. The security software created, can be employed in network infrastructure that are based on Linux and Unix operating systems.

The security software introduced by them was given the name as intelliagent. It worked as follows:

Step 1: A script whose task was to awaken the proposed software after every x minutes was installed in the host.
Step 2: The software when awakened will check for any anomaly or intrusion in the network.
Step 3: If there was any need for repair, the host was restored by using the recent backup data.
Step 4: In case of occurrence of attack, then intelliagent would take action after scanning and finding appropriate action from its attack library.

This approach was capable of informing the system administrator in case of any attack or any uncertain event occurring in the host.

This proposed system collected processes and system's state and created backup before going to sleep. Initially this approach was used by a mobile company that had around 650 servers. Before its deployment the attacks in the company were analyzed and then intelliagent was configured according to the company requirements. It took around a year to deploy and handle the attacks that were found in the company. After one year of deployment of intelliagent the security breaches in the company reduced from 1,000 to 0. Intelliagent was a "do it all" approach which had its own built in attack detection and attack response rules. It could handle any node that needs protection. It was customizable and its performance depended upon its built-in rules.

11.4.4 Self-Reproducing Machine Learning

The author in [38] proposed the use of self-reproducing ML in computer security and internet. Self-reproducing ML machine can be defined using the following terms:

Let, A: Factory system, E: Source program, P: System's characteristic. (A,E) was able to self-reproduce (B,F) if B had the characteristic of P and F had a subsystem of E [38]. This was an example of an approach where A was the learning environment and B was the internet environment.

The authors [38] proposed that this approach can be useful in internet and computer security. They also proposed a similar approach. In a given environment if A is a learning system, E is a virus database, then new variants of E can be self-reproduced in order to modify the virus database. They also proposed to use self-reproducing ML in firewall systems. In a learning system, if some set of rules are given some new rules can also be introduced to enhance the set of rules.

The authors gave only theoretical technique, they did not give any implementation. They mentioned that the ML methods and game theory can be used in the self-reproduction process.

11.4.5 Machine Learning in Reactive Security System

The author in [39] proposed the use of ML for making a reactive security system. He proposed to focus on dealing with unknown attackers in terms of cost instead of actions. He considered the computer or network as a game in which the participants were permitted to turn around in order to execute actions. The actions performed in the game changed the environment from one node to the other node of the graph. The attacker was rewarded in case it compromises a host present in the network, but it had to pay the cost in case of compromising with the host.

The aim of defender was to reduce rewards, maximize cost of any attacker that tries to compromise any host in the network. The defender was responsible for selecting the security software and security mechanism to be implemented at every host in the network. Every security mechanism has a cost related to it and the defender had a limited budget and it had to plan the cost according to the security mechanism.

The approach proposed in [40] permitted the attacker to have details about the defense strategy of the defender. The defender did not have any knowledge about the intention/of the attacker, but it was permitted to observe the actions performed by the attacker. The author proved that the reactive approach had an advantage over a proactive approach. Proactive approach was defined as a defense mechanism that was unchangeable and fixed security techniques. This approach had difficulty in designing as in this the intention of the attacker was not known before time. In this approach if the defense strategy designed fails to detect some attacks then making another defense strategy will incur cost higher than the reactive defense strategy. On the other hand, the reactive defense strategy had the capability of surviving multiple attacks while suffering catastrophic losses. This approach increased in case the defender tried to move the assets but was not penalized.

11.5   CONCLUSION

This chapter aims at describing the possibilities of using AI in computer security or computer-based intelligence and security. The tree data structure which is a context based and local regression opponent modeling can protect the computer network from attackers.

REFERENCES

1. Henry, W. P. and P. H. Winston (2014). *Artificial Intelligence*. Redwood City, CA: Addison Wesley Longman Publishing Co., Inc.
2. Rich, E. and K. Knight (2020). *Artificial Intelligence* (2nd ed.). McGraw-Hill Higher Education.
3. Webber, B. L. and N. J. Nilsson (Eds.). (2010). *Readings in Artificial Intelligence*. San Francisco, CA: Morgan Kaufmann Publishers Inc.
4. Barr, A. and E. A. Feigenbaum (Eds.). (2010). *The Handbook of Artificial Intelligence* (Vol. 1). Reading, MA: Addison Wesley Longman Publishing Co., Inc.
5. Shapiro, S. C. (2012). Editor's foreword. In *Encyclopedia of Artificial Intelligence* (Vol. 1, pp. 54–57).
6. Russell, S. J., P. Norvig, J. F. Candy, J. M. Malik, and D. D. Edwards (2016). *Artificial Intelligence: A Modern Approach*. Upper Saddle River, NJ: Prentice-Hall, Inc.
7. Guttman, B. and E. A. Roback (2005). An introduction to computer security: The Nist handbook. Technical Report. Washington, DC.
8. Taylor, R. N., N. Medvidovic, and E. M. Dashofy (2019). *Software Architecture: Foundations, Theory, and Practice*. Wiley Publishing.
9. Solomon, M. G. and M. Chapple (2015). *Information Security Illuminated*. Jones and Bartlett Publishers, Inc.
10. Oppliger, R. (2010). *Security Technologies for the World Wide Web*. Norwood, MA: Artech House, Inc.
11. Russell, D. and G. T. Gangemi, Sr. (2009). *Computer Security Basics*. Sebastopol, CA: O'Reilly & Associates, Inc.
12. TippingPoint. Tippingpoint. http://dvlabs.tippingpoint.com/.
13. Koziol, J. (2013). *Intrusion Detection with Snort* (1st ed.). Indianapolis, IN: Sams.
14. Wireshark. Wireshark. http://www.wireshark.org/.
15. Landwehr, C. (2018). Cyber security and artificial intelligence: From fixing the plumbing to smart water. In *Proceedings of the 1st ACM Workshop on Workshop on AISec, AISec '08* (pp. 51–52). New York, NY: ACM.
16. Tesauro, G., J. O. Kephart, and G. B. Sorkin (2006). Neural networks for computer virus recognition. *IEEE Expert Magazine*, 11(4), 5–6.
17. Du, Y., H. Wang, and Y. Pang (2014). A hidden markov models-based anomaly intrusion detection method. In *Fifth World Congress on Intelligent Control and Automation, 2004. WCICA 2004* (Vol. 5, pp. 4348–4351).

18. Wang, W., X. H. Guan, and X. L. Zhang (2014). Modeling program behaviors by Hidden Markov models for intrusion detection (Vol. 5).

19. Li, W. (2014). Using genetic algorithm for network intrusion detection. In *Proceedings of the United States Department of Energy Cyber Security Group 2004 Training Conference* (pp. 24–27).

20. Lu, W. and I. Traore (2014). Detecting new forms of network intrusion using genetic programming. *Computational Intelligence*, 475–494.

21. Hofmeyr, S. A. and S. A. Forrest (2010, December). Architecture for an artificial immune system. *Evolutionary Computation*, 8(4), 443–473.

22. Dal, D., S. Abraham, A. Abraham, S. Sanyal, and M. Sanglikar (2018). Evolution induced secondary immunity: An artificial immune system based intrusion detection system. In *Proceedings of the 2008 7th Computer Information Systems and Industrial Management Applications* (pp. 65–70). Washington, DC: IEEE Computer Society.

23. Dasgupta, D. and F. Gonzalez (2012). An immunity-based technique to characterize intrusions in computer networks. *IEEE Transactions on Evolutionary Computation*, 6(3), 281–291.

24. Lee, W. and S. J. Stolfo (2009). A data mining framework for building intrusion detection models. In *Proceedings of the 1999 IEEE Symposium on Security and Privacy* (pp. 120–132).

25. Kim, D. and J. Park (2013). Network-based intrusion detection with support vector machines. In H.-K. Kahng (Ed.), *Information Networking, Volume 2662 of Lecture Notes in Computer Science* (pp. 747–756). Berlin/Heidelberg: Springer.

26. Portnoy, L., E. Eskin, and S. Stolfo (2011). Intrusion detection with unlabelled data using clustering. In *Proceedings of the ACM CSS Workshop on Data Mining Applied to Security (DMSA-2001)* (pp. 5–8).

27. Pachghare, V., P. Kulkarni, and D. M. Nikam (2019, July). Intrusion detection system using self organizing maps. In 2009 International Conference on Intelligent Agent & Multi-Agent Systems (pp. 1–5).

28. Geib, C. W. and R. P. Goldman (2011). Plan recognition in intrusion detection systems. In *DARPA Information Survivability Conference and Exposition*.

29. Perkins, J. H., S. Kim, S. Larsen, S. Amarasinghe, J. Bachrach, M. Carbin, C. Pacheco, F. Sherwood, S. Sidiroglou, G. Sullivan, W.-F. Wong, Y. Zibin, M. D. Ernst, and M. Rinard (2019). Automatically patching errors in deployed software. In *Proceedings of the ACM SIGOPS 22nd Symposium on Operating Systems Principles, SOSP '09* (pp. 87–102). New York, NY: ACM.

30. Kumar, G. P. and P. Venkataram (2007). Artificial intelligence approaches to network management: Recent advances and a survey. *Computer Communications*, 20(15), 1313–1322.

31. Lin, Z., X. Jiang, D. Xu, B. Mao, and L. Xie (2017). Autopag: Towards automated software patch generation with source code root cause identification and repair. In *Proceedings of the 2nd ACM Symposium on Information, Computer and Communications Security*. New York, NY: ACM.

32. Cui, W., M. Peinado, H. Wang, and M. Locasto (2017, May). Shieldgen: Automatic data patch generation for unknown vulnerabilities with informed probing. In *IEEE Symposium on Security and Privacy*.

33. Chen, K., Y. Lian, and Y. Zhang (2020). Automatically generating patch in binary programs using attribute-based taint analysis. In *Proceedings of the 12th International Conference on Information and Communications Security* (pp. 367–382). Berlin, Heidelberg: Springer-Verlag.

34. Weimer, W., S. Forrest, C. Le Goues, and T. Nguyen (2020, May). Automatic program repair with evolutionary computation. *Communications of the ACM*, 53(5), 109–116.

35. Nathan, P. and W. Hurley (2014). Non-equilibrium risk models in enterprise network security. Symbiot, Inc. Publication. http://www.symbiot.com.

36. Harrop, W. and G. Armitage (2016). Modifying first person shooter games to perform real time network monitoring and control tasks. In *Proceedings of 5th ACM SIGCOMM Workshop on Network and System Support for Games*. New York, NY: ACM.

37. Corsava, S. and V. Getov (2013). Autonomous agents-based security infrastructure. In *Proceedings of the 2003 International Conference on Computational Science and Its Applications: Part II* (pp. 374–382). Berlin, Heidelberg: Springer-Verlag.

38. Huang, J. K. and B.-S. Chen (2017). Srml learning game theory with application to internet security and management systems. In *Proceedings of the 2007 IEEE International Conference on Granular Computing*. Washington, DC: IEEE Computer Society.

39. Rubinstein, B. I. P. (2020, May). Secure learning and learning for security: Research in the intersection. Ph.D. thesis, EECS Department, University of California, Berkeley.

40. Hunt, K., & Zhuang, J. (2023. A review of attacker-defender games: Current state and paths forward. *European Journal of Operational Research*.

12 Case Study: Artificial Intelligence and Machine Learning in Cybersecurity

Girija R, Abiram G, P. Durgadevi, and Savita

12.1 INTRODUCTION

The number of Advanced Persistent Threat (APT) assaults is growing each day. Unfortunately, it might be challenging to recognize [1–4]. This method involves systematically removing forms that focus on high-value industries such as government, military, or financial activities. The main goal of an APT assault is to take information from its host and not harm it. Once the hacker hooks on the system the aggressor introduces APT malware. A well-suited malware, for example, Trojan Pony, is tailor-made to infect the programming and firewalls [5–7] of the host's system. It hasn't been used for remotely controlling the traded-off machines yet, in addition to taking important data from infected host over an expanded time frame. Able malware can sidestep hostile to infection programs utilizing polymorphic code, and sidestep firewall utilizing conventions on permitted ports. Domain Name System (DNS) is a vital part of the Internet and is the main way of connecting something that you search for to its IP address. Shockingly, other than being used for essential services, web servers and mailing services are vulnerable to being used for vindictive purposes. To control the infected appliance, assailants construct an order and then switch channels. The order and control channel between the infected machine and the assailant is in charge of distributing directions and then exchanging information. Most malware, for example, Trojan, have indirect access and other inaccessible admittance apparatuses, utilize the field appellations to find their order and switch (C&C) servers and connect with assailants. Celebrated malware, like Ghost, PCShare, and Poison Ivy, train aggressors to find direction and mechanism servers.

12.2 PHISHING DOMAIN-DETECTION FEATURES

Currently, there is a wide assortment of information and research studies composed specifically for phishing identification for both academic and business purposes. A phishing URL and the comparing page have few highlights or features that can be used to separate a normal URL from a pernicious one. For instance, an aggressor can enrol tedious and confounding areas of information to conceal the genuine space name (Cybersquatting, Typosquatting) which prevents the user from identifying whether or not the site is reliable. Now aggressors can utilize coordinate IP addresses as opposed to utilizing the space name. However, it very well may be utilized for a similar reason. Assailants may use short URLs that are unnecessary for legitimate titles and do not require free URL expansion. These locations are included in our extension since they are more relevant to areas than phishing sites. Using Uniform Resource Locator-Based Features, multiple highlights/structures are used to recognize phishing sites by mechanism learning calculations [8, 9]. Highlights gathered from scholastic examinations of phishing space identification with machine-learning procedures are as follows:

DOI: 10.1201/9781003251781-12

1. Uniform Resource Locator-Based.
2. Domain-Based.
3. Page-Based.
4. Content-Based.

12.2.1 Uniform Resource Locator-Based Features

It is the principal object that near dissects to find out whether a site is phishing or not. As stated before, URLs of phishing spaces must have certain particular focus. When we handle the URL we get certain information that helps us determine whether the site is legit or not. Some specific varieties are specified below.

- Digitally.
- Overall dimension examination URL (e.g., google.com → goggle.com)
- Check to see if the corporate name is real (e.g., apple-icloud-login.com).
- Numeral of subdomains
- Is Uppermost Level Province (HLD) one of the normally utilized unique technique.

12.2.2 Domain Topographies

The main reason for the existence of Phishing Area Discovery is to recognize phishing space designations. Using this inactive inquiries can be identified with the space name, which we need to identify and categorize as phishing or not. Certain helpful domain- based features are prearranged below.

- Is area title or IP statement shunning a widely understood and known notoriety administration?
- How the days go by since the space was enlisted?
- Is the name of the registrant covered up, meaning could they be potentially hiding it?

12.2.3 Page-Based Features

Page-based features utilize data around sheets that stay computed by notoriety positioning administrations. A portion of these data gives us information about how legitimate a site is. Here are some of the page-based features:

- Worldwide Page Rank.
- Nation Sheet Rank.
- Place – Alexa Highest One Million Site.

Page-based types stretch the data around the client movement happening in a said board/selected place. A few of these points are listed below. Accessing this type of data isn't an easy ordeal. There are some paid systems which help us acquire this sort of information.

- Projected amount of appointments aimed at the area happening every day, week after week, or month to month.
- Average views on page per appointment.
- Mean call period.
- Web movement share per nation.
- Comparable sites and so on.

12.2.4 CONTENT-BASED FEATURES

In order to acquire this type of information, dynamic output to target area is required. Certain aspects of web page are used to distinguish whether space is utilized for phishing or sheet manipulation involves agreeing on specific locations. By investigating this data, certain evidence can be extracted.

All the types mentioned overhead are of utmost importance in determining whether a certain location is a phishing space or not. Like all things, there are certain times when using any of the above features don't make sense. For example, using content-based features for the growing quick recognition component which can dissect the quantity of areas somewhere in the range of 100.000 and 200.000 or if we need to examine new enrolled areas, page-based features aren't exactly useful. In this manner, the features that will be utilized by the location model rely entirely upon the motivation behind the identification instrument. What set of

features are to be used in the discovery system has to consider all of the factors and the most effective one should be used.

12.3 PROPOSED MODEL

Detection Process: Recognizing phishing domains is a specific and important issue that implies the requirement of specified information which has test cases as phishing area and genuine spaces in the preparation stage. The dataset which will be utilized in the preparation stage is a critical part to assemble effective discovery instrument. This calls for the employment of tests whose classes are unambiguously known, which implies that the instances which are marked as phishing must be indubitably distinguished as phishing. The instances marked as genuine must be completely recognized as real. On the off chance that we make use of tests that we don't know about, the framework doesn't work accurately. To avoid this, certain open datasets are made particularly for phishing. An outstanding example of this is Phish Tank. The information from these sources are utilized regularly in scholastic studies and research. Another major issue is the collection of legitimate areas. To solve this, we make use of site notoriety administrations. These administration systems not only examine the accessible sites but also rank them. Ranks might be given either on a global scale or country-wise. This positioning system relies upon wide assortment of highlights. The sites which have a higher rank on the scale are authentic locales which are utilized more. An example of such a notoriety positioning administration system is Alexa. Analysts are utilizing the best, most top-rated arrangements of Alexa positioning system for genuine sites. When we have unrefined and unreliable information for phishing and also authentic destinations in the same mix, this system helps process this information and refine important data from it which helps us recognize deceitful spaces thereby saving us a lot of trouble. The machine learning dataset which we choose to use for this particular process must comprise all of these highlights. We must also devise another dataset by processing the unreliable information which is gathered from Alexa, Phish Tank or other sources, to make a framework using machine learning calculations. The components ought to be chosen according to our requirements and purposes and have to be figured out separately for each one of them. Figure 12.1 shows detecting malicious and benign URL. Figure 12.2 result shows the the Jaro and Levenshtein distance in the domain names or in any website or URL. We can find out the malicious and benign URLs by giving any URL. So, here we have inserted our datasets which contain all the information about malicious and benign sites, and it gives the output according to those datasets, where it contains the port number, label, and URL of any website. Finally if we give any input it tells us if it is malicious or benign.

12.4 CONCLUSION

Malignant URL location assumes the basic job for some digital security applications and machine learning approaches are a promising way to solve issues. In this chapter, we have made a far-reaching

FIGURE 12.1   Result of malicious detection from URL

FIGURE 12.2   Finding the Jaro and Levenshtein distance

and deliberate study on the detection of malicious URL by using machine learning strategies. Categorically, we developed a distinctive plan of malicious URL identification from a machine learning point of view and also examined the essence of the dialogues of existing examinations for harmful URL locations.

REFERENCES

1. Yadav, S., Reddy, A. K. K., Reddy, A. L. N., & Ranjan, S. (2010). Detecting algorithmically generated malicious domain names. In *IMC '10: Proceedings Of The 10th ACM SIGCOMM Conference On Internet Measurement* (p. 4861).
2. Wolf, J. (2008). Technical details of Srizbi's domain generation algorithm [Online]. http://tinyurl.com/6mdasc.
3. Bilge, L., Kirda, E., Kruegel, C., & Balduzzi, M. (2011). Exposure: Finding malicious domains using passive DNS analysis. In *Proceedings of the Network and Distributed System Security Symposium*.
4. Stalmans, E., & Irwin, B. (2011, August). A framework for DNS based detection and mitigation of malware infections on a network. In *2011 Information Security for South Africa* (p. 18).

5. Ioannidis, S., Keromytis, A. D., Bellovin, S. M., & Smith, J. M. (2000, November). Implementing a distributed firewall. In *Proceedings of the 7th ACM Conference on Computer and Communications Security* (pp. 190–199).

6. Liu, A. X., & Gouda, M. G. (2008). Diverse firewall design. *IEEE Transactions on Parallel and Distributed Systems*, *19*(9), 1237–1251.

7. Pallavi, C., Girija, R., & Jayalakshmi, S. L. (2021, April). An analysis on network security tools and systems. In *Proceedings of the International Conference on Innovative Computing & Communication (ICICC)*.

8. Guru Prasad, U., Girija, R., Vedhapriyavadhana, R., & Jayalakshmi, S. L. (2022). Assessment of open source tools and techniques for network security. In *Cyber Security and Digital Forensics* (pp. 289–300). Springer.

9. Pallavi, C., Girija, R., Vedhapriyavadhana, R., Dey, B., & Vincent, R. (2021). A relative investigation of various algorithms for online financial fraud detection techniques. In *Recent Trends in Intensive Computing* (pp. 22–32). IOS Press.

Index

Account, 7, 27, 30, 31, 33, 35, 44, 58, 105, 113, 124
Accuracy, 3, 4, 8, 11, 12, 15, 76, 87, 113, 121, 130, 131, 135, 144
Adoptive, 8, 110, 143, 163
Adware, 24, 25
Algorithm, 1, 3, 4, 6, 10, 11, 14, 15, 38, 43, 48, 57, 66, 69, 76, 78, 83, 85
Analysis, 1, 4, 7, 11–13, 15, 35, 39, 44, 47–50, 54, 55, 57, 67, 69, 72, 74, 76, 95, 107, 115, 131, 138, 155
Application, 1, 7, 14, 25, 27, 32, 35, 43, 53, 55, 65, 67, 74, 85, 99
Approaches, 3, 4, 8, 9, 11, 14, 15, 23, 25, 33–35, 38, 47, 55, 56, 58, 81
Architecture, 12, 33, 53, 57, 72, 119, 124, 135, 145, 157
Artificial intelligence, 32, 41, 76, 113, 121
Artificial Neural Network (ANN), 3, 4
Attack, 1, 3–25, 32–36, 58, 64, 68, 73, 83, 99, 106
Attacker, 3, 5, 6, 11, 14, 24, 26, 27, 31, 33, 35, 39, 68, 73, 99, 138, 162, 169, 170
Authentication, 1, 66, 71, 103, 104
Automation, 30, 41, 55, 86, 131

Beehive Model, 73
Best, 3, 4, 8, 30, 31, 39, 43, 46, 66, 70, 81, 99, 101, 104, 106, 112, 117, 140
Big Data, 61, 74
Binary, 11–13, 39, 91, 164, 165, 167
Bioinspiration, 9, 10
Businesses, 3, 33, 34, 38, 48, 54, 57, 61, 67, 70, 80, 86, 88

Catastrophe, 117–119, 124
Channel, 11, 28, 33, 69, 118, 127, 172
Classification, 3–6, 12, 14, 22, 25, 43, 77, 127, 135, 136, 140, 144, 149, 150, 153, 163
Classifiers, 3, 4, 8, 36, 37, 39, 144, 151, 161, 165
Clustering, 4, 61, 68, 69, 127, 135, 145, 151, 153, 165, 166
Communication, 6–10, 13, 21, 29, 34, 49, 93, 118
Convolutional Neural Network (CNN), 3, 12, 43, 135, 136, 138, 146, 148–150, 153, 157
Criminal, 21, 22, 31, 38, 43–45, 56, 66, 76, 86, 87, 93
Cryptography, 64
Cyber-attacks, 21, 22, 29, 31, 39
Cyber crime, 119, 151
Cyber protection, 119
Cyber security, 98, 104, 116
Cyber threats, 1, 9, 30, 32, 33, 57, 72, 83, 108, 148

Database, 3, 7, 27, 51, 53, 71, 88, 104
Data security, 100, 103
Datasets, 1, 3–5, 10–12, 67, 70, 140, 144, 151
Deep learning, 131, 135, 146
Defender, 21, 35, 39, 83, 110, 168, 170
Defense, 14, 30, 32, 38, 39, 57, 68, 72, 99, 106, 107, 114, 121
Denial of service (DoS), 4, 138, 168
Detection, 68, 71, 74, 79, 81
Digital, 21, 24, 25, 28, 34, 43, 45–47, 50, 51, 53, 59, 79, 91–98, 110
Drawbacks, 12, 62, 69, 101, 114
Dynamic, 3, 4, 10–12, 14, 15, 38, 57, 93, 130, 138, 174

Encryption, 63, 104
Enterprise, 15, 112
Entomology, 43, 44
Environment, 3, 4, 6, 8, 9, 11, 13, 30–32, 38, 59, 96, 101, 107, 113, 132, 145, 163, 169
Exposure, 1, 127
Extraction, 3, 4, 39, 53, 54, 94, 106, 127, 152, 166

Facial recognition, 76, 87
Feature, 3, 4, 6, 8, 9, 43, 49, 69, 82, 113, 127, 145, 151, 163, 165, 172
Fight, 78, 99
Firewall, 1, 6, 24, 34, 38, 63, 68, 102, 105, 113, 142, 155
Forecasting, 43, 149
Forensics, 41, 148
Frameworks, 24, 27–29, 50, 53, 57, 72, 110, 114, 116, 118, 124, 125, 142
Future, 7, 14, 32, 35–37, 54, 55, 57–59, 73, 80–82, 86, 87, 100, 106, 108, 115, 119, 132
Fuzzing, 115, 132
Fuzzy, 11, 125

Gaussian, 14
Google, 63, 130–131, 173
Government, 62, 172

Hackers, 21, 138
Healthcare, 42, 119
Hype, 8

Identification, 7, 11, 14, 15, 45, 48, 49, 65, 68, 69, 72, 81, 92, 94, 104, 123, 128, 138, 143
Improve, 8, 13, 15, 41, 43, 49–51, 65, 67, 73, 99, 110, 113
Industry, 65, 97
Instance, 10, 13, 46, 59, 93, 99, 172
Intelligence, 32
Intelligent System, 1, 14, 150
Internet of Things, 1, 64, 112
Intimidation, 112, 155
Intrusion, 1, 3–9, 12, 15, 34, 38–39, 65, 68–69, 71, 98, 99, 101, 102, 106–108
Investigation, 24, 35, 41, 43–46, 49–52, 54, 56, 78, 83, 87, 91, 96, 118, 136, 140
IP addresses, 29, 172

KDD, 3–5, 7, 12, 151, 154, 165
Knowledge, 3, 11, 12, 14, 15, 21, 25, 29, 31, 33, 35, 41, 45, 48, 50, 51, 61, 73, 77, 81, 95, 112, 115, 124, 132

Legal, 103, 111
LiDAR, 127, 128
Limitations, 15, 57, 62, 63, 70, 83, 100, 119, 130, 151
Location, 6, 7, 33, 36, 37, 51, 53, 67, 76, 92, 94, 97, 99

Machine learning, 1, 3, 6, 8, 10, 12, 14, 35, 37–39, 41, 42, 46, 48, 55, 62, 76, 81, 99
Malware, 3, 24, 39
Market, 67, 79

Message, 9–10, 25, 91, 92, 99, 118, 136, 144
Metric, 3, 15

Natural language processing, 79, 113, 135
Neural network, 3, 54, 138, 167
Novel, 3, 11, 12, 14, 45, 56, 101, 143

Offense, 76, 91, 110, 138, 139, 151
Optimization, 4, 8, 10, 47, 48, 104, 154

Password, 7, 25, 29–31, 37, 66, 92, 93, 97, 98, 102, 155, 162
Pattern recognition, 161, 166
Permission, 66, 92, 98, 103, 124, 136, 137, 142, 161, 168
Phishing, 22, 24, 27, 29, 83, 98, 105, 136–138, 143, 151, 156, 172, 173
Platforms, 9, 31, 39, 74, 79, 93, 107, 155
Police, 110, 157
Policies, 27, 29, 48, 71, 77, 79, 101, 103, 138, 145
Prediction, 10, 155
Private, 7, 8, 34, 46, 63, 66, 94, 103, 136, 155
Protocol, 6, 94
Public, 5, 24, 34, 50, 56, 65–67, 81, 94, 111, 118, 139, 155

Random forest (RF), 14, 154, 155
Recurrent neural networks (RNN), 3, 12, 14, 138, 139, 142, 150, 153, 157
Regression, 3, 4, 8, 61, 135, 143, 144, 150, 170
Remote, 5, 7, 25–27, 33, 93, 94, 112, 113, 116, 117, 127, 151
Remote-sensing, 127
Research, 9, 123, 172
Residual neural net (ResNet), 136, 157
Risk, 11, 15, 32, 33, 35, 38, 39, 47, 48, 55–57, 59, 61, 65, 70, 72, 99, 100, 102, 103, 113, 116, 168
Robot, 26, 140, 161

Security, 14, 73
Sensors, 7, 9, 11, 13–14, 62, 67, 71, 73, 93, 102, 117, 127, 128, 151
Snake oil, 79, 80, 88
Social, 9, 24, 26, 30, 31, 33, 62, 67, 79, 88, 93, 97
Spoofing, 136, 162
Statistical, 42, 50, 142
Statistics, 6, 13, 36, 47, 50, 106, 114, 136, 152
Strategic, 32, 33, 131
Support Vector Machine (SVM), 3, 4, 8, 12, 14, 135, 150, 151, 165
Surveillance, 81, 151

TCP, 4, 7, 165
Technology, 1, 21, 42, 61
Tensor Flow, 37, 142
Threat, 1, 22, 32, 68, 83
Threat intelligence, 1, 32, 34, 37
Threshold, 4, 153, 163–165
Traffic, 1, 4, 6, 8, 9, 13, 68, 72, 83, 88, 100, 139, 148
Trust, 26, 27, 31, 79, 88, 101, 105, 111, 112, 117, 157

VGGNet, 136, 146, 147, 149, 150, 153, 157
Virtual, 3, 6, 26, 27, 96, 103, 111, 115
Vulnerability, 6, 7, 13, 34, 62, 99, 115, 132, 168

Weapon, 24, 38, 49, 76, 121, 124
Website, 6, 7, 28, 29, 65, 67, 68, 100, 102, 137, 138, 156, 174
Writing, 46, 49, 79, 88

You Only Look Once (YOLO), 136, 146, 148, 149, 153, 157